Japanese Homes and Their Surroundings

Reserved

JAPANESE HOMES

AND

THEIR SURROUNDINGS

JAPANESE HOMES

AND

THEIR SURROUNDINGS

BY

EDWARD S. MORSE

DIRECTOR OF THE PEABODY ACADEMY OF SCIENCE;

LATE PROFESSOR OF ZOÖLOGY, UNIVERSITY OF TOKIO, JAPAN; MEMBER OF THE NATIONAL ACADEMY OF SCIENCE;
FELLOW OF THE AMERICAN ACADEMY OF ARTS AND SCIENCES; ETC.

WITH ILLUSTRATIONS

BY THE AUTHOR

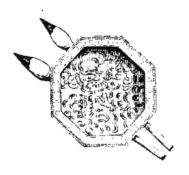

BOSTON

TICKNOR AND COMPANY

1886

SECOND EDITION.

University Press:
JOHN WILSON AND SON, CAMBRIDGE

TO

WILLIAM STURGIS BIGELOW, M.D.

IN MEMORY OF THE DELIGHTFUL EXPERIENCES IN THE

"𝕳eart of 𝕵apan"

THIS VOLUME IS AFFECTIONATELY INSCRIBED

BY THE

AUTHOR

PREFACE.

IN an exceedingly interesting article on the early study of the Dutch in Japan, by Professor K. Mitsukuri,[1] the author has occasion to refer to the uncle of one of the three famous Japanese scholars who translated into Japanese a Dutch book on anatomy. He says this uncle "Miyada was almost eccentric in his disposition. He held it to be a solemn duty to learn any art or accomplishment that might be going out of the world, and then describe it so fully that it might be preserved to posterity." The nephew was faithful to his uncle's instructions, and "though following medicine for his profession, he took it upon himself to learn 'hitoyogiri,'—a certain kind of music which was well-nigh forgotten,—and even went so far as to study a kind of dramatic acting."

Though not animated by Miyada's spirit when I set about the task of collecting the material embodied in this work, I feel now that the labor has not been altogether in vain, as it may result in preserving many details of the Japanese house,—some of them trivial, perhaps,—which in a few decades of years may be difficult, if not impossible, to obtain. Whether this has been accomplished or not, the praiseworthy ambition of the old Japanese scholar might well be imitated by the ethnological student in his investigations,—since nothing can be of greater importance than the study of those nations and

---

[1] Transactions of the Asiatic Society of Japan, vol. v. part i. p. 207.

peoples who are passing through profound changes and readjustments as a result of their compulsory contact with the vigorous, selfish, and mercantile nations of the West, accompanied on their part by a propagandism in some respects equally mercenary and selfish.

Thanks to the activity of a number of students of various nationalities in the employ of the Japanese government, and more especially to the scholarly *attachés* of the English legation in Japan, much information has been obtained concerning this interesting people which might otherwise have been lost. If investigators and students would bear in mind the precept of Miyada, and seize upon those features in social life — forms of etiquette, games, ceremonies, and other manners and customs — which are the first to change in any contact with alien races, a very important work would be accomplished for the future sociologist. The native Japanese student might render the greatest service in this work by noting down from the older persons, before it is too late, the social features and habits of his own people as they were before the late Revolution. Profound changes have already taken place in Japan, and other changes are still in progress. As an indication of the rapidity of some of these changes, reference might be made to an interesting memoir, by Mr. McClatchie, on "The Feudal Mansions of Yedo;" and though this was written but ten years after the revolution of 1868, he speaks of the *yashiki,* or fortified mansions where dwelt the feudal nobles of Japan, as in "many cases deserted, ruined, and fallen into decay;" and he describes observances and manners connected with the *yashiki,* such as "etiquette of the gates," "exchange of yashiki," "rules relating to fires," etc., which were then obsolete at the time of his writing, though in full force but a few years before.

I shall be particularly grateful for any facts concerning the Japanese house beyond those recorded in this book, or which may be already in my possession, as also for the correction of any errors which may have unavoidably been made in the text. Should a second edition of this work be called for, such new information and corrections will be incorporated therein, with due acknowledgments.

I wish to express my gratitude to Dr. W. S. Bigelow, whose delightful companionship I enjoyed during the collection of many of the facts and sketches contained in this volume, and whose hearty sympathy and judicious advice were of the greatest service to me. To Professor and Mrs. E. F. Fenollosa, also, my thanks are especially due for unnumbered kindnesses during my last visit to Japan.

I would also here return my thanks to a host of Japanese friends who have at various times, in season and out of season, granted me the privilege of sketching their homes and examining their dwellings from top to bottom in quest of material for this volume; who furthermore have answered questions, translated terms, hunted up information, and in many ways aided me, — so that it may be truly said, that had this assistance been withheld, but little of my special work could have been accomplished. Any effort to recall the names of all these friends would lead to the unavoidable omission of some; nevertheless, I must specially mention Mr. H. Takamine, Director of the Tokio Normal School; Dr. Seiken Takenaka; Mr. Tsunejiro Miyaoka; Mr. S. Tejima, Director of the Tokio Educational Museum; Professors Toyama, Yatabe, Kikuchi, Mitsukuri, Sasaki, and Kozima, and Mr. Ishikawa and others, of the University of Tokio; Mr. Isawa and Mr. Kodzu, Mr. Fukuzawa, the distinguished teacher and author; Mr. Kashiwagi, Mr. Kohitsu, and Mr. Masuda. I must also acknowledge my indebtedness to Mr. H. Kato, Director of the University of Tokio, to Mr. Hattori, Vice-director, and to Mr. Hamao and other officers of the Educational Department, for many courtesies, and for special accommodations during my last visit to Japan. Nor must I omit to mention Mr. Tachibana, Director of the nobles' school; Mr. Kikkawa, Mr. Tahara, Mr. Kineko, Mr. Ariga, Mr. Tanada, Mr. Nakawara, Mr. Yamaguchi, Mr. Negishi of Kabutoyama, and many others, who supplied me with various notes of interest. In this country I have been specially indebted to Mr. A. S. Mihara and Mr. S. Fukuzawa, for valuable assistance during the preparation of the text; and to Mr. Arakawa, Mr. Shiraishi, Mr. Shugio, and Mr. Yamada of New York, for timely aid.

To the Board of Trustees of the Peabody Academy of Science, who, recognizing the ethnological value of the work I had in hand, granted me a release from my duties as Director until I could complete it; and to Professor John Robinson, Treasurer of the Academy, and Mr. T. F. Hunt, for friendly suggestions and helpful interest, as also to Mr. Percival Lowell for numerous courtesies, — my thanks are due. I must not forget to record here my indebtedness to Mr. A. W. Stevens, chief proof-reader of the University Press, for his invaluable assistance in the literary part of my labors, and for his faithful scrutiny of the proof-sheets. At the same time I desire to thank Miss Margarette W. Brooks for much aid given to me in my work; my daughter, Miss Edith O. Morse, for the preliminary tracings of the drawings from my journals; Mr. L. S. Ipsen, who drew the unique and beautiful design for the cover of this book; Mr. A. V. S. Anthony for judicious supervision of the process-work in the illustrations; the University Press for its excellent workmanship in the printing of the book; and the Publishers for the generous manner in which they have supported the undertaking. I will only add, that the excellent Index to be found at the end of this book was prepared by Mr. Charles H. Stevens.

EDWARD S. MORSE.

SALEM, MASS., U. S. A.
November, 1885.

CONTENTS.

CHAPTER IV.

INTERIORS — (*Continued*).

CHAPTER V.

ENTRANCES AND APPROACHES.

CHAPTER VI.

GARDENS.

CHAPTER VII.

MISCELLANEOUS MATTERS.

CHAPTER VIII.

THE ANCIENT HOUSE.

CHAPTER IX.

THE NEIGHBORING HOUSE.

LIST OF ILLUSTRATIONS.

VIEWS OF CITY AND VILLAGE.

HOUSE CONSTRUCTION.

SHINGLED ROOFS, ETC.

TILED ROOFS, ETC.

THATCHED ROOFS, ETC.

INTERIORS, PLANS, MATS, SLIDING SCREENS, ETC.

INTERIORS SHOWING TOKONOMA AND CHIGAI-DANA.

TEA-ROOMS.

KURA INTERIORS, DOORS, ETC.

CEILING, RAMMA, WINDOWS.

PORTABLE SCREENS, CURTAINS, ETC.

KITCHENS, STAIRWAYS, ETC.

BATHING CONVENIENCES.

PILLOWS, HIBACHI, AND TABAKO-BON.

INTRODUCTION.

WITHIN twenty years there has gradually appeared in our country a variety of Japanese objects conspicuous for their novelty and beauty, — lacquers, pottery and porcelain, forms in wood and metal, curious shaped boxes, quaint ivory carvings, fabrics in cloth and paper, and a number of other objects as perplexing in their purpose as the inscriptions which they often bore. Most of these presented technicalities in their work as enigmatical as were their designs, strange caprices in their ornamentation which, though violating our hitherto recognized proprieties of decoration, surprised and yet delighted us. The utility of many of the objects we were at loss to understand; yet somehow they gradually found lodgment in our rooms, even displacing certain other objects which we had been wont to regard as decorative, and our rooms looked all the prettier for their substitution. We found it difficult to formulate the principles upon which such art was based, and yet were compelled to recognize its merit. Violations of perspective, and colors in juxtaposition or coalescing that before we had regarded as inharmonious, were continually reminding us of Japan and her curious people. Slowly our methods of decoration became imbued with these ways so new to us, and yet so many centuries old to the people among whom these arts had originated. Gradually yet surely, these arts, at first so little understood, modified our own methods of ornamentation, until frescos and wall-papers, wood-work and carpets, dishes and table-cloths, metal work and book-covers, Christmas cards and even railroad advertisements were decorated, modelled, and designed after the Japanese style.

It was not to be wondered at that many of our best artists, — men like Coleman, Vedder, Lafarge, and others, — had long before recognized the transcendent merit of Japanese decorative art. It was however somewhat remarkable that the public at large should come so universally to recognize it, and in so short a time. Not only our own commercial nation, but art-loving France, musical Germany, and even conservative England yielded to this invasion. Not that new designs were evolved by us; on the contrary, we were content to adopt Japanese designs outright, oftentimes with a mixture of incongruities that would have driven a Japanese decorator stark mad. Designs appropriate for the metal mounting of a sword blazed out on our ceilings; motives from a heavy bronze formed the theme for the decoration of friable pottery; and suggestions from light crape were woven into hot carpets to be trodden upon. Even with this mongrel admixture, it was a relief by any means to have driven out of our dwelling the nightmares and horrors of design we had before endured so meekly, — such objects, for example, as a child in dead brass, kneeling in perpetual supplication on a dead brass cushion, while adroitly balancing on its head a receptacle for kerosene oil; and a whole regiment of shapes equally monstrous. Our walls no longer assailed us with designs that wearied our eyes and exasperated our brains by their inanities. We were no longer doomed to wipe our feet on cupids, horns of plenty, restless tigers, or scrolls of architectural magnitudes. Under the benign influence of this new spirit it came to be realized that it was not always necessary to tear a flower in bits to recognize its decorative value; and that the simplest objects in Nature — a spray of bamboo, a pine cone, a cherry blossom — in the *right place* were quite sufficient to satisfy our craving for the beautiful.

The Japanese exhibit at the Centennial exposition in Philadelphia came to us as a new revelation; and the charming onslaught of that unrivalled display completed the victory. It was then that the Japanese craze took firm hold of us. Books on Japan rapidly multiplied, especially books on decorative art; but it was found that such rare art could be properly represented only in the most costly fashion, and with plates of marvellous elaboration. What the Japanese were able to do with their primitive methods of block-printing and a few colors, required the highest genius of our artists and chromo-lithographers; and even then the subtile spirit which the artist sought for could not be caught.

The more intelligent among our collectors soon recognized that the objects from Japan divided themselves into two groups, — the one represented by a few objects having great intrinsic merit, with a refinement and reserve of decoration; the other group, characterized by a more florid display and less delicacy of treatment, forming by far the larger number, consisting chiefly of forms in pottery, porcelain, lacquer and metal work. These last were made by the Japanese expressly for the foreign market, many of them having no place in their economy, and with few exceptions being altogether too gaudy and violent to suit the Japanese taste. Our country became flooded with them; even the village grocery displayed them side by side with articles manufactured at home for the same class of customers, and equally out of place in the greater marts of the country. To us, however, these objects were always pretty, and were moreover so much cheaper, with all their high duties and importer's profits, than the stuff to which we had been accustomed, that they helped us out amazingly at every recurring Christmas. Of the better class of objects, nearly all of them were originally intended either for personal use or adornment, — such as metal clasps, little ivory carvings, sectional lacquer-boxes, fans, etc. ; or mere objects of household use, such as hanging flower-holders, bronze and pottery vases, incense burners, lacquer cabinets, dishes, etc.

Naturally great curiosity was awakened to know more about the social life of this remarkable people ; and particularly was it desirable to know the nature of the house that sheltered such singular and beautiful works of art. In response to the popular demand, book after book appeared ; but with some noteworthy exceptions they repeated the same information, usually prefaced by an account of the more than special privileges accorded to their authors by the Japanese government, followed by a history of the Japanese empire from its first emperor down to the present time, — apparently concise enough, but interminable with its mythologies, wars, decays, restorations, etc. Then we had the record of an itinerary of a few weeks at some treaty port, or of a brief sojourn in the country, where, to illustrate the bravery of the author, imaginary dangers were conjured up ; a wild guess at the ethnical enigma, erroneous conceptions of Japanese character and customs, — the whole illustrated by sketches derived from previous works on the same subject, or from Japanese sources, often without due credit being given ; and finally we were given a forecast of the future of Japan, with an account of the progress its public were making in adopting outside customs, with no warning of the acts of *hara-kiri* their arts would be compelled to perform in the presence of so many influences alien to their nature. As an illustration of this, could the force of absurdity go further than the attempt to introduce the Italian school of painting, — and this in the land of a Kano ; or the melancholy act of a foreign employé of one of the colleges in Tokio, in inducing or compelling all its pupils to wear hot woollen Scotch caps, — converting a lot of handsome dark-haired boys, with graceful and picturesque dress, into a mob of ridiculous monkeys?

In these books on Japan we look in vain for any but the most general description of what a Japanese home really is; even Rein's work, so apparently monographic, dismisses the house and garden in a few pages.[1] The present work is an attempt to fill this deficiency, by describing not only the variety of dwellings seen in Japan, but by specializing more in detail the variety of structure seen within the building.

In the following pages occasion has often led to criticism and comparison. Aside from any question of justice, it would seem as if criticism, to be of any value, should be comparative; that is to say, in any running commentary on Japanese ways and conditions the parallel ways and conditions of one's own people should be as frankly pointed out, or at least recognized. When

---

[1] It may be well to state here that most of the good and reliable contributions upon Japan are to be found in the Transactions of the English and German Asiatic Societies published in Yokohama; also in the pages of the Japan "Mail," in the now extinct Tokio "Times," and in a most excellent but now defunct magazine called the "Chrysanthemum," whose circulation becoming vitiated by the theological sap in its tissues, finally broke down altogether from the dead weight of its dogmatic leaves.

Among the many valuable papers published in these Transactions of the Asiatic Society of Japan, is one by Thomas R. H. McClatchie, Esq., on "The Feudal Mansions of Yedo," vol. vii. part iii. p. 157, which gives many important facts concerning a class of buildings that is rapidly disappearing, and to which only the slightest allusion has been made in the present work. The reader is also referred to a Paper in the same publication by George Cawley, Esq., entitled "Some Remarks on Constructions in Brick and Wood, and their Relative Suitability for Japan," vol. vi. part ii. p. 291; and also to a Paper by R. H. Brunton, Esq., on "Constructive Art in Japan," vol. ii. p. 64; vol. iii. part ii. p. 20.

Professor Huxley has said in one of his lectures, that if all the books in the world were destroyed, with the exception of the Philosophical Transactions, "it is safe to say that the foundations of Physical Science would remain unshaken, and that the vast intellectual progress of the last two centuries would be largely though incompletely recorded." In a similar way it might almost be said of the Japan "Mail," that if all the books which have been written by foreigners upon Japan were destroyed, and files of the Japan "Mail" alone preserved, we should possess about all of value that has been recorded by foreigners concerning that country. This journal not only includes the scholarly productions of its editor, Capt. F. Brinkley, as well as an immense mass of material from its correspondents, but has also published the Transactions of the Asiatic Society of Japan in advance of the Society's own publications.

one enters your city, — which is fairly clean and tidy, — and
complains of its filthy streets, the assumption is that the streets
of his own city are clean; and when these are found to be
dirty beyond measure, the value of the complaint or criticism is
at once lost, and the author immediately set down as a wilful
maligner. Either we should follow the dictum of the great
moral Teacher, and hesitate to behold the mote in others' eyes,
or else in so doing we should consider the beam in our own.

This duty, however, even to fair and unprejudiced minds,
becomes a matter of great difficulty. It is extraordinary how
blind one may be to the faults and crimes of his own people,
and how reluctant to admit them. We sing heroic soldier-songs
with energy and enthusiasm, and are amazed to find numbers
in a Japanese audience disapproving, because of the bloody
deeds celebrated in such an exultant way. We read daily in
our papers the details of the most blood-curdling crimes, and
often of the most abhorrent and unnatural ones; and yet we
make no special reflections on the conditions of society where
such things are possible, or put ourselves much out of the way to
arouse the people to a due sense of the degradation and stain on
the community at large because of such things. But we go
to another country and perhaps find a new species of vice; its
novelty at once arrests our attention, and forthwith we howl
at the enormity of the crime and the degradation of the nation
in which such a crime could originate, send home the most
exaggerated accounts, malign the people without stint, and then
prate to them about Christian charity!

In the study of another people one should if possible look
through colorless glasses; though if one is to err in this respect, it were better that his spectacles should be rose-colored than
grimed with the smoke of prejudice. The student of Ethnology
as a matter of policy, if he can put himself in no more generous attitude, had better err in looking kindly and favorably

at a people whose habits and customs he is about to study. It is human nature the world over to resist adverse criticism; and when one is prowling about with his eyes darkened by the opaquest of uncorrected provincial glasses, he is repelled on all sides; nothing is accessible to him; he can rarely get more than a superficial glance at matters. Whereas, if he tries honestly to seek out the better attributes of a people, he is only too welcome to proceed with any investigation he wishes to make; even customs and ways that appear offensive are freely revealed to him, knowing that he will not wilfully distort and render more painful what is at the outset admitted on all hands to be bad.

We repeat that such investigation must be approached in a spirit of sympathy, otherwise much is lost or misunderstood. This is not only true as to social customs, but also as to studies in other lines of research as well. Professor Fenollosa, the greatest authority on Japanese pictorial art, says most truthfully that " it is not enough to approach these delicate children of the spirit with the eye of mere curiosity, or the cold rigid standard of an alien school. One's heart must be large enough to learn to love, as the Japanese artist loves, before the veil can be lifted to the full splendor of their hidden beauties."

In this spirit I have endeavored to give an account of Japanese homes and their surroundings. I might have dealt only with the huts of the poorest, with the squalor of their inmates, and given a meagre picture of Japanese life; or a study might have been made of the homes of the wealthy exclusively, which would have been equally one-sided. It seemed to me, however, that a description of the homes of the middle classes, with occasional reference to those of the higher and lower types, would perhaps give a fairer picture of the character and structure of Japanese homes and houses, than had I pursued either of the other courses. I may have erred in looking through spectacles

tinted with rose; but if so, I have no apology to make. Living
for some time among a people with whom I have had only the
most friendly relations, and to whom I still owe a thousand debts
of gratitude, it would be only a contemptible and jaundiced
temperament that could under such circumstances write otherwise than kindly, or fail to make generous allowance for what
appear to others as grave faults and omissions.

In regard to Japanese houses, there are many features not
to my liking; and in the ordinary language of travellers I
might speak of these houses as huts and hovels, cold and cheer-
less, etc., and give such a generic description of them as would
include under one category all the houses on the Pacific coast
from Kamtchatka to Java. Faults these houses have; and in
criticising them I have endeavored to make my reflections comparative; and I have held up for comparison much that is objectionable in our own houses, as well as the work done by
our own artisans. But judging from the rage and disgust expressed in certain English publications, where one writer speaks
of "much of the work for wage as positively despicable," and
another of the miseries entailed by the unscientific builder, my
comparison may legitimately extend to England also.[1]

In the present volume the attempt has been made to describe the Japanese house and its immediate surroundings in
general and in detail. No one realizes better than the author
the meagreness in certain portions of this work. It is believed,
however, that with the many illustrations, and the classification
of the subject-matter, much will be made clear that before was
vague. The figures are in every case fac-similes by one of the

---

[1] Still another English writer says: "It is unpleasant to live within ugly walls;
it is still more unpleasant to live within unstable walls: but to be obliged to live in
a tenement which is both unstable and ugly is disagreeable in a tenfold degree." He
thinks it is quite time to evoke legislation to remedy these evils, and says: "An
Englishman's house was formerly said to be his castle; but in the hands of the spec-
ulating builder and advertising tradesman, we may be grateful that it does not oftener
become his tomb."

relief processes of the author's pen-and-ink drawings, and with few exceptions are from his own sketches made on the spot; so that whatever they lack in artistic merit, they make up in being more or less accurate drawings of the objects and features depicted. The material has been gleaned from an illustrated daily journal, kept by the author during three successive residences in that delightful country, embracing travels by land from the northwest coast of Yezo to the southernmost parts of Satsuma.

The openness and accessibility of the Japanese house are a distinguishing feature of Japan; and no foreigner visits that country without bringing away delightful memories of the peculiarly characteristic dwellings of the Japanese.

On the occasion of the author's last visit to Japan he also visited China, Anam, Singapore, and Java, and made studies of the houses of these various countries, with special reference to the Japanese house and its possible affinities elsewhere.

JAPANESE HOMES

AND

THEIR SURROUNDINGS.

CHAPTER I.

THE HOUSE.

A BIRD'S-EYE view of a large city in Japan presents an appearance quite unlike that presented by any large assemblage of buildings at home. A view of Tokio, for example, from some elevated point reveals a vast sea of roofs, — the gray of the shingles and dark slate-color of the tiles, with dull reflections from their surfaces, giving a sombre effect to the whole. The even expanse is broken here and there by the fire-proof buildings, with their ponderous tiled roofs and ridges and pure white or jet-black walls. These, though in color adding to the sombre appearance, form, with the exception of the temples, one of the most conspicuous features in the general monotony. The temples are indeed conspicuous, as they tower far above the pigmy dwellings which surround them. Their great black roofs, with massive ridges and ribs, and grand sweeps and white or red gables, render them striking objects from whatever point they are viewed. Green

1

masses of tree-foliage springing from the numerous gardens add some life to this gray sea of domiciles.

It is a curious sight to look over a vast city of nearly a million inhabitants, and detect no chimney with its home-like streak of blue smoke. There is of course no church spire, with its usual architectural inanities. With the absence of chimneys and the almost universal use of charcoal for heating purposes, the cities have an atmosphere of remarkable clearness and purity; so clear, indeed, is the atmosphere that one may look over the city and see distinctly revealed the minuter details of the landscape beyond. The great sun-obscuring canopy of smoke and fumes that forever shroud some of our great cities is a feature happily unknown in Japan.

Having got such a bird's-eye view of one city, we have seen them all, — the minor variations consisting, for the most part, in the inequalities of the sites upon which they rest. A view of Kioto, for example, as seen from some high point, is remarkably beautiful and varied, as the houses creep out between the hills that hem it in. In Nagasaki the houses literally rise in tiers from the water's edge to the hills immediately back, there to become blended with the city of the dead which caps their summits. A view of Nagasaki from the harbor is one of surpassing interest and beauty. Other large cities, such as Sendai, Osaka, Hiroshima, and Nagoya present the same uniform level of roofs.

The compact way in which in the cities and towns the houses are crowded together, barely separated by the narrow streets and lanes which cross like threads in every direction, and the peculiarly inflammable material of which most of the buildings are composed, explains the lightning-like rapidity with which a conflagration spreads when once fairly under way.

In the smaller villages the houses are stretched along the sides of a single road, nearly all being arranged in this way,

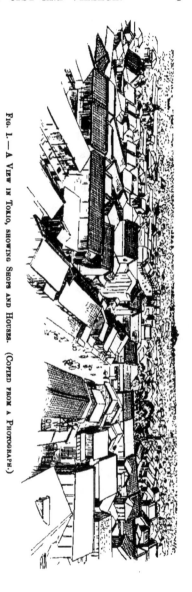

FIG. 1.—A VIEW IN TOKIO, SHOWING SHOPS AND HOUSES. (COPIED FROM A PHOTOGRAPH.)

FIG. 2.—A VIEW IN TOKIO, SHOWING TEMPLES AND GARDENS. (COPIED FROM A PHOTOGRAPH.)

sometimes extending for a mile or more. Rarely ever does one see a cross street or lane, or evidences of compactness, save that near the centre of this long street the houses and shops often abut, while those at the end of the streets have ample space between them. Some villages, which from their situation have no chance of expanding, become densely crowded: such for example is the case of Enoshima, near Yokohama, wherein the main street runs directly from the shore, by means of a series of steps at intervals, to a flight of stone steps, which lead to the temples and shrines at the summit of the island. This street is flanked on both sides by hills; and the ravine, of which the street forms the central axis, is densely crowded with houses, the narrowest of alley-ways leading to the houses in the rear. A fire once started would inevitably result in the destruction of every house in the village.

It is a curious fact that one may ride long distances in the country without passing a single dwelling, and then abruptly enter a village. The entrance to a village is often marked by a high mound of earth on each side of the road, generally surmounted by a tree; or perhaps the evidences of an old barrier are seen in the remains of gate-posts or a stone-wall. Having passed through the village one enters the country again, with its rice-fields and cultivated tracts, as abruptly as he had left it. The villages vary greatly in their appearance: some are extremely trim and pretty, with neat flower-plats in front of the houses, and an air of taste and comfort everywhere apparent; other villages present marked evidences of poverty, squalid houses with dirty children swarming about them. Indeed, the most striking contrasts are seen between the various villages one passes through in a long overland trip in Japan.

It is difficult to imagine a more dreary and dismal sight than the appearance of some of these village streets on a rainy night. No brightly-lighted window cheers the traveller; only

dim lines of light glimmer through the chinks of the wooden
shutters with which every house is closed at night. On pleasant
evenings when the paper screens alone are closed, a ride through
a village street is often rendered highly amusing by the grotesque
shadow-pictures which the inmates are unconsciously projecting
in their movements to and fro.

Fig. 3. — View of Enoshima. (Copied from a Photograph.)

In the cities the quarters for the wealthier classes are not
so sharply defined as with us, though the love for pleasant
outlooks and beautiful scenery tends to enhance the value of
certain districts, and consequently to bring together the wealthier
classes. In nearly all the cities, however, you will find the
houses of the wealthy in the immediate vicinity of the habitations of the poorest. In Tokio one may find streets, or narrow

alleys, lined with a continuous row of the cheapest shelters; and here dwell the poorest people. Though squalid and dirty as such places appear to the Japanese, they are immaculate in comparison with the unutterable filth and misery of similar quarters in nearly all the great cities of Christendom. Certainly a rich man in Japan would not, as a general thing, buy up the land about his house to keep the poorer classes at a distance, for the reason that their presence would not be objectionable, since poverty in Japan is not associated with the impossible manners of a similar class at home.

Before proceeding with a special description of Japanese homes, a general description of the house may render the chapters that are to follow a little more intelligible.

The first sight of a Japanese house, — that is, a house of the people, — is certainly disappointing. From the infinite variety and charming character of their various works of art, as we had seen them at home, we were anticipating new delights and surprises in the character of the house; nor were we on more intimate acquaintance to be disappointed. As an American familiar with houses of certain types, with conditions among them signifying poverty and shiftlessness, and other conditions signifying refinement and wealth, we were not competent to judge the relative merits of a Japanese house.

The first sight, then, of a Japanese house is disappointing; it is unsubstantial in appearance, and there is a meagreness of color. Being unpainted, it suggests poverty; and this absence of paint, with the gray and often rain-stained color of the boards, leads one to compare it with similar unpainted buildings at home, — and these are usually barns and sheds in the country, and the houses of the poorer people in the city. With one's eye accustomed to the bright contrasts of American houses with their white, or light, painted surfaces; rectangular windows, black from the shadows within, with glints of light reflected from the glass; front door with its pretentious steps and portico; warm red chimneys surmounting all, and a general trimness of appearance outside, which is by no means always correlated with like conditions within, — one is too apt at the outset to form a low estimate of a Japanese house. An American finds it difficult indeed to consider such a structure as a dwelling, when so many features are absent that go to make up a dwelling at home, — no doors or windows such as he had been familiar with; no attic or cellar; no chimneys, and within no fire-place, and of course no customary mantle; no permanently enclosed rooms; and as for furniture, no beds or tables, chairs or similar articles, — at least, so it appears at first sight.

One of the chief points of difference in a Japanese house as compared with ours lies in the treatment of partitions and outside walls. In our houses these are solid and permanent; and when the frame is built, the partitions form part of the framework. In the Japanese house, on the contrary, there are two or more sides that have no permanent walls. Within, also, there are but few partitions which have similar stability; in their stead are slight sliding screens which run in appropriate grooves in the floor and overhead. These grooves mark the limit of each room. The screens may be opened by sliding them back, or they may be entirely removed, thus throwing a number of rooms into one great apartment. In the same way the whole side of a house may be flung open to sunlight and air. For communication between the rooms, therefore, swinging doors are not necessary. As a substitute for windows, the outside screens, or *shōji*, are covered with white paper, allowing the light to be diffused through the house.

Where external walls appear they are of wood unpainted, or painted black; and if of plaster, white or dark slate colored. In certain classes of buildings the outside wall, to a height of several feet from the ground, and sometimes even the entire wall, may be tiled, the interspaces being pointed with white plaster. The roof may be either lightly shingled, heavily tiled, or thickly thatched. It has a moderate pitch, and as a general thing the slope is not so steep as in our roofs. Nearly all the houses have a verandah, which is protected by the widely-overhanging eaves of the roof, or by a light supplementary roof projecting from beneath the eaves.

While most houses of the better class have a definite porch and vestibule, or *genka*, in houses of the poorer class this entrance is not separate from the living room; and since the interior of the house is accessible from two or three sides, one may enter it from any point. The floor is raised a foot and a half or more from the ground, and is covered with thick straw mats, rectangular in shape, of uniform size, with sharp square edges, and so closely fitted that the floor upon which they rest is completely hidden. The rooms are either square or rectangular, and are made with absolute reference to the number of mats they are to contain. With the exception of the guest-room few rooms have projections or bays. In the guest-room there is at one side a more or less deep recess divided into two bays by a slight partition; the one nearest the verandah is called the *tokonoma*. In this place hang one or more pictures, and upon its floor, which is slightly raised above the mats, rests a flower vase, incense burner, or some other object. The companion bay has shelves and a low closet. Other rooms also may have recesses to accommodate a case of drawers or shelves. Where closets and cupboards occur, they are finished with sliding screens instead of swinging doors. In tea-houses of two stories the stairs, which often ascend from the vicinity of the kitchen, have beneath them a closet; and this is usually closed by a swinging door.

The privy is at one corner of the house, at the end of the verandah; sometimes there are two at diagonal corners of the house. In the poorer class of country houses the privy is an isolated building with low swinging door, the upper half of the door-space being open.

In city houses the kitchen is at one side or corner of the house; generally in an L, covered with a pent roof. This apartment is often towards the street, its yard separated from other areas by a high fence. In the country the kitchen is nearly always under the main roof. In the city few out-buildings such as sheds and barns are seen. Accompanying the houses of the better class are solid, thick-walled, one or two storied, fire-proof buildings called *kura*, in which the goods and chattels are stored away at the time of a conflagration. These buildings, which are known to the foreigners as "godowns," have one or two small windows and one door, closed by thick and ponderous shutters. Such a building usually stands isolated from the dwelling, though often in juxtaposition; and sometimes, though rarely, it is used as a domicile.

In the gardens of the better classes summer-houses and shelters of rustic appearance and diminutive proportions are often seen. Rustic arbors are also to be seen in the larger gardens. Specially constructed houses of quaint design and small size are not uncommon; in these the ceremonial tea-parties take place. High fences, either of board or bamboo, or solid walls of mud or tile with stone foundations, surround the house or enclose it from the street. Low rustic fences border the gardens in the suburbs. Gateways of various styles, some of imposing design, form the entrances; as a general thing they are either rustic and light, or formal and massive.

Whatever is commonplace in the appearance of the house is towards the street, while the artistic and picturesque face is turned towards the garden, which may be at one side or in the rear of the house, — usually in the rear. Within these plain and unpretentious houses there is often to be seen marvels of exquisite carving, and the perfection of cabinet work; and surprise follows surprise, as one becomes more fully acquainted with the interior finish of these curious and remarkable dwellings.

In the sections which are to follow, an attempt will be made by description and sketches to convey some idea of the details connected with the structure and inside finish of the Japanese house.

There is no object in Japan that seems to excite more diverse and adverse criticism among foreigners than does the Japanese house; it is a constant source of perplexity and annoyance to most of them. An Englishman particularly, whom Emerson says he finds "to be him of all men who stands firmest in his shoes," recognizes but little merit in the apparently frail and perishable nature of these structures. He naturally dislikes the anomaly of a house of the lightest description oftentimes sustaining a roof of the most ponderous character, and fairly loathes a structure that has no king-post, or at least a queen-post, truss; while the glaring absurdity of a house that persists in remaining upright without a foundation, or at least without his kind of a foundation, makes him furious. The mistake made by most writers in criticising Japanese house-structure, and indeed many other matters connected with that country, is that these writers do not regard such matters from a Japanese stand-point. They do not consider that the nation is poor, and that the masses are in poverty; nor do they consider that for this reason a Japanese builds such a house as he can afford, and one that after all is as thoroughly adapted to his habits and wants as ours is to our habits and wants.

The observation of a Japanese has shown him that from generation to generation the houses of his people have managed to sustain themselves; and if in his travels abroad he has chanced to visit England, he will probably recall the fact that he saw more dilapidated tenements, tumble-down shanties, broken-backed farm-houses, cracked walls, and toppling fences in a single day in that virtuous country where there are no typhoons or earthquakes, than he would see in a year's travel in his own country.

When one of these foreign critical writers contemplates the framework of a Japanese house, and particularly the cross-beams of the roof, and finds no attempt at trussing and bracing, he is seized with an eager desire to go among these people as a missionary of trusses and braces, — it is so obvious that much wood might be saved! In regard to the Japanese house-frame, however, it is probable that the extra labor of constructing braces and trusses would not compensate for the difference saved in the wood.

Rein, in his really admirable book on Japan, says "the Japanese house lacks chiefly solidity and comfort." If he means comfort for himself and his people, one can understand him; if he means comfort for the Japanese, then he has not the faintest conception of the solid comfort a Japanese gets out of his house. Rein also complains of the evil odors of the closet arrangements, though his complaints refer more particularly to the crowded inns, which are often in an exceedingly filthy condition as regards these necessary conveniences, — and one is led to inquire what the Japanese would think of similar features in Germany, where in the larger cities the closet may be seen opening directly into the front hall, and in some cases even from the dining-room! Bad as some of these conditions are in Japan, they are mild in comparison with like features in Germany. The filthy state of the larger cities, in this respect, may be indicated by the fact that the death-rate of Munich a few years ago was forty-four, and Kaulbach died of cholera in that city in mid-winter! Indeed, the presence of certain features in every bed-chamber at home and abroad are looked upon as surpassingly filthy by every Japanese, — as they truly are.

Rein and other writers speak of the want of privacy in Japanese dwellings, forgetting that privacy is only necessary in the midst of vulgar and impertinent people, — a class of which Japan has the minimum, and the so-called civilized races — the English and American particularly — have the maximum.

For my part, I find much to admire in a Japanese house, and some things not to my comfort. The sitting posture on the floor is painful until one gets accustomed to it; and, naturally, I find that our chairs are painful to the Japanese, until they become accustomed to them.   I found the Japanese house in winter extremely cold and uncomfortable; but I question whether their cold rooms in winter are not more conducive to health than are our apartments with our blistering stoves, hot furnaces or steam-heaters ; and as to the odors arising from the closet in certain country inns, who does not recall similar offensive features in many of our country inns at home, with the addition of slovenly yards and reeking piggeries? I question, too, whether these odors are more injurious to the health than is the stifling air from a damp and noisome cellar, which not only filters through our floors, but is often served to us hot through scorching furnaces. Whittier's description of the country house, —

> " The best room
> Stifling with cellar-damp, shut from the air
> In hot midsummer," —

is only too true of many of our American houses both in the country and city.

Whether the Japanese house is right or wrong in its plan and construction, it answers admirably the purposes for which it was intended. A fire-proof building is certainly beyond the means of a majority of this people, as, indeed, it is with us; and not being able to build such a dwelling, they have from necessity gone to the other extreme, and built a house whose very structure enables it to be rapidly demolished in the path of a conflagration. Mats, screen-partitions, and even the board ceilings can be quickly packed up and carried away. The roof is rapidly denuded of its tiles and boards, and the skeleton framework left makes but slow fuel for the flames. The efforts of the firemen in checking the progress of a conflagration consist mainly in tearing down these adjustable structures; and in this connection it may be interesting to record the curious fact that oftentimes at a fire the streams are turned, not upon the flames, but upon the men engaged in tearing down the building!

The improvements, however, that are imperatively demanded in Japanese house-structure are such modifications as shall render the building less inflammable. While these inflammable houses may be well enough in the suburbs or in country villages, they are certainly quite out of place in cities; and here, indeed, the authorities are justified in imposing such restrictions as shall not bear too heavily upon the people.

The Japanese should clearly understand that insuperable difficulties are to be encountered in any attempt to modify their style of dwellings, and that many of such proposed modifications are neither judicious nor desirable. That slight changes for safety may be effected, however, there can be no doubt. Through the agency of science, means may be found by which outside woodwork may be rendered less inflammable, — either by fire-proof paint or other devices.

The mean path of Tokio conflagrations has been ingeniously worked out by Professor Yamakawa, from data extending back two hundred years; and in this path certain areas might be left open with advantage. Fire-proof blocks in foreign style, such as now exist on the Ginza, may be ultimately constructed in this path. Since the last great conflagration, the Tokio authorities have specified certain districts within which shingled roofs shall not be made; and where such roofs existed, the authorities have compelled the substitution of tin, zinc, or tiled roofs. Above all,

let there be a reorganization, under Government, of the present
corrupt fire-brigades. Such changes will certainly lead to good
results; but as to altering the present plan of house-building and
present modes of living, it is not only impracticable but well-nigh
impossible. If such changes are effected, then will perish many of
the best features of true Japanese art, which has been the surprise and admiration of Western nations, and of which in the
past they have been the unwitting cause of the modification and
degradation it has already undergone.

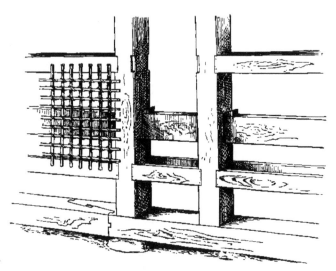

Fig. 4. — Side Framing.

The frame-work of an ordinary Japanese dwelling is simple
and primitive in structure; it consists of a number of upright
beams which run from the ground to the transverse beams and
inclines of the roof above. The vertical framing is held together
either by short strips which are let in to appropriate notches
in the uprights to which the bamboo lathing is fixed, or by

longer strips of wood which pass through mortises in the uprights
and are firmly keyed or pinned into place (fig. 4). In larger
houses these uprights are held in position by a frame-work near
the ground. There is no cellar or excavation beneath the house,
nor is there a continuous stone foundation as with us. The uprights rest directly, and without attachment, upon single uncut or
rough-hewn stones, these in turn resting upon others which have

Fig. 5. — POUNDING DOWN FOUNDATION STONES.

been solidly pounded into the earth by means of a huge wooden
maul worked by a number of men (fig. 5). In this way the house
is perched upon these stones, with the floor elevated at least a foot
and a half or two feet above the ground. In some cases the space
between the uprights is boarded up; this is generally seen in
Kioto houses. In others the wind has free play beneath; and
while this exposed condition renders the house much colder and
more uncomfortable in winter, the inmates are never troubled by
the noisome air of the cellar, which, as we have said, too often

infects our houses at home. Closed wooden fences of a more
solid character are elevated in this way; that is, the lower rail
or sill of the fence rests directly upon stones placed at intervals
apart of six or eight feet. The ravages of numerous ground-
insects, as well as larvae, and the excessive dampness of the
ground at certain seasons of the year, render this method of
building a necessity.

The accurate way in which the base of the uprights is
wrought to fit the inequalities of the stones upon which they
rest, is worthy of notice. In the
Emperor's garden we saw a two-
storied house finished in the most
simple and exquisite manner. It
was, indeed, like a beautiful cabinet, though disfigured by a
bright-colored foreign carpet upon its lower floor. The uprights
of this structure rested on large
oval beach-worn stones buried
endwise in the ground; and upon the smooth rounded portions
of the stones, which projected
above the level of the ground
to a height of ten inches or more,
the uprights had been most accur-

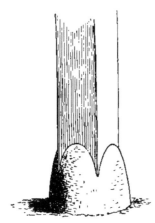

Fig 6. — Foundation Stone.

ately fitted (fig. 6). The effect was extremely light and buoyant,
though apparently insecure to the last degree; yet this building
had not only withstood a number of earthquake shocks, but also
the strain of severe typhoons, which during the summer months
sweep over Japan with such violence. If the building be very
small, then the frame consists of four corner-posts running to
the roof. In dwellings having a frontage of two or more rooms,
other uprights occur between the corner-posts. As the rooms

increase in number through the house, uprights come in the corners of the rooms, against which the sliding-screens, or *fusuma,* abut. The passage of these uprights through the room to the

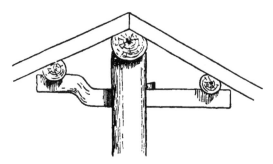

FIG. 7. — SECTION OF FRAMING.

roof above gives a solid constructive appearance to the house. When a house has a verandah, — and nearly every house possesses this feature on one or more of its sides, — another row of uprights starts in a line with the outer edge of the verandah. Unless the verandah be very long, an upright at each end is sufficient to support the supplementary roof which shelters it. These uprights support a cross-beam, upon which the slight rafters of the supplementary roof rests.

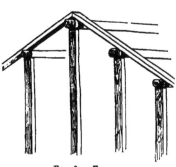

FIG. 8. — FRAMING.

This cross-beam is often a straight unhewn stick of timber from which the bark has been removed (fig. 49). Indeed, most of the horizontal framing-timbers, as well as the rafters, are usually unhewn, — the rafters often having the bark on, or perhaps being accurately squared sticks; but in either case they are always visible as they project from the sides of the house, and run out to support the overhanging eaves. The larger beams and girders are but slightly hewn; and it is not unusual to see

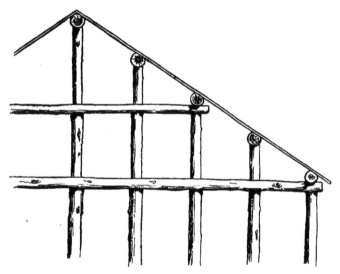

FIG. 9. — END-FRAMING OF LARGE BUILDING.

irregular-shaped beams worked into the construction of a frame, often for their quaint effects (fig. 7), and in many cases as a matter of economy (fig. 39).

For a narrow house, if the roof be a gable, a central upright at each end of the building gives support to the ridge-pole from which the rafters run to the eaves (fig. 8). If the building be wide, a transverse beam traverses the end of the building on a level with the eaves, supported at intervals by uprights from the ground; and upon this short uprights rest, supporting

another transverse beam above, and often three or more tiers
are carried nearly to the ridge. Upon these supports rest the
horizontal beams which run parallel with the ridge-pole, and
which are intended to give support to the rafters (fig. 9).

In the case of a wide gable-roof there are many ways to
support the frame, one of which is illustrated in the following
outline (fig. 10). Here a stout stick of timber runs from one
end of the house to the other on a vertical line with the
ridge-pole, and on a level with the eaves. This stick is always
crowning, in order to give additional strength. A few thick
uprights start from this to support the ridge-pole above; from

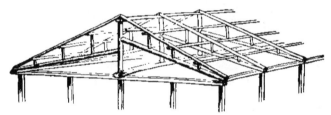

Fig. 10. — Roof-frame of large Building.

these uprights beams run to the eaves; these are mortised into
the uprights, but at different levels on either side in order
not to weaken the uprights by the mortises. From these beams
run short supports to the horizontal rafters above.

The roof, if it be of tile or thatch, represents a massive
weight, — the tiles being thick and quite heavy, and always
bedded in a thick layer of mud. The thatch, though not so
heavy, often becomes so after a long rain. The roof-framing
consequently has oftentimes to support a great weight; and
though in its structure looking weak, or at least primitive in
design, yet experience must have taught the Japanese carpenter
that their methods were not only the simplest and most economical, but that they answered all requirements. One is amazed

to see how many firemen can gather upon such a roof without
its yielding. I have seen massive house-roofs over two hundred
years old, and other frame structures of a larger size and of
far greater age, which presented no visible signs of weakness.
Indeed, it is a very unusual sight to see a broken-backed roof
in Japan.

The beams that support the roofs of the fire-proof buildings, or
kura, are usually rough-hewn and of ponderous dimensions. It

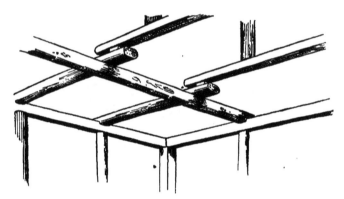

FIG. 11. — ROOF-FRAMING OF KURA.

would seem that here, at least, the foreign method of trussing
might be an economy of material, besides giving much greater
strength; and yet the expense of reducing these beams to
proper dimensions, in the absence of saw-mills and other labor-
saving machinery, with the added expense of iron rods, bolts, etc.,
would more than counterbalance the saving of material (fig. 11).
In Fig. 11 is shown the universal method of roof support;
namely, horizontal beams resting upon perpendicular walls, these
in turn supporting vertical beams, which again give support to
horizontal beams. That the Japanese have been familiar with the
arch is seen in some of their old stone bridges; but they seem as

averse to using this principle in their house-architecture as were the Egyptians and Hindus. Furgusson, in his illustrated Hand-book of Architecture, page xxxv, says: "So convinced were the Egyptians and Greeks of this principle, that they never used any other construction-expedient than a perpendicular wall or prop, supporting a horizontal beam; and half the satisfactory effect of their buildings arises from their adhering to this simple though expensive mode of construction. They were perfectly acquainted with the use of the arch and its properties, but they knew that its employment would introduce complexity and confusion into their designs, and therefore they wisely rejected it. Even to the present day the Hindus refuse to use the arch, though it has long been employed in their country by the Mahometans. As they quaintly express it, 'an arch never sleeps;' and it is true that by its thrusting and pressure it is always tending to tear a building to pieces. In spite of all counterpoises, whenever the smallest damage is done it hastens the ruin of a building which, if more simply constructed, might last for ages."

When the frame is mortised, the carpenter employs the most elaborate methods of mortising, of which there are many different formulas; yet I was informed by an American architect that their ways had no advantage as regards strength over those employed by our carpenters in doing the same work. There certainly seems to be much unnecessary work about many of their framing-joints. This same gentleman greatly admired the way in which the Japanese carpenter used the adze, and regretted that more of this kind of work was not done in America. In scarfing beams a common form of joint is made, precisely similar to that made by our carpenters (fig. 4). This joint is called a *Samisen tsugi*, it being similar to the joint in the handle of a guitar-like instrument called a *samisen*.[1]

[1] Fig. 12 represents the frame-work of an ordinary two-storied house. It is copied from a Japanese carpenter's drawing, kindly furnished the writer by Mr. Fukusawa, of Tokio, proper corrections in perspective having been made. The various parts have been

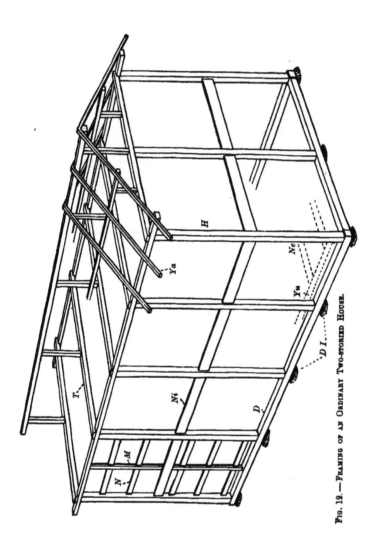

Fig. 12.—Framing of an Ordinary Two-storied House.

Diagonal bracing in the frame-work of a building is never seen. Sometimes, however, the uprights in a weak frame are supported by braces running from the ground at an acute angle, and held in place by wooden pins (fig. 13). Outside diagonal braces are sometimes met with as an ornamental feature. In the province of Ise one often sees a brace or bracket made out of an un-hewn piece of timber, generally the proximal portion of some big branch. This is fastened to an upright, and appears to be a brace to hold up the end of a horizontal beam that projects beyond the eaves. These braces, however, are not even notched

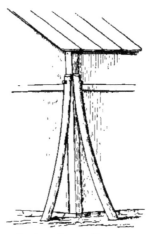

FIG. 13.—OUTSIDE BRACES.

lettered, and the dimensions given in Japanese feet and inches. The Japanese foot is, within the fraction of an inch, the same as ours, and is divided into ten parts, called *sun*. The wood employed in the frame is usually cedar or pine. The corner posts, as well as the other large upright posts, called *hashira* (*H*), are square, and five *sun* in thickness; these are tenoned into the plate upon which they rest. This plate is called *do-dai* (*D*); it is made of cedar, and sometimes of chestnut. The *do-dai* is six *sun* square, and rests directly on a number of stones, which are called *do-dai-ishi* (*D*, 1). Between the *hashira* come smaller uprights, called *ma-bashira* (*M*) (*hashira* changed to *bashira* for euphony); these are two *sun* square. Through these pass the cross-pieces called *nuki*; these are four *sun* wide and one *sun* thick. To these are attached the bamboo slats as substitutes for laths. The horizontal beam to support the second-story floor is called the *nikaibari* (*Ni*); this is of pine, with a vertical thickness of one foot two *sun*, and a width of six tenths of a *sun*. The rafters of the roof, called *yane-shita* (*Ya*), in this frame are nine feet long, three *sun* wide, and eight tenths of a *sun* in thickness. Cross-beams (*T*), from the upper plate from which spring posts to support the ridge-pole, are called *taruki*. The first floor is sustained by posts that rest on stones embedded in the ground, as well as by a beam called *yuka-shita* (*Yu*); this is secured to the upright beams at the height of one and one-half or two feet above the *do-dai*. The upper floor-joists are of pine, two inches square; the flooring boards are six tenths of a *sun* in thickness, and one foot wide. The lower floor-joists, called *neda-maruta* (*Ne*), are rough round sticks, three *sun* in diameter, hewn on opposite sides. On top of these rest pine boards six tenths of a *sun* in thickness.

into the upright, but held in place by square wooden pins, and are
of little use as a support for the building, though answering well
to hold fishing-rods and other long poles, which find here convenient lodgment (fig. 14).

In the village of Naruge, in Yamato, I noticed in an old inn
a diagonal brace which made a pleasing ornamental feature to a

solid frame-work, upon which
rested a ponderous supplementary roof, heavily tiled. As the
horizontal beams were supported
by uprights beyond the ends
of the brackets, no additional
strength was gained by these
braces in question, except as they
might prevent fore and aft displacement. They were placed
here solely for their ornamental
appearance; or at least that was
all the function they appeared to
perform (fig. 15).

FIG. 14. — OUTSIDE BRACE.

The frame-work of a building
is often revealed in the room in
a way that would delight the heart of an Eastlake. Irregularities in the form of a stick are not looked upon as a hindrance in
the construction of a building. From the way such crooked
beams are brought into use, one is led to believe that the builder
prefers them. The desire for rustic effects leads to the selection
of odd-shaped timber. Fig. 7 represents the end of a room,
wherein is seen a crooked cross-piece passing through a central
upright, which sustains the ridge-pole.

In the finish of the rooms great care is shown in the selection
and preparation of the wood. For the better rooms the wood is

selected as follows : First, a stick of timber is sawed (fig. 16), — the central piece (*A*) being rejected as liable to split. Second,

in the round upright post that in most instances forms the front of the shallow partition that divides one end of the best room into two bays or recesses, a deep groove is cut, to admit the edge of the partition (fig. 17). By this treatment the wood is not so apt to check or split.

Special details of the room will be described in other chapters. It may be well to state here, however, that in the finish of

Fig. 15. — ORNAMENTAL BRACE.

the interior the *daiku,* or carpenter, has finished his work, and a

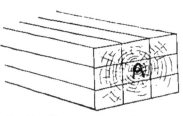

Fig. 16. — METHOD OF CUTTING TIMBER FOR HOUSE-FINISH.

new set of workmen, the *sashimono ya,* or cabinet-makers, come in, — the rough framing and similar work being done by the carpenter proper. Great care is taken to secure wood that matches in grain and color; and this can be done only by getting material that has come from the same log. In the lumber-yard one notices boards of uniform lengths tied up in bundles, — in fact tied up in precisely the same position that the wood occupied in the trunk before it was sawed into boards (fig. 18). So with other wood material, — the pieces are kept together in the same manner.   One never sees in a lumber-yard a promis-

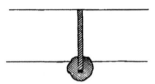

cuous pile of boards, but each log having been cut into boards is securely tied without displacement.

As the rooms are made in sizes corresponding to the number of mats they are to contain, the beams, uprights, rafters, flooring-boards, boards for the ceiling, and

FIG. 17. — SECTION OF POST GROOVED
FOR PARTITION.

all strips are got out in sizes to accommodate these various dimensions.   The dimensions of the mats from one end of the Empire to the other are approximately three feet wide and six feet long; and these are fitted compactly on the floor.   The

architect marks on his plan the number of mats each room is to contain, — this number defining the size of the room; hence the lumber used must be of definite lengths, and the carpenter is sure to find these lengths at the lumber-yard.   It

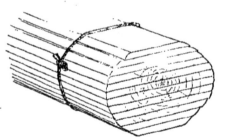

FIG. 18. — BUNDLE OF BOARDS.

follows from this that but little waste occurs in the construction of a Japanese house.   Far different is it with us in our extravagant and senseless methods of house-building.   In our country, a man after building a wooden house finds his cellar and shed choked to repletion with the waste of his new house, and for a year or more at least has the grim comfort of feeding his fireplaces and kitchen stove with rough and finished woods which have cost him at the rate of four to eight cents per square foot !

The ordinary ceiling in a Japanese house consists of wide thin boards, with their edges slightly overlapping. These boards at first sight appear to be supported by narrow strips of wood like slender beams, upon which the boards rest (fig. 96). On reflection, however, it soon becomes apparent that these diminu-

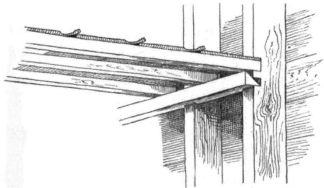

Fig. 19. — Section of Ceiling.

tive cross-beams, measuring in section an inch square or less, are altogether inadequate to support the ceiling, thin and light as the boards composing it really are. As one examines the ceiling, he finds no trace of pin or nail, and finally comes to wonder how the strips and boards are held in place, and why the whole ceiling does not sag.[1] The explanation is that the strips upon which the boards are to rest are first stretched across the room at distances apart varying from ten to eighteen

[1] The accompanying sketches will illustrate the various stages in the construction of the ceiling.

inches. The ends of these strips are supported by a moulding which is secured to the uprights of the wall. In cheap houses this moulding in section is angular; notches are cut in the uprights, and into these notches the sharp edge of the angular moulding rests and is secured (fig. 19). The moulding is cut in this way to economize material. The strips having been adjusted,

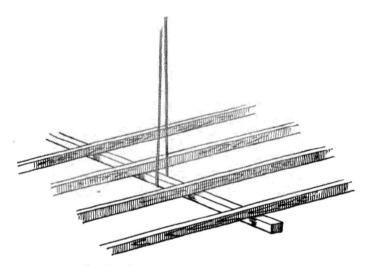

FIG. 20. — CEILING-RAFTERS SUPPORTED TEMPORARILY.

they are brought to a uniform level, but crowning slightly, — that is, the centre is a little higher than the sides, — and are held in place either by a long board being placed temporarily beneath them, and propped up from the floor below; or else a long stick is placed beneath them, which is supported by a stout string from the rafters above (fig. 20). A low staging is then erected on the floor (the stud of the room rarely being over seven or eight feet); and the carpenter standing between the cross-strips, while elevated upon the staging, adjusts the boards, one after the other, as they are passed up to him. The first board is placed against the wall, its edge fitting into a groove in the uprights; the next board is placed with its edge on the first board, and then nailed from above, with wooden or bamboo pegs, to the cross-strips. Thus it is that no nail or peg holes appear in the ceiling from below. Board after board is thus placed in position, each board lapping slightly over the one before it, and each in turn being slightly nailed to the strips. Each board has a deep wide groove ploughed out near its lapping edge, so that it bends very readily, and is thus

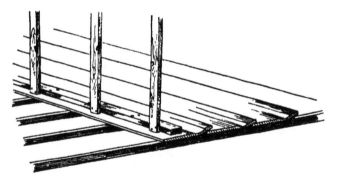

FIG. 21. — METHOD OF SUSPENDING CEILING AS SEEN FROM ABOVE.

brought down on the strip below. When the boards are carried in this manner half way across the room, a long, narrow, and thick piece of wood, say six feet in length, is placed on the last board laid, within an inch of its free edge and parallel to it. This piece is firmly nailed to the board upon which it rests, and into the cross-strips below. To the edge of this piece two or three long strips of wood are nailed vertically, the upper ends being nailed to the nearest rafters above. In this way is the ceiling suspended (fig. 21). After this has been done, the remaining boards of the ceiling are placed in position and secured, one after another, until the last is reached.   To secure the last one in position the carpenter gets down from his position and adopts other methods.   One method is to place this board on

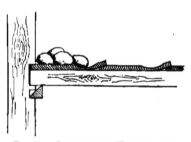

the last one secured and weight it with a few heavy stones, and then it is moved along from below and placed in position, where it remains quite as firm as if it had been lightly nailed (fig. 22).   In case there is a closet in the room or a recess, the last board is sawed into

FIG. 22. — CEILING-BOARD WEIGHTED WITH STONES.

two or three lengths, and these are placed in position, one after another, and nailed from above to the cross-strips, — care being taken to have these sections come directly over the cross-strips, so that from below the appearance is that of a continuous board.

The sections are so arranged, as to length, that the last piece comes in the closet; and this may either be weighted with stones or left out altogether (fig. 23).

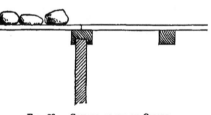

FIG. 23. — CEILING-BOARD IN CLOSET.

We have been thus explicit in describing the ceiling, because so few even among the Japanese seem to understand precisely the manner in which it is suspended.

In long rooms one is oftentimes surprised to see boards of great width composing the ceiling, and apparently continuous from one end of the room to the other.   What appears to be a single board is in fact composed of a number of short lengths. The matching of the grain and color is accomplished by taking two adjacent boards in a bundle of boards, as previously figured and described, and placing them so that the same ends come together (fig. 24), — care being taken, of course, to have the joints come directly over the cross-pieces. The graining of the wood becomes continuous, each line of the grain and the color being of course duplicated and matched in the other board. Sometimes a number of lengths of board may be continued in this way, and yet from below the appearance is that of a single long piece.

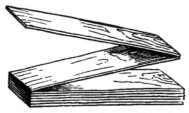

FIG. 24. — METHOD OF REMOVING BOARDS FROM BUNDLE TO PRESERVE UNIFORMITY OF GRAIN.

The advantage of keeping all the boards of a given log in juxta-position will be readily understood. In our country a carpenter has to ransack a lumber-yard to find wood of a similar grain and color; and even then he generally fails to get wood of precisely the same kind.

The permanent partitions within the house are made in various ways. In one method, bamboo strips of various lengths take the place of laths. Small bamboos are first nailed in a vertical position to the wooden strips, which are fastened from one upright to another; narrow strips of bamboo are then secured across these bamboos by means of coarse cords of straw, or bark fibre (fig. 4). This partition is not unlike our own plaster-and-lath partition. Another kind of partition may be of boards; and against these small bamboo rods are nailed quite close together, and upon this the plaster is put. Considerable pains are taken as to the plastering. The plasterer brings to the house samples of various-colored sands and clays, so that one may select from these the color of his wall. A good coat of plaster comprises three layers. The first layer, called *shita-nuri*, is composed of mud, in which chopped straw is mixed; a second layer, called *chu-nuri*, of rough lime, mixed with mud; the third layer, called *uwa-nuri*, has the colored clay or sand mixed with lime, — and this last layer is always applied by a skilful workman. Other methods of treating this surface will be given in the chapter on interiors.

Many of the partitions between the rooms consist entirely of light sliding screens, which will be specially described farther on. Often two or more sides of the house are composed entirely of these simple and frail devices. The outside permanent walls of a house, if of wood, are made of thin boards nailed to the frame horizontally, — as we lay clapboards on our houses. These may be more firmly held to the house by long strips nailed against the boards vertically. The boards may also be secured to the house vertically, and weather-strips nailed over the seams, — as is commonly the way with certain of our houses. In the southern provinces a rough house-wall is made of wide slabs of bark, placed vertically, and held in place by thin strips of bamboo nailed cross-wise. This style is common among the poorer houses in Japan; and, indeed, in the better class of houses it is often used as an ornamental feature, placed at the height of a few feet from the ground.

Outside plastered walls are also very common, though not of a durable nature. This kind of wall is frequently seen in a dilapidated condition. In Japanese picture-books this broken condition is often shown, with the bamboo slats exposed, as a suggestion of poverty.

In the cities, the outside walls of more durable structures, such as warehouses, are not infrequently covered with square tiles, a board wall being first made, to which the tiles are secured by being nailed at their corners. These may be placed in diagonal or horizontal rows, — in either case an interspace of a quarter of an inch being left between the tiles, and the seams closed with white plaster, spreading on each side to the width of an inch or more, and finished with a rounded surface. This work is done in a very tasteful and artistic manner, and the effect of the dark-gray tiles crossed by these white bars of plaster is very striking (fig. 25).

As the fire-proof buildings, or *kura,* are often used as dwelling - places, a brief mention of their structure may be proper here. These buildings are specially designed for fire-proof store-houses. They are generally two stories in height, with walls eighteen inches to two feet or more in thickness, composed of mud plastered on

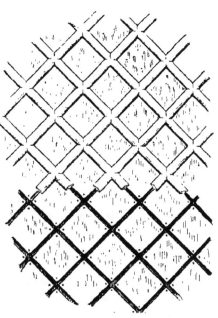

Fig. 25. — ARRANGEMENT OF SQUARE TILES ON SIDE OF HOUSE.

to a frame-work of great strength and solidity. The beams are closely notched, and bound with a coarse-fibred rope; and small bamboos are closely secured to the beams. Short coarse-fibred ropes, a foot in length, are secured in close rows to the cross-beams and uprights. All these preparations are made for the purpose of more securely holding the successive layers of mud

3

to be applied. As a preliminary to this work a huge and ample staging is erected to completely envelop the building. The staging, indeed, forms a huge cage, and upon this straw mattings are hung . so that the mud plastering shall not dry too quickly. This cage is sufficiently ample to allow the men to work freely around and beneath it. Layer after layer is applied, and a long time elapses between these applications, in order that each layer may dry properly. Two years or more are required in the proper construction of one of these fire-proof buildings. The walls having been finished, a coat of plaster, or a plaster mixed with lamp-black, is applied, and a . fine polished surface, like black lacquer, is produced. This polished black surface is made by first rubbing with a cloth, then with silk, and finally with the hand.

A newly-finished *kura* presents a remarkably solid and imposing appearance. The roofs are of immense thickness, with enormous ridges ornamented with artistic designs in stucco, and the ridges terminating with ornamental tiles in high-relief. The fine polish of these buildings soon becomes impaired, and they finally assume a dull black or slaty color; sometimes a coat of white plaster is applied. Upon the outside of the wall a series of long iron hooks are seen; these are to hold an adjustable wooden casing which is often used to cover the walls, and thus to protect them from the eroding action of the elements. These wooden casings are placed against the buildings, proper openings being left through which the iron hooks project, and long slender bars of wood stretch across the wall, held in place by the upturned ends of the iron hooks, and in turn holding the wooden casing in place.

The windows of the buildings are small, and each is closed either by a sliding-door of great thickness and solidity, or by double-shutters swinging together. The edges of these shutters have a series of rabbets, or steps, precisely like those seen in the heavy doors of a bank-safe. At the time of a fire, additional precautions are taken by stopping up the chinks of these closed shutters with mud, which is always at hand, ready mixed for such an emergency. These buildings, when properly constructed, seem to answer their purpose admirably; and after a conflagration, when all the surrounding territory is absolutely flat, — for there are no tottering chimneys or cavernous cellars and walls to be seen, as with us, — these black, grimy *kura* stand conspicuous in the general ruin. They do not all survive, however, as smoke is often seen issuing from some of them, indicating that, as in our own country, safes are not always fire-proof.

A somewhat extended experience with the common every-day carpenter at home leads me to say, without fear of contradiction, that in matters pertaining to their craft the Japanese carpenters are superior to American. Not only do they show their superiority in their work, but in their versatile ability in making new things. One is amazed to see how patiently a Japanese carpenter or cabinet-maker will struggle over plans, not only drawn in ways new and strange to him, but of objects equally new, — and struggle successfully. It is a notorious fact that most of the carpenters in our smaller towns and villages are utterly incompetent to carry out any special demand made upon them, outside the building of the conventional two-storied house and ordinary roof. They stand bewildered in the presence of a window-projection or cornice outside the prescribed ruts with which they and their fathers were familiar. Indeed, in most cases their fathers were not carpenters, nor will their children be; and herein alone the Japanese carpenter has an immense advantage over the American, for his trade, as well as other trades, have been perpetuated through generations of families. The little children have been brought up amidst the odor of fragrant shavings, — have with childish hands performed the duties of an adjustable vise or clamp; and with the same tools which when children they have handed to their fathers, they have in later days earned their daily rice.

When I see one of our carpenters' ponderous tool-chests, made of polished woods, inlaid with brass decorations, and filled to repletion with several hundred dollars' worth of highly polished and elaborate machine-made implements, and contemplate the work often done with them, — with everything binding that should go loose, and everything rattling that should be tight, and much work that has to be done twice over, with an indication everywhere of a poverty of ideas, — and then recall the Japanese carpenter with his ridiculously light and flimsy tool-box containing a meagre assortment of rude and primitive tools, — considering the carpentry of the two people, I am forced to the conviction that civilization and modern appliances count as nothing unless accompanied with a moiety of brains and some little taste and wit.

It is a very serious fact that now-a-days no one in our country is acquiring faithfully the carpenter's trade. Much of this lamentable condition of things is no doubt due to the fact that machine-work has supplanted the hand-work of former times.[1] Doors, blinds, sashes, mouldings are now turned out by the cord and mile, and all done in such greedy haste, and with the greenest of lumber, that if it does not tumble to pieces in transportation it is sure to do so very soon after entering into the house-structure. Nevertheless, the miserable truth yet remains that any man who has nailed up a few boxes, or stood in front of a circular

[1] General Francis A. Walker, in his Lowell Lectures on the United States Census for 1880, shows that carpenters constitute the largest single body of artisans working for the supply of local wants. He shows that the increase of this body from decade to decade is far behind what it should be if it increased in the ratio of the population; and though this fact might excite surprise, he shows that it is due to the enormous increase in machine-made material, such as doors, sashes, blinds, etc.; in other words, to the making of those parts which in former times trained a man in delicate work and accurate joinery.

saw for a few months, feels competent to exercise all the duties of that most honorable craft, — the building of a house.[1]

It may be interesting, in this connection, to mention a few of the principal tools one commonly sees in use among the Japanese carpenters. After having seen the good and serviceable carpentry, the perfect joints and complex mortises, done by good Japanese workmen, one is astonished to find that they do their work without the aid of certain appliances considered indispensable by similar craftsmen in our country. They have no bench, no vise, no spirit-level, and no bit-stock; and as for labor-saving machinery, they have absolutely nothing. With many places which could be utilized for water-power, the old country saw-mill has not occurred to them.[2] Their tools appear to be roughly made, and of primitive design, though evidently of the best-tempered steel. The only substitute for the carpenter's bench is a plank

[1] There is no question but that in England apprentices serve their time at trades more faithfully than with us; nevertheless, the complaints that go up in the English press in regard to poor and slovenly work show the existence of a similar class of impostors, who defraud the public by claiming to be what they are not. The erratic Charles Reade, in a series of letters addressed to the "Pall Mall Gazette," on builders' blunders, inveighs against the British workmen as follows: "When last seen, I was standing on the first floor of the thing they call a house, with a blunder under my feet, — unvarnished, unjoined boards; and a blunder over my head, — the oppressive, glaring plaster-ceiling, full of the inevitable cracks, and foul with the smoke of only three months' gas." In regard to sash windows, he says: "This room is lighted by what may be defined 'the unscientific window.' Here, in this single structure, you may see most of the intellectual vices that mark the unscientific mind. The scientific way is always the simple way; so here you have complication on complication, — one half the window is to go up, the other half is to come down. The maker of it goes out of his way to struggle with Nature's laws; he grapples insanely with gravitation, and therefore he must use cords and weights and pulleys, and build boxes to hide them in. He is a great hider. His wooden frames move up and down wooden grooves, open to atmospheric influence. What is the consequence? The atmosphere becomes humid; the wooden frame sticks in the wooden box, and the unscientific window is jammed. What, ho! Send for the CURSE OF FAMILIES, the British workman! On one of the cords breaking (they are always breaking), send for the CURSE OF FAMILIES to patch the blunder of the unscientific builder."

[2] A Government bureau called the *Kaitakushi*, now fortunately extinct, established in Yezo, the seat of its labors, one or two saw-mills; but whether they are still at work I do not know.

on the floor, or on two horses; a square, firm, upright post is the nearest approach to a bench and vise, for to this beam a block of wood to be sawed into pieces is firmly held (fig. 26). A big wooden wedge is bound firmly to the post with a stout rope, and this driven down with vigorous blows till it pinches the block which is to be cut into the desired proportions.

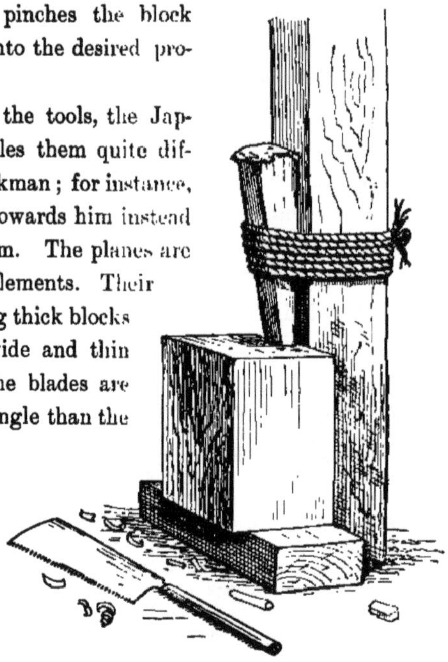

In using many of the tools, the Japanese carpenter handles them quite differently from our workman; for instance, he draws the plane towards him instead of pushing it from him. The planes are very rude-looking implements. Their bodies, instead of being thick blocks of wood, are quite wide and thin (fig. 27, *D, E*), and the blades are inclined at a greater angle than the blade in our plane. In some planes, however, the blade stands vertical; this is used in lieu of the steel scrapers in giving wood a smooth finish, and might be used with advantage

Fig. 26. — A Japanese Carpenter's Vise.

by our carpenters as a substitute for the piece of glass or thin plate of steel with which they usually scrape the surface of the wood. A huge plane is often seen, five or six feet long. This plane, however, is fixed in an inclined position, upside down; that is, with the blade uppermost. The board, or piece to be planed, is moved back and forth upon it.

Draw-shaves are in common use. The saws are of various kinds, with teeth much longer than those of our saws, and cut in different ways. Some of these forms reminded me of the teeth seen in certain recently patented saws in the United States. Some saws have teeth on the back as well as on the front, one edge being used as a cross-cut saw (fig. 27 *B*, *C*). The hand-saw, instead of having the curious loop-shaped handle made to accommodate only one hand as with us, has a simple

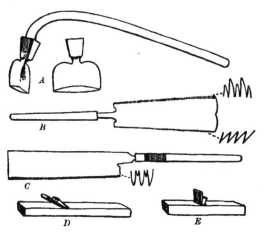

Fig. 27. — Carpenters' Tools in Common Use.

straight cylindrical handle as long as the saw itself, and sometimes longer. Our carpenters engage one hand in holding the stick to be sawed, while driving the saw with the other hand ; the Japanese carpenter, on the contrary, holds the piece with his foot, and stooping over, with his two hands drives the saw by quick and rapid cuts through the wood. This style of working and doing many other things could never be adopted in this country without an importation of Japanese backs. It was an extraordinary sight to see the attitudes these people assumed in doing work of various kinds. A servant girl, for example, in wiping up the floor or verandah with a wet cloth, does not get down on her knees to do her work, but bending over while still on her feet, she pushes the cloth back and forth, and thus in this trying position performs her task.

The adze is provided with a rough handle bending considerably at the lower end, not unlike a hockey-stick (fig. 27, *A*). In summer the carpenters work with the scantiest clothing possible, and nearly always barefooted. It is a startling sight to a nervous man to see a carpenter standing on a stick of timber, hacking away in a furious manner with this crooked-handled instrument having an edge as sharp as a razor, and taking off great chips of the wood within an inch of his naked toes. Never having ourselves seen a toeless carpenter, or one whose feet showed the slightest indication of his ever having missed the mark, we regarded as good evidence of the unerring accuracy with which they use this serviceable tool.

For drilling holes a very long-handled awl is used. The carpenter seizing the handle at the end, between the palms of his hands, and moving his hands rapidly back and forth, pushing down at the same time, the awl is made rapidly to rotate back and forth; as his hands gradually slip down on the handle he quickly seizes it at the upper end again, continuing the motion as before. One is astonished to see how rapidly holes are drilled in this simple, yet effective way. For large holes, augers similar to ours are used. Their chisel is also much like ours in shape. For nailing in places above the easy reach of both hands they use a hammer, one end of which is prolonged to a point; holding, then, a nail between the thumb and finger with the hammer grasped in the same hand, a hole is made in the wood with the pointed end of the hammer, the nail inserted and driven in.

A portable nail-box is used in the shape of a round basket, to which is attached a short cord with a button of wood or bamboo at the end; this is suspended from a sash or cord that encircles the waist (fig. 28). The shingler's nail-box has the bottom prolonged and perforated, so that it may be temporarily nailed to the roof (fig. 64).

There are three implements of the Japanese carpenter which are inseparable companions; these are the *magari-gane*, *sumi-sashi*, and *sumi-tsubo*. The *magari-gane* is an iron square rather narrower than our square. The *sumi-sashi* is a double-ended brush made out of fibrous wood, rounded at one end, and having a wide sharp edge at the other (fig. 29). The carpenter always

FIG. 28. — A JAPANESE NAIL-BASKET.

has with him a box containing cotton saturated with ink; by

FIG. 29. — A CARPENTER'S MARKING-BRUSH MADE OF WOOD.

means of the *sumi-sashi* and ink the carpenter can mark characters and signs with the rounded end, or fine black lines with the sharp edge. One advantage attending this kind of a brush is that the carpenter can make one at a moment's notice. The *sumi-tsubo* (fig. 30, *A*, *B*) is the substitute for our carpenter's chalk-line; it is made of wood, often curiously wrought, having at one end a cavity scooped out and filled with cotton saturated with ink, and the other end has a reel with a little crank. Upon the reel is wound a long cord, the free end of which passes through the cotton and out through a hole at the end of the instrument. To the end of the cord is secured an object resembling an awl. To make a line on a plank or board the awl is driven into the wood, the cord is unreeled, and in this act it becomes blackened with ink; by snapping the cord in the usual way, a clear black line is left upon the surface of the wood. It is then quickly reeled up again by means of a little crank. This instrument is an improvement in every way over the

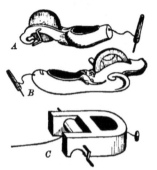

chalk-line, as it is more convenient, and by its use a clear black line is left upon the wood, instead of the dim chalk-line which is so easily effaced. This implement is often used as a plumb-line by giving a turn to the cord about the handle, thus holding it firmly, and suspending the instrument by means of the awl.

A plumb-line is made with a strip of wood four or five feet in length, to each end of which is

FIG. 30. — THE SUMI-TSUBO.

nailed, at right angles, a strip of wood four or five inches long, projecting an inch on one side. These two transverse strips are of exactly the same length, and are so adjusted to the longer strip as to project the same distance. From the longer arm of one of these pieces is suspended a cord with a weight at the lower end. In plumbing a wall, the short ends of the transverse pieces are brought against the wall or portion to be levelled, and an adjustment is made till the cord just touches the edge of the lower arm. The accompanying sketch (fig. 31) will make clear the appearance and method of using this simple device.

FIG. 31.
THE JAPANESE
PLUMB-LINE.

In gluing pieces of wood together, more especially veneers, the Japanese resort to a device which is common with American cabinet-makers, — of bringing into play a number of elastic or bamboo rods, one end coming against a firm ceiling or support, and the other end pressing on the wood to be united. In polishing and grinding, the same device is used in getting pressure.

This necessarily brief description is not to be regarded in any way as a catalogue of Japanese carpenters' tools, but is intended simply to describe those more commonly seen as one watches them at their work. The chief merit of many of these tools is that they can easily be made by the users; indeed, with the exception of the iron part, every Japanese carpenter can and often does make his own tools.

By an examination of old books and pictures one gets an idea of the antiquity of many objects still in use in Japan. I was shown, at the house of a Japanese antiquary, a copy of a very old *maki-mono* (a long scroll of paper rolled up like a roll of wall-paper, on which continuous stories or historical events are written or painted). This *maki-mono* in question was painted by Takakana, of Kioto, five hundred and seventy years ago, and represented the building of a temple, from the preliminary exercises to its completion. One sketch showed the carpenters at work

FIG. 32. — ANCIENT CARPENTER. (COPIED FROM AN OLD PAINTING.)

hewing out the wood and making the frame. There were many men at work; a few were eating and drinking; tools were lying about. In all the tools represented in the picture, — of which there were chisels, mallets, hatchets, adzes, squares, and saws, — there was no plane or long saw. A piece of timber was being cut longitudinally with a chisel. The square was the same as that in use to-day. The tool which seemed to take the place of a

plane was similar to a tool still used by coopers, but I believe by
no other class of workmen, though I remember to have seen a
man and a boy engaged in stripping bark from a long pole with
a tool similar to the one seen in the sketch (fig. 32).

The *sumi-tsubo* was much more simple and primitive in form
in those times, judging from the sketch given on page 42
(fig. 30, *C*). A carpenter's tool-box is shown quite as small
and light as similar boxes in use to-day. To the cover of this
box (fig. 32) is attached a curious hand-saw with a curved edge.
Large saws with curved edges, having handles at both ends,
to be worked by two men, are in common use; but I have never
seen a hand-saw of this shape. All the saws represented in the
picture had the same curved edge.

Nothing is more to be commended than the strong, durable,
and sensible way in which the Japanese carpenter erects his
staging. The various parts of a staging are never nailed together, as this would not only weaken the pieces through which
spikes and nails have been driven, but gradually impair its in-
tegrity. All the pieces, upright and transverse, are firmly tied
together with tough, strong rope. The rope is wound about,
again and again, in the tightest possible manner. Buddhist temples of lofty proportions are reared and finished, and yet one
never hears of the frightful accidents that so often occur at home
as the results of stagings giving way in the erection of similar
lofty structures. How exceedingly dull and stupid it must appear
to a Japanese carpenter when he learns that his Christian brother
constructs a staging that is liable, sooner or later, to precipitate
him to the ground.

CHAPTER II.

TYPES OF HOUSES.

City and Country Houses. — Fishermen's Houses. — Kura. — A Study of Roofs. — Shingled Roofs. — Tiled Roofs. — Stone Roofs. — Thatched Roofs.

WRITERS on Japan have often commented upon the absence of any grand or imposing architectural edifices in that country; and they have offered in explanation, that in a country shaken by frequent earthquakes no stately structures or·buildings of lofty proportions can endure. Nevertheless, many such structures do exist, and have existed for centuries, — as witness the old temples and lofty pagodas, and also the castles of the Daimios, notably the ones at Kumamoto and Nagoya. If the truth were known, it would be found that revolution and rebellion have been among the principal destructive agencies in nearly obliterating whatever may have once existed of grand architectural structures in Japan.

Aimé Humbert finds much to admire in the castles of the Daimios, and says, with truth : " In general, richness of detail is less aimed at than the general effect resulting from the grandeur and harmony of the proportions of the buildings. In this respect some of the seigniorial residences of Japan deserve to figure among the architectural monuments of Eastern Asia."

In regard to the architecture of Japan, as to other matters, one must put himself in an attitude of sympathy with her people, or at least he must become awakened to a sympathetic appreciation of their work and the conditions under which it

has arisen. Above all, he must rid himself of· all preconceived
ideas as to what a house should be, and judge the work of
a Japanese builder solely from the Japanese stand-point. Architectural edifices, such as we recognize as architectural, do not
exist outside her temples and castles. Some reason for this
condition of things may be looked for in the fact that the vast
majority of the Japanese are poor, — very poor ; and further, in
the fact that the idea of co-operative buildings, with the exception
of the Yashiki barracks, has never entered a Japanese mind, —
each family, with few exceptions, managing to have a house of its
own. As a result of this, a vast number of the houses are shelters merely, and are such from necessity ; though even among
these poorer shelters little bits of temple architecture creep in, —
quite as scanty, however, in that respect as are similar features in
our two-storied wooden boxes at home, which may have a bit of
Grecian suggestion in the window caps, or of Doric in the front
door-posts.

In considering the temples of the Japanese, moreover, one
should take into account their methods of worship, and precisely
what use .the worshippers make of these remarkable edifices. And
so with intelligent sympathy finally aroused in all these matters,
they begin to wear a new aspect ; and what appeared grotesque
and unmeaning before, now becomes full of significance and beauty.
We see that there is something truly majestic in the appearance
of the broad and massive temples, with the grand upward sweep
of their heavily-tiled roofs and deep-shaded eaves, with intricate
maze of supports and carvings beneath ; the whole sustained on
colossal round posts locked and tied together by equally massive
timbers. Certainly, to a Japanese the effect must be inspiring
beyond description ; and the contrast between these structures
and the tiny and perishable dwellings that surround them renders the former all the more grand and impressive. Foreigners,
though familiar with the cathedral architecture of Europe, must

yet see much to admire in these buildings. Even in the smaller towns and villages, where one might least expect to find such structures, the traveller sometimes encounters these stately edifices. Their surroundings are invariably picturesque; no sterile lot, or worthless sand-hill outside the village, will suit these simple people, but the most charming and beautiful place is always selected as a site for their temples of worship.

Whatever may be said regarding the architecture of Japan, the foreigner, at least, finds it difficult to recognize any distinct types of architecture among the houses, or to distinguish any radical differences in the various kinds of dwellings he sees in his travels through the country. It may be possible that these exist, for one soon gets to recognize the differences between the ancient and modern house. There are also marked differences between the compact house of the merchant in the city and the country house; but as for special types of architecture that would parallel the different styles found in our country, there are none. Everywhere one notices minor details of finish and ornament which he sees more fully developed in the temple architecture, and which is evidently derived from this source; and if it can be shown, as it unquestionably can, that these features were brought into the country by the priests who brought one of the two great religions, then we can trace many features of architectural detail to their home, and to the avenues through which they came.

In connection with the statement just made, that it is difficult to recognize any special types of architecture in Japanese dwellings, it may be interesting to mention that we found it impossible to get books in their language treating of house architecture. Doubtless books of this nature exist, — indeed, they must exist; but though the writer had a Japanese bookseller, and a number of intelligent friends among the Japanese, looking for such books, he never had the good fortune to

secure any. Books in abundance can be got treating of temple
architecture, from the plans of the framing to the completed
structure; also of *kura*, or go-downs, gateway, *tori-i*, etc. Plans
of buildings for their tea-ceremonies, and endless designs for
the inside finish of a house, — the recesses, book-shelves, screens,
and indeed all the delicate cabinet-work, — are easily obtainable; but a book which shall show the plans and elevations
of the ordinary dwelling the writer has never yet seen. A
number of friends have given him the plans of their houses
as made by the carpenter, but there were no elevations or
details of outside finish represented. It would seem as if, for
the ordinary houses at least, it were only necessary to detail
in plan the number and size of the rooms, leaving the rest of
the structure to be completed in any way by the carpenter, so
long as he contrived to keep the rain out.

If there is no attempt at architectural display in the dwelling-
houses of Japan the traveller is at least spared those miserable
experiences he so often encounters in his own country, where
to a few houses of good taste he is sure to pass hundreds of
perforated wooden boxes with angular roofs and red chimneys
unrelieved by a single moulding; and now and then to meet
with one of those cupola-crowned, broad-brimmed, corinthian-
columned abominations, as well as with other forms equally grotesque and equally offending good taste.

Owing to the former somewhat isolated life of the different
provinces, the style of building in Japan varies considerably;
and this is more particularly marked in the design of the
roof and ridge. Though the Japanese are conservative in many
things concerning the house, it is worthy of note that changes
have taken place in the house architecture within two hundred
and fifty years; at all events, houses of the olden times have
much heavier beams in their frame and wider planks in their
structure, than have the houses of more recent times. A prob-

able reason is that wood was much cheaper in past times; or it is possible that experience has taught them that sufficiently strong houses can be made with lighter material.

The Japanese dwellings are always of wood, usually of one story and unpainted. Rarely does a house strike one as being specially marked or better looking than its neighbors; more substantial, certainly, some of them are, and yet there is a sameness about them which becomes wearisome. Particularly is this the case with the long, uninteresting row of houses that border a village street; their picturesque roofs alone save them from becoming monotonous. A closer study, however, reveals some marked differences between the country and city houses, as well as between those of different provinces.

The country house, if anything more than a shelter from the elements, is larger and more substantial than the city house, and with its ponderous thatched roof and elaborate ridge is always picturesque. One sees much larger houses in the north, — roofs of grand proportions and an amplitude of space beneath, that farther south occurs only under the roofs of temples. We speak now of the houses of the better classes, for the poor farm-laborer and fisherman, as well as their prototypes in the city, possess houses that are little better than shanties, built, as a friend has forcibly expressed it, of "chips, paper, and straw." But even these huts, clustered together as they oftentimes are in the larger cities, are palatial in contrast to the shattered and filthy condition of a like class of tenements in many of the cities of Christian countries.

In travelling through the country the absence of a middle class, as indicated by the dwellings, is painfully apparent. It is true that you pass, now and then, large comfortable houses with their broad thatched roofs, showing evidences of wealth and abundance in the numerous *kura* and outbuildings surrounding them; but where you find one of these you pass hundreds

4

which are barely more than shelters for their inmates; and within, the few necessary articles render the evidences of poverty all the more apparent.

Though the people that inhabit such shelters are very poor, they appear contented and cheerful notwithstanding their poverty. Other classes, who though not poverty-stricken are yet poor in every sense of the word, occupy dwellings of the simplest character. Many of the dwellings are often diminutive in size; and as one looks in at a tiny cottage containing two or three rooms at the most, the entire house hardly bigger than a good-sized room at home, and observes a family of three or four persons living quietly and in a cleanly manner in this limited space, he learns that in Japan, at least, poverty and constricted quarters are not always correlated with coarse manners, filth, and crime.

Country and city houses of the better class vary as greatly as with us, — the one with its ponderous thatched roof and smoke-blackened interior, the other with low roof neatly tiled, or shingled, and the perfection of cleanliness within.

In Tokio, the houses that abut directly on the street have a close and prison-like aspect. The walls are composed of boards or plaster, and perforated with one or two small windows lightly barred with bamboo, or heavily barred with square wood-gratings. The entrance to one of these houses is generally at one corner, or at the side. The back of the house and one side, at least, have a verandah. I speak now of the better class of houses in the city, but not of the best houses, which almost invariably stand back from the street and are surrounded by gardens.

The accompanying sketch (fig. 33) represents a group of houses bordering a street in Kanda Ku, Tokio. The windows are in some cases projecting or hanging bays, and are barred with bamboo or square bars of wood. A sliding-screen covered with stout white paper takes the place of our glass-windows. Through these gratings the inmates of the house do their bargaining with the street venders. The entrance to these houses is usually by means of a gate common to a number. This entrance consists of a large gate used for vehicles and heavy loads, and by the side of this is a smaller gate used by the people. Sometimes the big gate has a large square opening in it, closed by a sliding-door or grating, — and through this the inmates have ingress and egress.

The houses, if of wood, are painted black; or else, as is more usually the case, the wood is left in its natural state,

FIG. 33. — STREET IN KANDA KU, TOKIO.

and this gradually turns to a darker shade by exposure. When painted, a dead black is used; and this color is certainly agreeable to the eyes, though the heat-rays caused by this black surface become almost unendurable on hot days, and must add greatly to the heat and discomfort within the house. With a plastered outside wall the surface is often left white, while the frame-work of the building is painted black, — and this treatment gives it a decidedly funereal aspect.

In fig. 34 two other houses in the same street are shown, one having a two-storied addition in the rear. The entrance to this house is by means of a gate, which in the sketch is open. The farther house has the door on the street.

It is not often that the streets are bordered by such well-constructed ditches on the side, as is represented in the last two figures; in these cases the ditches are three or four feet

Fig. 34. — Street in Kanda Ku, Tokio.

wide, with well-built stone-walls and stone or wooden bridges spanning them at the doors and gateways. Through these ditches the water is running, and though vitiated by the water from the kitchen and baths is yet sufficiently pure to support quite a number of creatures, such as snails, frogs, and even fishes. In the older city dwellings of the poorer classes a number of tenements often occur in a block, and the entrance is by means of a gateway common to all.

Since the revolution of 1868 there has appeared a new style of building in Tokio, in which a continuous row of tenements is under one roof, and each tenement has its own separate entrance directly upon the street. Fig. 35 gives a sketch of a row of these tenements. These blocks, nearly always of one story, are now quite common in various parts of Tokio. In the rear is provided a small plot for each tenement, which may be used for a garden. People of small means, but by no means the poorer classes, generally occupy these dwellings. I was informed by an old resident of Tokio that only since

Fig. 35. — BLOCK OF CHEAP TENEMENTS IN TOKIO.

the revolution have houses been built with their doors or main entrances opening directly on the street. This form of house is certainly convenient and economical, and is destined to be a common feature of house-building in the future.

On the business streets similar rows of buildings are seen, though generally each shop is an independent building, abutting directly to the next; and in the case of all the smaller shops, and indeed of many of the larger ones, the dwelling and shop are one, the goods being displayed in the room on the street, while the family occupy the back rooms. While one is bartering at a shop, the whole front being open, he may often catch a glimpse of the family in the back room at dinner, and may look entirely through a building to a garden beyond. It is a source of amazement to a foreigner to find in the rear of a row of dull and sombre business-houses independent dwellings, with rooms of exquisite taste and cleanliness. I remember, in one of the busiest streets of Tokio, passing through a lithographer's establishment, with the inky presses and inky workmen in full activity, and coming upon the choicest of tiny gardens and, after crossing a miniature foot-bridge, to a house of rare beauty and finish.

Fig. 36. — Street View of Dwelling in Tokio.

It is customary for the common merchant to live under the same roof with the shop, or in a closely contiguous building; though in Tokio, more than elsewhere, I was informed it is the custom among the wealthy merchants to have their houses in the suburbs of the city, at some distance from their place of business.

The sketch shown in Fig. 36 is a city house of one of the better classes. The house stands on a new street, and the lot on one side is vacant; nevertheless, the house is surrounded on all sides by a high board-fence, — since, with the open character of a Japanese house, privacy, if desired, can be secured only by high fences or thick hedges. The house is shown as it appears from the street. The front-door is near the gate, which is shown on the left of the sketch. There is here no display of an architectural front; indeed, there is no display anywhere. The largest and best rooms are in the back of the house; and what might be called a back-yard, upon which the kitchen opens, is parallel with the area in front of the main entrance to the house, and

Fig. 37. — View of Dwelling from Garden, in Tokio.

separated from it by a high fence. The second story contains one room, and this may be regarded as a guest-chamber. Access to this chamber is by means of a steep flight of steps, made out of thick plank, and unguarded by hand-rail of any kind. The roof is heavily tiled, while the walls of the house are outwardly composed of broad thin boards, put on vertically, and having strips of wood to cover the joints. A back view of this house is shown in Fig. 37. Here all the rooms open directly on the garden. Along the verandah are three rooms *en suite*. The

balcony of the second story is covered by a light supplementary
roof, from which hangs a bamboo screen to shade the room from
the sun's rays.   Similar screens are also seen hanging below.

The verandah is quite spacious; and in line with the division
between the rooms is a groove for the adjustment of a wooden
screen or shutter when it is desired to separate the house into
two portions temporarily.   At the end of the verandah to the

FIG. 38. — DWELLING NEAR KUDAN, TOKIO.

left of the sketch is the latrine.   The house is quite open beneath, and the air has free circulation.

Another type of a Tokio house is shown in Fig. 38.   This is a
low, one-storied house, standing directly upon the street, its tiled
roof cut up into curious gables.   The entrance is protected by
a barred sliding door.   A large hanging bay-window is also
barred.   Just over the fence a bamboo curtain may be seen,
which shades the verandah.   The back of the house was open,
and probably looked out on a pretty garden, — though this I did

not see, as this sketch, like many others, was taken somewhat hastily.

From this example some idea may be got of the diminutive character of many of the Japanese dwellings, in which, nevertheless, families live in all cleanliness and comfort.

In the northern part of Japan houses are often seen which possess features suggestive of the picturesque architecture of

Fig. 39. — COUNTRY INN IN RIKUZEN.

Switzerland, — the gable ends showing, in their exterior, massive timbers roughly hewn, with all the irregularities of the tree-trunk preserved, the interstices between these beams being filled with clay or plaster. The eaves are widely overhanging, with projecting rafters. Oftentimes delicately-carved wood is seen about the gable-ends and projecting balcony. As a still further suggestion of this resemblance, the main roof, if shingled, as well as the roof that shelters the verandah, is weighted with stones of various sizes to prevent its being blown away by the high

winds that often prevail. This feature is particularly common
in the Island of Yezo.

Fig. 39 gives a house of this description near Matsushima, in
Rikuzen. An opening for the egress of smoke occurs on the
side of the roof, in shape not unlike that of a round-topped
dormer window. This opening in almost every instance is found
on the gable end, directly beneath the angle formed at the peak
of the roof.

Another house of this kind, seen in the same province, is
shown in fig. 40. Here the smoke-outlet is on the ridge in

Fig. 40. — Country Inn in Rikuzen.

the shape of an angular roof, with its ridge running at right
angles to the main ridge; in this is a latticed window. This
ventilator, as well as the main roof, is heavily thatched, while
the supplementary ridge is of boards and weighted with stones.
A good example of a heavily-tiled and plastered wooden fence
is seen on the left of the sketch. In the road a number
of laborers are shown in the act of moving a heavy block
of stone.

Another house, shown in fig. 41, was seen on the road to Mororan, in Yezo. Here the smoke-outlet was in the form of a low supplementary structure on the ridge. The ridge itself was flat, and upon it grew a luxuriant mass of lilies. This roof was unusually large and capacious.

At the place where the river Kitakami empties into the Bay of Sendai, and where we left our boat in which we had

FIG. 41. — HOUSE NEAR MORORAN, YEZO.

come down the river from Morioka, the houses were all of the olden style, — a number of these presenting some good examples of projecting windows. Fig. 42 represents the front of a house in this place. This shows a large gable-roof, with broad overhanging eaves in front, — the ends of the rafters projecting to support the eaves and the transverse-beams of the gable ends being equally in sight. The projecting window, which might perhaps be called a bay, runs nearly the entire length of the gable. The panels in the frieze were of dark wood, and bore perforated designs of pine and bamboo alternating.

The larger houses of this description are always inns. They usually abut directly upon the road, and have an open appearance and an air of hospitality about them which at once indicates their character. One encounters such places so frequently in Japan, that travelling in the interior is rendered a matter of ease and comfort as compared with similar experiences in neigh-

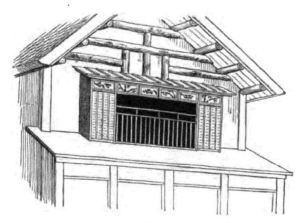

Fig. 42. — Bay-window, Village of Odzuka, Rikuzen.

boring countries. The larger number of these inns in the north are of one-story, though many may be seen that are two-storied. Very rarely does a three-storied building occur. Fig. 43 represents one of this nature, that was seen in a small village north of Sendai.

Houses of the better classes stand back from the road, and have bordering the road high and oftentimes ponderous ridged walls, with gateways of similar proportions and character, or fences of various kinds with rustic gateways. Long, low outbuildings, for servants' quarters, also often form portions of the boundary wall. In the denser part of larger cities it is rare to find an old house, — the devastating conflagrations that so often sweep across the cities rendering the survival of old houses almost an impossibility. In the suburbs of cities and in the country, however, it is not difficult to find houses one hundred, and even two or three hundred years old. The houses age as rapidly as the people, and new houses very soon turn gray from the weather ; the poorer class of

FIG. 43. — THREE-STORIED HOUSE IN RIKUCHIU.

houses in particular appear much older than they really are.

In entering Morioka, at the head of navigation on the Kitakami River, the long street presents a remarkably pretty appear-

FIG. 44. — STREET IN THE SUBURBS OF MORIOKA.

ance, with its odd low - roofed houses (fig. 44), each standing with its end to the street, — the peak of the thatched roof overhanging the smoke-outlet like a hood. The street is bordered by a high, rustic, bamboo fence ; and between the houses are little plats filled with bright-colored flowers, and shrubbery clustering within the fences, even sending its sprays into the footpath bordering the road.

The country house of an independent *samurai*, or rich farmer, is large, roomy, and thoroughly comfortable. I recall with the keenest pleasure the delightful days enjoyed under the roof of one of these typical mansions in Kabutoyama, in the western part of the province of Musashi. The residence consisted of a group of buildings shut in from the road by a high wall. Passing through a ponderous gateway, one enters a spacious court-yard, flanked on either side by long, low buildings used

FIG. 45. — OLD FARM-HOUSE IN KABUTOYAMA.

as store-houses and servants' quarters. At the farther end of the yard, and facing the entrance, was a comfortable old farm-house, having a projecting gable-wing to its right (fig. 45). The roof was a thatched one of unusual thickness. At the end of the wing was a triangular latticed opening, from which thin blue wreaths of smoke were curling. This building contained a few rooms, including an unusually spacious kitchen, — a sketch of which is given farther on. The kitchen opened directly into a larger and unfinished portion of the house, having the earth for its floor, and used as a wood-shed. The owner informed me that the farm-house was nearly three hundred years old. To the left of the building was a high wooden fence, and passing through a gateway one came into a smaller yard and garden. In this area was another house quite independent of the farm-house; this was the house for guests. Its conspicuous feature consisted of a newly-thatched roof, surmounted by an elaborate and picturesque ridge, — its design derived from temple architecture. Within were two large rooms opening upon a narrow verandah. These rooms were unusually high in stud, and the mats and all the appointments were most scrupulously clean. Communication with the old house was by means of a covered passage. Back of this dwelling, and some distance from it, was still another house, two stories in height, and built in the most perfect taste; and here lived the grandfather of the family, — a fine old gentleman, dignified and courtly in his manners.

The farm-house yard presented all the features of similar areas at home. A huge pile of wood cut for the winter's supply was piled up against the L. Basket-like coops, rakes, and the customary utensils of a farmer's occupation were scattered about. The sketch of this old house gives but a faint idea of the massive and top-heavy appearance of the roof, or of the large size of the building. The barred windows below, covered by a narrow tiled roof, were much later additions to the structure.

In the city houses of the better class much care is often taken to make the surroundings appear as rural as possible, by putting here and there quaint old wells, primitive and rustic arbors, fences, and gateways. The gateways receive special attention in this way, and the oddest of entrances are often seen in thickly-settled parts of large cities.

Houses with thatched roofs, belonging to the wealthiest classes, are frequently seen in the suburbs of Tokio and Kioto, and, strange as it may appear, even within the city proper. One might be led to suppose that such roofs would quickly fall a prey to the sparks of a conflagration ; but an old thatched roof gets compacted with dust and soot to such an extent that plants and weeds of various kinds, and large clumps of mosses, are often seen flourishing in luxuriance upon such surfaces, offering a good protection against flying sparks.   In Kioto we recall a house of this description which was nearly three centuries old ; and since we made sketches

FIG. 46. — ENTRANCE TO COURT-YARD OF OLD HOUSE IN KIOTO.

of its appearance from the street, from just within the gateway, and from the rear, we will describe these views in sequence.

The first view, then (fig. 46), is from the street, and represents a heavily-roofed gateway, with a smaller gateway at the side.   The big gates had been removed, and the little gateway was permanently closed.   This ponderous structure was flanked on one side by a low stretch of buildings, plastered on the outside, having small barred windows on the street, and a barred look-out commanding the gateway both outside and within.   On the other side of the gateway was a high, thick wall, also furnished with a window or lookout. The outer walls rose directly from the wall forming the gutter, or, more properly speaking, a diminutive moat that ran along the side of the street. Blocks of worked stone formed a bridge across this moat, by which access was gained to the enclosure. The old dwelling, with its sharp-ridged roof, may be seen above the buildings just described.

FIG. 47. — OLD HOUSE IN KIOTO. COURT-YARD VIEW.

Fig. 47 represents the appearance of this old house from just within the gateway. The barred window to the right of the sketch may be seen through the open gateway in fig. 46, and the tree which showed over the top of the gateway in that sketch is now in full view. The old house has a thatched roof with a remarkably steep pitch, surmounted by a ridge of tiles; a narrow tiled roof runs about the house directly below the eaves of the thatched roof. Suspended below this roof is seen a ladder and fire-engine, to be ready in case of emergency. The truth must be

5

told, however, that these domestic engines are never ready; for when they are wanted, it is found that the square cylinders are so warped and cracked by the hot summers that when they are brought into action their chief accomplishment consists in squirting water through numerous crevices upon the men who are frantically endeavoring to make these engines do their duty properly.

FIG. 48. — OLD HOUSE IN KIOTO. GARDEN VIEW.

The yard was well swept, and quite free from weeds, though at one side a number of shrubs and a banana tree were growing in a luxuriant tangle. A single tree, of considerable age, rose directly in a line with the entrance to the yard.

The. house, like all such houses, had its uninteresting end toward the street; and here, attached to the house, was a "lean-to," or shed, with a small circular window. This was probably a kitchen, as a gateway is seen in the sketch, which led to the kitchen-garden.

In Fig. 48 a sketch of this house is given from the garden in the rear. The house is quite open behind, and looks out on the garden and fish-pond, which is seen in the foreground. The tiled roof which covers the verandah, and the out-buildings as well, was a subsequent addition to the old house. The sole occupants consisted of the mother and maiden sister of the famous antiquarian Ninagawa Noritani. The garden, with its shrubs, plats of flowers, stepping-stones leading to the fish-pond filled with lotus and lilies, and the bamboo trellis, is a good specimen of an old garden upon which but little care has been bestowed.

In the cities nothing is more surprising to a foreigner than to go from the dust and turmoil of a busy street directly into a rustic yard and the felicity of quiet country life. On one of the busy streets of Tokio I had often passed a low shop, the barred front of which was never opened to traffic, nor was there ever any one present with whom to deal. I used often to peer between the bars; and from the form of the wooden boxes on the step-like shelves within, I knew that the occupant was a dealer in old pottery. One day I called through the bars several times, and finally a man pushed back the screen in the rear of the shop and bade me come in by way of a narrow alley a little way up the street. This I did, and soon came to a gate that led me into one of the neatest and cleanest little gardens it is possible to imagine. The man was evidently just getting ready for a tea-party, and, as is customary in winter, the garden had been liberally strewn with pine-needles, which had then been neatly swept from the few paths and formed in thick mats around some of the shrubs and trees. The master had already accosted me from the verandah, and after bringing the customary *hibachi*, over which I warmed my hands, and tea and cake, he brought forth some rare old pottery.

FIG. 49. — HOUSE IN TOKIO.

The verandah and a portion of this house as it appeared from the garden are given in fig. 49. At the end of the verandah is seen a narrow partition, made out of the planks of an old ship; it is secured to the side of the house by a huge piece of bamboo. One is greatly interested to see how curiously, and oftentimes artistically, the old worm-eaten and blackened fragments of a shipwreck are worked into the various parts of a house, — this being an odd fancy of the Japanese house-builder. Huge and irregular shaped logs will often form the cross-piece to a gateway; rudder-posts fixed in the ground form the support of bronze or pottery vessels to hold water. But fragments of a shipwreck are most commonly seen. This wood is always rich in color, and has an antique appearance, — these qualities commending it at once to the Japanese eye, and rendering it, with its associations, an attractive object for their purposes.

In the house above mentioned a portion of a vessel's side or bottom had been used bodily for a screen at the end of the verandah, — for just beyond was the latrine, from the side of which is seen jutting another wing, consisting of a single weather-worn plank bordered by a bamboo-post. This was a screen to shut out the kitchen-yard beyond. Various stepping-stones of irregular shape, as well as blackened planks, were arranged around the yard in picturesque disorder. The sketch conveys, with more or less accuracy, one of the many phases of Japanese taste in these matters.

The wood-work from the rafters of the verandah roof above, to the planks below, was undefiled by oil, paint, wood-filling, or varnish of any kind. The carpentry was light, yet durable and thoroughly constructive; while outside and inside every feature was as neat and clean as a cabinet. The room bordering this verandah is shown in fig. 125.

Fig. 50 gives a view from the L of a gentleman's house in Tokio, from which was seen the houses and gardens of the neighborhood. The high and close fence borders a roadway which runs along the bank of the Sumida-gawa. A short fence of brush juts out obliquely from the latrine, and forms a screen

between the house and the little gate. From this sketch some
idea may be formed of the appearance of the balcony and verandah, and how well they are protected by the overhanging
roofs.

FIG. 50. — VIEW FROM SECOND STORY OF DWELLING IN IMADO, TOKIO.

The inns, particularly the country inns, have a most cosey
and comfortable air about them. One always has the freedom
of the entire place; at least a foreigner generally makes himself
at home everywhere about the public houses, and in this respect

must impress a Japanese with his boorish ways, since the native guests usually keep to their own rooms. The big, capacious kitchen, with its smoke-blackened rafters overhead, its ruddy glow of wood-fire (a sight rarely seen in the cities, where charcoal is the principal fuel), and the family busy with their various domestic duties, is a most cosey and agreeable region.

Fig. 51.— Old Inn in Mishima, Suruga.

On the ride across Yezo, from Otarunai to Mororan, one passes a number of inns of the most ample proportions; and their present deserted appearance contrasts strangely with their former grandeur, when the Daimio of the province, accompanied by swarms of *samurai* and other attendants, made his annual pilgrimage to the capital.

At Mishima, in the province of Suruga, a curious old inn was seen (fig. 51). The second story overhung the first story in front, and the eaves were very widely-projecting. At the sides of the building a conspicuous feature was the verge boards, which were very large, with their lower margins cut in curious sweeps. This may have been intended for an architectural adornment, or possibly for a wind or sun screen; at all events it was, as we saw it, associated with buildings of considerable antiquity. In the middle and southern provinces of Japan the feature of an overhanging second story is by no means uncommon.

Fig. 52. — Village Street in Nagaike, Yamashiro.

A group of houses in a village street is shown in fig. 52. The nearest house is a resting-place for travellers; the next is a candle-shop, where the traveller and *jinrikisha* man may replenish their lanterns; the third is a *jinrikisha* stand, and beyond this is a light board-structure of some kind. All of these are dwellings as well. This street was in the village of Nagaike, between Nara and Kioto.

The country houses on the east coast of Kagoshima Gulf, in the province of Osumi, as well as in the province of Satsuma, have thatched roofs of ponderous proportions, while the walls supporting them are very low. These little villages along the coast present a singular aspect, as one distinguishes only the high and thick roofs. Fig. 53 is a sketch of Mototaru-midsu as seen from the water, and fig. 54 repre- sents the appearance of a group of houses seen in the same vil- lage, which is on the road running along the gulf coast of Osu-

FIG. 53. — SHORE OF OSUMI.

mi. The ridge is covered by a layer of bamboo; and the ends of the ridge, where it joins the hip of the roof, are guarded by

FIG. 54. — FARMERS' HOUSES IN MOTOTARUMIDSU, OSUMI.

a stout matting of bamboo and straw. In this sketch a regular New England well-sweep is seen, though it is by no means an uncommon object in other parts of Japan. Where the well is under cover, the well-sweep is so arranged that the well-pole goes through a hole in the roof.

The fishermen's houses are oftentimes nothing more than the roughest shelters from the elements, and being more closed than the peasants' houses are consequently darker and dirtier. In

FIG. 55. — FISHERMEN'S HUTS IN HAKODATE.

the neighborhood of larger towns, where the fishermen are more prosperous, their houses compare favorably with those of the peas-

ant class. Fig. 55 shows a group of fishermen's huts on the neck of sand which connects Hakodate with the main island. The high stockade fences act as barriers to the winds which blow so furiously across the bar at certain seasons. Fig. 56 represents a few fishermen's huts at Enoshima, a famous resort a little south of

FIG. 56. — FISHERMEN'S HOUSES AT ENOSHIMA.

Yokohama. Here the houses are comparatively large and comfortable, though poor and dirty at best. The huge baskets seen in the sketch are used to hold and transport fish from the boat to the shore.

In the city no outbuildings, such as sheds and barns, are seen. Accompanying the houses of the better class are solid, thick-walled, fire-proof buildings called *kura*, in which the goods and chattels are stowed away in times of danger from conflagrations. These buildings, which are known to the foreigner as " go-downs,"

Fig. 57. — Kura in Tokio.

are usually two stories in height, and have one or two small windows, and one door, closed by thick and ponderous shutters. Such a building usually stands isolated from the dwelling, and sometimes, though rarely, they are converted into domiciles. Of such a character is the group of buildings in Tokio represented in fig. 57, belonging to a genial antiqua- ry, in which he has stored a rare collec- tion of old books, manuscripts, paint- ings, and other an- tique objects.

Fig. 58. — Kura, or Fire-proof Buildings in Tokio.

Fig. 58, copied from a sketch made by Mr. S. Koyama, represents another group of these buildings in Tokio. These *kura* belonged to the famous

antiquarian Ninagawa Noritane.   In these buildings were stored
his treasures of pottery and painting.   Often light wooden exten-
sions are built around the *kura*, and in such cases the family live
in the outside apartments.   An example of this kind is shown
in fig. 59, which is an old house in a poor quarter of the city
of Hakodate.   The central portion represents the two-storied
kura, and around it is built an additional shelter having a tiled
roof.   In case of fire the contents of the outer rooms are hur-
riedly stowed within the fire-proof portion, the door closed, and
the crevices chinked with mud.   These buildings usually survive

Fig. 59. — Old House in Hakodate.

in the midst of a wide-spread conflagration, while all the outer
wooden additions are consumed.   Further reference will be made
to these structures in other portions of the work.   It may be
proper to state, however, that nearly every shop has connected
with it a fire-proof building of this nature.

It hardly comes within the province of this work to describe or
figure buildings which are not strictly speaking homes; for this
reason no reference will be made to the monotonous rows of buildings so common in Tokio, which form portions of the boundary-

wall of the *yashiki*; and, indeed, had this been desirable, it would have been somewhat difficult to find the material, in their original condition, for study. Many of the *yashikis* have been destroyed by fire; others have been greatly modified, and are now occupied by various Government departments. In Tokio, for example, the *yashiki* of the Daimio of Kaga is used by the educational department, the Mito *yashiki* for the manufacture of war material, and still others are used for barracks and other Government purposes. As one rides through the city he often passes these *yashikis*, showing from the street as long monotonous rows of buildings, generally two stories in height, with heavy tiled roofs. The wall of the first story is generally tiled or plastered. The second-story wall may be of wood or plaster. This wall is perforated at intervals with small heavily-barred windows or hanging bays. The entrance, composed of stout beams, is closed by ponderous gates thickly studded with what appear to be massive-headed bolts, but which are, however, of fictitious solidity. The buildings rest on stone foundations abutting directly on the street, or interrupted by a ditch which often assumes the dignity of a castle moat. These buildings in long stretches formed a portion of the outer walls of the *yashikis* within which were the separate residences of the Daimios and officers, while the buildings just alluded to were used by the soldiers for barracks.

The great elaboration and variety in the form and structure of the house-roof almost merits the dignity of a separate section. For it is mainly to the roof that the Japanese house owes its picturesque appearance; it is the roof which gives to the houses that novelty and variety which is so noticeable among them in different parts of the country. The lines of a well-made thatched roof are something quite remarkable in their proportions. A great deal of taste and skill is displayed in the proper trimming of the eaves; and the graceful way in which the eaves of the gable are made to join the side eaves is always attractive and a noticeable feature in Japanese architecture, and the admirable way in which a variety of gables are made to unite with the main roof would excite praise from the most critical architect.

The elaborate structure of the thatched and tiled roofs, and the great variety in the design and structure of the ridges show what might be done by a Japanese architect if other portions of the house-exterior received an equal amount of ingenuity and attention.

Japanese roofs are either shingled, thatched, or tiled. In the country, tiled roofs are the exception, the roofs being almost exclusively thatched, — though in the smaller houses, especially in the larger country villages, the shingled and tiled roofs are often seen. In the larger towns and cities the houses are usually tiled; yet even here shingled roofs are not uncommon, and though cheaper than the tiled roofs, are by no means confined to the poorer houses. In the suburbs, and even in the outskirts of the cities, thatched roofs are common: in such cases the thatched roof indicates either the presence of what was at one time an old farm-house to which the city has extended, or else it is the house of a gentleman who prefers such a roof on account of its picturesqueness and the suggestions of rural life that go with it.

The usual form of the roof is generally that of a hip or gable. In the thatched roof, the portion coming directly below the ridge-pole is in the form of a gable, and this blends into a hip-roof. A curb-roof is never seen. Among the poorer classes a simple pent roof is common; and additions or attachments to the main building are generally covered with a pent roof. A light, narrow, supplementary roof is often seen projecting just below the eaves of the main roof; it is generally made of wide thin boards (fig. 60). This roof is called *hisashi.*

It commonly shelters from the sun and rain an open portion of the house or a verandah. It is either supported by uprights from the ground, or by slender brackets which are framed at right angles to the main uprights of the building proper. Weak and even flimsy as this structure often appears to be, it manages to sup-

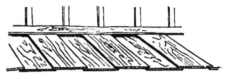

FIG. 60. — HISASHI.

port itself, in violation of all known laws of structure and gravitation. After a heavy fall of damp snow one may see thick accumulations covering these slight roofs, and yet a ride through the city reveals no evidences of their breaking down. One recalls similar structures at home yielding under like pressure, and wonders whether gravitation behaves differently in this land of anomalies.

In the ordinary shingled roof a light boarding is first nailed to the rafters, and upon this the shingles are secured in close courses. The shingles are always split, and are very thin, — being about the thickness of an ordinary octavo book-cover, and not much larger in size, and having the same thickness throughout. They come in square bunches (fig. 61, *A*), each bunch containing about two hundred and twenty shingles, and costing about forty cents.

Bamboo pins, resembling attenuated shoe-pegs, are used as shingle-nails. The shingler takes a mouthful of these pegs, and with quick motions works precisely and in the same rapid manner as a similar class of workmen do at home. The shingler's hammer is a curious implement (fig. 61, *B, C*). The iron portion is in the shape of a square block, with its roughened face nearly on a level with its handle. Near the end of the handle, and below, is inserted an indented strip of brass (fig. 61, *b*). The shingler in grasping the handle brings the thumb and fore-

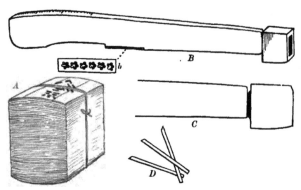

FIG. 61.— BUNCH OF SHINGLES, NAILS, AND HAMMER.

finger opposite the strip of brass; he takes a peg from his mouth with the same hand with which he holds the hammer. and with the thumb and forefinger holding the peg against

FIG. 62. — SHINGLER'S HAND.

the brass strip (fig. 62), he forces it into the shingle by a pushing blow. By this movement the peg is forced half-way down; an oblique blow is then given it with the hammer-head, which bends the protruding portion of the peg against the shingle, — this broken-down portion representing the head of our shingle-nail. The bamboo being tough and fibrous can easily be broken down without separating. In this way is the shingle held to the roof. The hammer-handle has marked upon it the smaller divisions of a carpenter's measure, so that the courses of shingles may be properly aligned. The work is done very rapidly, — for with one hand the shingle is adjusted, while the other hand is busily driving the pegs.

That the shingles are not always held firmly to the roof by this method of shingling is seen in the fact that oftentimes long narrow strips of bamboo are nailed obliquely across the

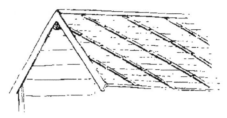

FIG. 63. — BAMBOO STRIPS ON SHINGLE-ROOF.

roof, from the ridge-pole to the eaves (fig. 63). These strips are placed at the distance of eighteen inches or two feet apart. Yet even in spite of this added precaution, in violent gales the roof is often rapidly denuded of its shingles, which fill the air at such times like autumn leaves.

Fig. 64, *A*, represents a portion of a shingled roof with courses of shingles partially laid, and a shingler's nail-box held to the roof. The box has two compartments, — the larger compartment holding the bamboo pegs; and the smaller containing iron nails, used for nailing down the boards and for other purposes.

There are other methods of shingling, in which the courses of shingles are laid very closely together, and also in many layers. Remarkable examples of this method may be seen in some of the temple roofs, and particularly in the roofs of certain temple gateways in Kioto, where layers of the thinnest shingles, forming a mass a foot or more in thickness, are compactly laid, with the many graceful contours of the roof delicately preserved. The edges of the roof are beautifully rounded, and the eaves squarely and accurately trimmed. On seeing one of these roofs

6

one is reminded of a thatched roof, which this style seems
evidently intended to imitate. The rich brown bark of the
hinoké tree is also used in a similar way; and a very compact
and durable roof it appears to make. In better shingled house-
roofs it is customary to secure a wedge-shaped piece of wood
parallel to the eaves, to which the first three or four rows
of shingles are nailed; other courses of shingles are then laid

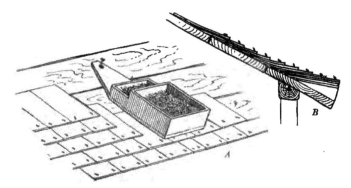

FIG. 64. — ROOF WITH SHINGLES PARTLY LAID.

on very closely, and thus a thicker layer of shingles is secured
(fig. 64, *B*).

But little variety of treatment of the ridge is seen in a
shingled roof. Two narrow weather-strips of wood nailed over
the ridge answer the purpose of a joint, as is customary in
our shingled roofs. A more thorough way is to nail thin strips
of wood of a uniform length directly over the ridge and at
right angles to it. These strips are thin enough to bend readily.
Five or six layers are fastened in this way, and then, more
firmly to secure them to the roof, two long narrow strips of
wood or bamboo are nailed near the two edges of this mass,
parallel to the ridge (fig. 65).

The shingled roof is the most dangerous element of house-structure in the cities. The shingles are nothing more than thick shavings, and curved and warped by the sun are ready to spring into a blaze by the contact of the first spark that falls upon them, and then to be sent flying by a high wind to scatter the fire for miles.

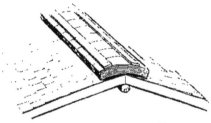

FIG. 65. — RIDGE OF SHINGLE-ROOF IN MUSASHI.

A very stringent law should be passed, prohibiting the use of such material for roofing in cities and large villages.

FIG. 66. — WATER-CONDUCTOR.

The usual form of gutter for conveying water from the roof consists of a large bamboo split lengthwise, with the natural partitions broken away. This is held to the eaves by iron hooks, or by long pieces of wood nailed to the rafters, — their upper edges being notched, in which the bamboo rests. This leads to a conductor, consisting also of a bamboo, in which the natural partitions have likewise been broken through. The upper end of this bamboo is cut away in such a manner as to leave four long spurs; between these spurs a square and tapering tunnel of thin wood is forced, — the elasticity of the bamboo holding the tunnel in place (fig. 66).

Attention has so often been drawn, in books of travels, to the infinite variety of ways in which Eastern nations use the bamboo, that any reference to the subject here would be superfluous. I can only say that the importance of this wonderful plant in their domestic economy has never been exaggerated. The more one studies the ethnographical peculiarities of the Japanese, as displayed in their houses, utensils, and countless other fabrications, the more fully is he persuaded that they could more easily surrender the many devices and appliances adopted from European nations, than to abandon the ubiquitous bamboo.

In tiling a roof, the boarded roof is first roughly and thinly shingled, and upon this surface is then spread a thick layer of mud, into which the tiles are firmly bedded. The mud is scooped up from some ditch or moat, and is also got from the canals. In the city one often sees men getting the mud for this purpose from the deep gutters which border many of the streets. This is kneaded and worked with hoe and spade till it acquires the consistency of thick dough. In conveying this mass to the roof no hod is used. The material is worked into large lumps by the laborer, and these are tossed, one after another, to a man who stands on a staging or ladder, who in turn pitches it to the man on the roof, or, if the roof be high, to another man on a still higher staging. The mud having been got to the roof, is then spread over it in a thick and even layer. Into this the tiles are then bedded, row after row. There seems to be no special adhesion of the tiles to this substratum of mud, and high gales often cause great havoc to a roof of this nature. In the case of a conflagration, when it becomes necessary to tear down buildings in its path, the firemen appear to have no difficulty in shovelling the tiles off a roof with ease and rapidity.

The ridge-pole often presents an imposing combination of tiles and plaster piled up in square ridges and in many ornamental ways. In a hip-roof the four ridges are also made thick and ponderous by successive layers of tiles being built up, and forming great square ribs. In large fire-proof buildings the ridge may be carried up to a height of three or four feet. In such ridges white plaster is freely used, not only as a cement, but as a medium in which the artist works out various designs in high-relief. One of the most favorite subjects selected is that of dashing and foaming waves. A great deal of art and

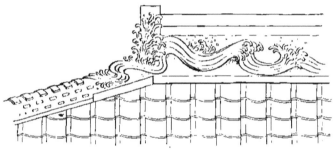

FIG. 67. — RIDGE OF TILED ROOF.

skill is often displayed in the working out of this design, — which is generally very conventional, though at times great freedom of expression is shown in the work. It certainly seems an extraordinary design for the crest of a roof, though giving a very light and buoyant appearance to what would otherwise appear top-heavy. Fig. 67 is a very poor sketch of the appearance of this kind of a ridge. From the common occurrence of this design, it would seem as if some sentiment or superstition led to using this watery subject as suggesting a protection from fire; whether this be so or not, one may often notice at the end of the ridge in the thatched roofs in the country the Chinese character for water deeply cut in the straw and blackened (fig. 82), — and this custom, I was told, originated in a superstition that the character for water afforded a protection against fire.

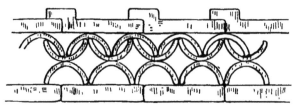

FIG. 68. — ORNAMENTAL COPING OF TILES.

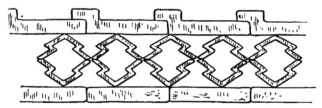

FIG. 69. — ORNAMENTAL COPING OF TILES.

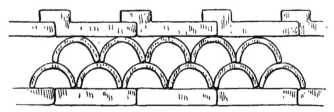

FIG. 70. — ORNAMENTAL COPING OF TILES.

The tiled ridges always terminate in a shouldered mass of tiles specially designed for the purpose. The smaller ribs of tiles that run down to the eaves, along the ridges in a hip-roof, or border the verge in a gable-roof, often terminate in some ornamental tile in high-relief. The design may be that of a mask, the head of a devil, or some such form. In the heavier ridges much ingenuity and art is shown in the arrangement of semi-cylindrical or other shaped tiles in conventional pattern. Figs. 68, 69, 70 will illustrate some of the designs made in this way. These figures, however, represent copings of walls in Yamato.

Many of the heavier ridges are deceptive, the main body consisting of a frame of wood plastered over, and having the appearance externally of being a solid mass of tile and plaster. The tiles that border the eaves are specially designed for the purpose. The tile has the form of the ordinary tile, but its free edge is turned down at right angles and ornamented with some conventional de-

sign. Fig. 71 illustrates this form of tile. In the long panel a design of flowers or conventional scrolls in relief is often seen. The circular portion generally contains the

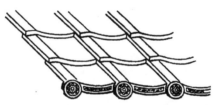

Fig. 71. — Eaves of Tiled Roof.

crest of some family : the crest of the Tokugawa family is rarely seen on tiles (see fig. 73).

In the better class of tiled roof it is common to point off with white mortar the joints between the rows of tiles near the eaves, and also next the ridge; and oftentimes the entire roof is treated in this manner. In some photographs of Korean houses taken by Percival Lowell, Esq., the same method of closing the seams of the bordering rows of tiles with white plaster is shown.

The older a tile is, the better it is considered for roofing purposes. My attention was called to this fact by a friend stating to me with some pride that the tiles used in his house,

just constructed, were over forty years old.   Second-hand tiles
therefore are always in greater demand.   A new tile, being very
porous and absorbent, is not considered so good as one in which

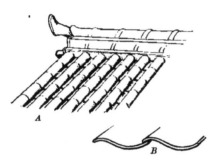

time has allowed the
dust and dirt to fill
the minute interstices,
thus rendering it a
better material for
shedding water.

A tiled roof cannot
be very expensive, as
one finds it very com-
mon in the cities and
larger villages.   The
price of good tiles for

FIG. 72. — NAGASAKI TILED ROOF.

roofing purposes is five *yen* for one hundred (one *yen* at par
equals one dollar).   Cheap ones can be got for from two and
one-half *yen* to three *yen* for one hundred.   In another measure-

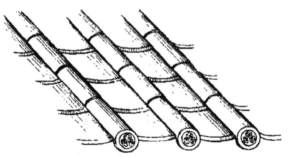

FIG. 73. — HON-GAWARA, OR TRUE TILE.

ment, a *tsubo* of tiles, which covers an area of six feet square,
can be laid for from two and one-half to three *yen*.

The form of tile varies in different parts of Japan.   The
tile in common use in Nagasaki (fig. 72, *A*) is similar in form

to those used in China, Korea, Singapore, and Europe. These
tiles are slightly curved, and are laid with their convex surface
downwards. Another form of tile, narrower and semi-cylindrical
in section, is laid with its convex
side upwards, covering the seams
between the lower rows of tiles.
This is evidently the most ancient
form of tile in the East, and in

FIG. 74. — YEDO-GAWARA, OR YEDO-TILE
EAVES.

Japan is known by the name of *hon-gawara*, or true tile. Fig.
73 represents the form of the *hon-gawara* used in Tokio.

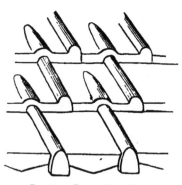

FIG. 75. — FRENCH TILE EAVES

The most common form
of tile used in Tokio is represented in fig. 71, called the
yedo-gawara, or *yedo* tile.
With this tile the upper convex tile is dispensed with,
as the tile is constructed in
such a way as to lap over
the edge of the one next to
it. Fig. 74 illustrates the
eaves of a roof in which a
yedo tile is used, having the
bordering tiles differing in
form from those shown in fig. 71. A modification of this form
is seen farther south in Japan (fig. 72, *B*), and also in Java.

A new form of
tile, called the French
tile, has been intro-
duced into Tokio
within a few years
(fig. 75). It is not

FIG. 76. — IWAMI TILE FOR RIDGE.

in common use, however; and I can recall only a few buildings roofed with this tile. These are the warehouses of the

Mitsu Bishi Steamship Company near the post-office, a building back of the Art Museum at Uyeno, and a few private houses.

Other forms of tiles are made for special purposes. In the province of Iwami, for example, a roof-shaped tile is made specially for covering the ridge of thatched roofs (fig. 76, *A*). The true tile is also used for the same purpose (fig. 76, *B*).

In this province the tiles are glazed, — the common tiles being covered with a brown glaze, while the best tiles are glazed with iron sand. In digging the foundations for a library building at Uyeno Park, a number of large glazed tiles were dug up which were supposed to have been brought from the province of Bizen two hundred years ago. These were of the *hon-gawara* pattern.

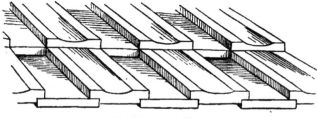

Fig. 77. — Stone Roof.

In the province of Shimotsuke, and doubtless in adjacent provinces, stone *kura* (fire-proof store-houses) are seen; and these buildings often have roofs of the same material. The stone appears to be a light-gray volcanic tufa, and is easily wrought. The slabs of stone covering the roof are wrought into definite shapes, so that the successive rows overlap and interlock in a way that gives the appearance of great solidity and strength. Fig. 77 illustrates a portion of a roof of this description seen on the road to Nikko. I was told by a Korean friend that stone roofs were also to be found in the northern part of Korea, though whether made in this form could not be ascertained.

The thatched roof is by far the most common form of roof in Japan, outside the cities. The slopes of the roof vary but little; but in the design and structure of the ridge the greatest variety of treatment is seen. South of Tokio each province seems to have its own peculiar style of ridge; at least, as the observant traveller passes from one province to another his attention is attracted by a new form of ridge, which though occasionally seen in other provinces appears to be characteristic of that particular province. This is probably due to the partially isolated life of the provinces in feudal times; for the same may be said also in regard to the pottery and many other products of the provinces.

For thatching, various materials are employed. For the commonest thatching, straw is used; better kinds of thatch are made of a grass called *Kaya*. A kind of reed called *yoshi* is used for this purpose, and also certain species of rush. The roof requires no special preparation to receive the thatch, save that the rafters and frame-work shall be close enough together properly to secure and support it. If the roof be small, a bamboo frame-work is sufficient for the purpose.

The thatch is formed in suitable masses, combed with the fingers and otherwise arranged so that the straws all point in the same direction. These masses are then secured to the rafters and bound down to the roof by bamboo poles (fig. 78, *A*), which are afterwards removed. While the thatch is bound down in this way it is beaten into place by a wooden mallet of peculiar shape (fig. 78, *B*). The thatch is then trimmed into shape by a pair of long-handled shears (fig. 78, *C*) similar to the shears used for trimming grass in our country.

This is only the barest outline of the process of thatching; there are doubtless many other processes which I did not see. Suffice it to say, however, that when a roof is finished it presents a clean, trim, and symmetrical appearance, which seems surprising when the nature of the material is considered. The eaves are trimmed off square or slightly rounding, and are often very thick, — being sometimes two feet or more in thickness. This does not indicate, however, that the thatch is of the same thickness throughout. The thatch trimmed in these various ways is thus seen in section, and one will often notice at this section successive layers of light and dark thatch. Whether

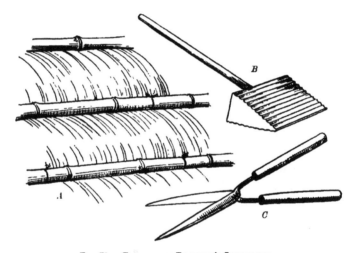

FIG. 78. — THATCH, AND THATCHER'S IMPLEMENTS.

it is old thatch worked in with the new for the sake of economy, or different kinds of thatching material, I did not ascertain.

In old roofs the thatch becomes densely filled with soot and dust, and workmen engaged in repairing such roofs have the appearance of coal-heavers. While a good deal of skill and patience is required to thatch a roof evenly and properly, vastly more skill must be required to finish the ridge, which is often very intricate in its structure; and of these peculiar ridges there are a number of prominent types. In presenting these types, more reliance will be placed on the sketches to convey a general idea of their appearance than on descriptions.

In that portion of Japan lying north of Tokio the ridge is much more simple in its construction than are those found in the southern part of the Empire. The roofs are larger, but their ridges, with some exceptions, do not show the artistic features, or that variety in form and appearance, that one sees in the ridges of the southern thatched roof. In many cases the ridge is flat, and this area is made to support a luxuriant growth of *iris*, or the red lily (fig. 41). A most striking feature is often seen in the appearance of a brown sombre-colored village, wherein all the ridges are aflame with the bright-red blossoms of the lily; or farther south, near Tokio, where the purer colors of the blue and white iris form floral crests of exceeding beauty.

In some cases veritable ridge-poles, with their ends freely projecting beyond the gable and wrought in a gentle upward curve, are seen (fig. 39). This treatment of the free ends of beams in

FIG. 79. — END OF ROOF IN FUJITA, IWAKI.

ridge-poles, gateways, and other structures, notably in certain forms of *tori-i*,[1] is a common feature in Japanese architecture, and is effective in giving a light and buoyant appearance to what might otherwise appear heavy and commonplace.

At Fujita, in Iwaki, and other places in that region, a roof is often seen which shows the end of a round ridge-pole

---

[1] A structure of stone or wood, not unlike the naked frame-work of a gate, erected in front of shrines and temples.

projecting through the thatch at the gable-peak; and at this point a flat spur of wood springs up from the ridge, to which is attached, at right angles, a structure made of plank and painted black, which projects two feet or more beyond the gable. This appears to be a survival of an exterior ridge-pole, and is retained from custom. Its appearance, however, is decidedly flimsy and insecure, and from its weak mode of attachment must be at the mercy of every high gale (fig. 79). After getting south of Sendai,

FIG. 80. — TILED RIDGE OF THATCHED ROOF IN IWAKI.

ridges composed of tile are often to be seen, — becoming more common as one approaches Tokio. The construction of this kind of ridge is very simple and effective; semi-cylindrical tiles, or the wider forms of *hon-gawara*, are used for the crest, and these in turn cap a row of similar tiles placed on either side of the ridge (fig. 80). The tiles appear to be bedded in a layer of clay or mud and chopped straw, which is first piled on to the thatched ridge. In some cases a large bamboo holds the lower row of tiles in place (fig. 81). What

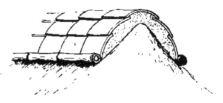

FIG. 81. — TILED RIDGE OF THATCHED ROOF IN MUSASHI.

other means there are of holding the tiles I did not learn. They must be fairly secure, however, as it is rare to see them displaced, even in old roofs.

A very neat and durable ridge (fig. 82) is common in Musashi and neighboring provinces. This ridge is widely rounded. It is first covered with a layer of small bamboos; then narrow bands of bamboo or bark are bent over the ridge at short intervals, and these are kept in place by long bamboo-strips or entire bamboos, which run at intervals parallel to the ridge. These are firmly bound down to the thatch. In some cases these outer bamboos form a continuous layer. The ends of the ridge, showing a mass of projecting thatch in section, is abruptly cut vertically, and the free border is rounded in a bead-like moulding and closely bound by bamboo, appearing like the edge of a thick basket. This finish is done in the

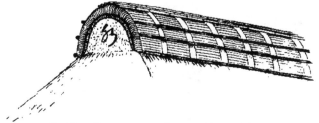

Fig. 82. — Bamboo-ridge of Thatched Roof in Musashi.

most thorough and workman-like manner. It is upon the truncate end of this kind of a ridge that the Chinese character for water is often seen, allusion to which has already been made.

When there is no window at the end of the roof for the egress of smoke, the roof comes under the class of hip-roofs. In the northern provinces the opening for the smoke is built in various ways upon the ridge or side of the roof. By referring to figs. 39, 40, 41, various methods of providing for this window may be seen.

Smoke-outlets do occur at the ends of the roof in the north, as may be seen by referring to fig. 44. The triangular opening for the outlet of smoke is a characteristic feature of the thatched

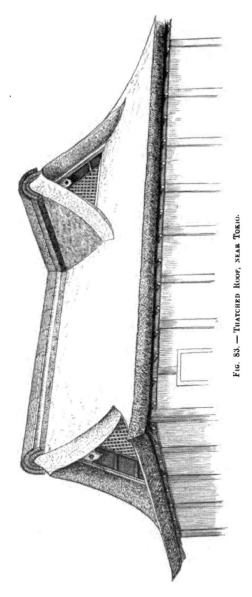

FIG. 83. — THATCHED ROOF, NEAR TOKIO.

roofs south of Tokio; on some of them a great deal of study and skill is bestowed by the architect and builder. Sometimes an additional gable is seen, with its triangular window (fig. 83). This sketch represents the roof of a gentleman's house near Tokio, and is a most beautiful example of the best form of thatched roof in Musashi. Another grand old roof of a different type is shown in fig. 84. Where these triangular windows occur the opening is protected by a lattice of wood. The roof partakes of the double nature of a gable and hip roof combined, — the window being in the gable part, from the base of which runs the slope of the hip-roof.

Great attention is given to the proper and symmetrical trimming of the thatch at the eaves and at the edges of the gable. By referring to figs. 83 and 84 some idea may be got of the clever way in which this is managed. Oftentimes, at the peak of the gable, a cone-like enlargement with a circular depression is curiously shaped out of the thatch (fig. 84). A good deal of skill is also shown in bringing the thick edges of the

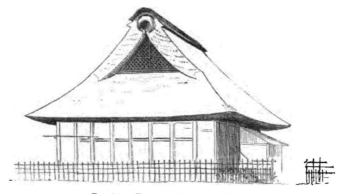

Fig. 84. — Thatched Roof, near Tokio.[1]

eaves, which are on different levels, together in graceful curves. An example of this kind may be seen in fig. 39.

In Musashi a not uncommon form of ridge is seen, in which there is an external ridge-pole wrought like the upper transverse beam of a *tori-i*. This beam has a vertical thickness of twice or three times its width; resting transversely upon it, and at short intervals, are a number of wooden structures shaped like the letter X, — the lower ends of these pieces resting on the

[1] This sketch was made from a photograph taken for this work, at the suggestion of Dr. W. S. Bigelow, by Percival Lowell, Esq.

slopes of the roof, the upper ends projecting above the ridge-pole. The ridge at this point is matted with bark ; and running parallel with the ridge a few bamboos are fastened, upon which these cross-beams rest, and to which they are secured (fig. 45).

Modifications of this form of ridge occur in a number of southern provinces, and ridges very similar to this I saw in Saigon and Cholon, in Anam. The curious Shin-tō temple, at Kamijiyama, in Ise, said to be modelled after very ancient types of roof, has the end-rafters of the gable continuing through the roof and

FIG. 85.— RIDGE OF THATCHED ROOF AT KABUTOYAMA, MUSASHI.

beyond the peak to a considerable distance. It was interesting to see precisely the same features in some of the Malay houses in the neighborhood of Singapore. In Musashi, and farther south, a ridge is seen of very complex structure, — the entire ridge forming a kind of supplementary roof, its edges thick and squarely trimmed, and presenting the appearance of a smaller roof having been made independently and dropped upon the large roof like a saddle. This style of roof, with many modifications, is very common in Yamashiro, Mikawa, and neighboring provinces. A very elaborate roof of this description is shown in fig. 85. This roof was sketched in Kabutoyama, a village nearly fifty miles west of Tokio. In this ridge the appearance of a supplementary roof is rendered more apparent by the projection beneath of what appears to be a ridge-pole, and also parallel sticks of the roof proper. This roof had a remarkably picturesque and substantial appearance. This style of roof is derived from temple architecture.

A very simple form of ridge is common in the province of Omi; this is made of thin pieces of board, three feet or more in length, secured on each slope of the roof and at right angles to the ridge; and these are bound down by long strips of wood, two

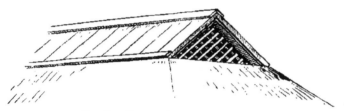

Fig. 86. — Crest of Thatched Roof in Omi.

resting across the ridge, and another strip resting on the lower edge of the boards (fig. 86). In the provinces of Omi and Owari tiled ridges are often seen, and some ridges in which wood and tile are combined. At Takatsuki-mura, in Setsu, a curious ridge prevails. The ridge is very steep, and is covered by a close mat of bamboo, with saddles of tiles placed at intervals along the ridge (fig. 87). A very picturesque form of ridge occurs in the province of Mikawa; the roof is a hip-roof, with the ridge-roof having a steep slope trimmed off squarely at the eaves. On this portion strips of brown bark are placed across the ridge, resting on the slopes of the roof; a number of bamboos rest on the bark, parallel to the ridge; on the top of these, stout, semi-cylindrical saddles, sometimes sheathed with bark, rest across the ridge, with an interspace of three or four feet between them.   Fig. 88 represents a roof with three of these saddles, which is the usual number. These saddles are firmly bound to the roof, and on their crests and directly over the ridge a long bamboo is secured by a black-fibred cord, which is tied to the ridge between each saddle.   The smoke-outlet at the end of the ridge-gable is protected by a mass of straw hanging down from the apex of the window, in shape

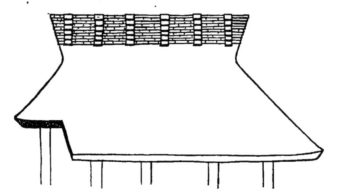

FIG. 87.—TILE AND BAMBOO RIDGE OF THATCHED ROOF, TAKATSUKI, SETSU.

and appearance very much like a Japanese straw rain-coat.   The smoke filters out through this curtain, though the rain cannot beat in.

Roofs of a somewhat similar construction may be seen in other provinces.   In the suburbs of Kioto a form of roof and ridge, after a similar design, may be often seen.   In this form the supplementary roof is more sharply defined; the corners of it are slightly turned up as in the temple-roof.   To be more definite, the main roof, which is a hip-roof, has built upon it a low upper-roof, which is a gable; and upon this rests, like a separate structure, a continuous saddle of thatch, having upon its back a few bamboos running longitudinally, and across the whole a number of thick narrow saddles of thatch sheathed with bark, and over all a long bamboo bound to the ridge with cords (fig. 89). These roofs, broad and thick eaved,

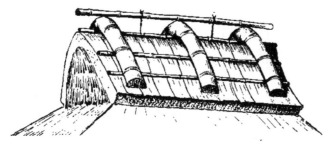

Fig. 88. — Crest of Thatched Roof in Mikawa.

with their deep-set, heavily latticed smoke-windows, and the warm brown thatch, form a pleasing contrast to the thin-shingled roofs of the poorer neighboring houses.

Fig. 89. — Crest of Thatched Roof in Kioto.

Another form of Mikawa roof, very simple and plain in structure, is shown in fig. 90. Here the ridge-roof is covered with a continuous sheathing of large bamboos, with rafter-poles at the ends coming through the thatch and projecting beyond the peak.

In the provinces of Kii and Yamato the forms of ridges

are generally very simple. In one form, common in the province of Kii, the ridge-roof, which has a much sharper incline than

the roof proper, is covered with bark, this being bound down by parallel strips, or whole rods of bamboo; and spanning the ridge at intervals are straw saddles sheathed with bark.

Fig. 90. — CREST OF THATCHED ROOF IN MIKAWA.

These are very narrow at the ridge, but widen at their extremities.

The smoke-outlet is a small triangular opening (fig. 91). In the province of Yamato there are two forms of roof very common. In one of these the roof is a gable, the end-walls, plastered

FIG. 91. — CREST OF THATCHED ROOF IN KII.

with clay and chopped straw, projecting above the roof a foot or more, and capped with a simple row of tiles (fig. 92), — the ridge in this roof being made as in the last one described. In another form of roof with a similar ridge, the thatch on the slopes of the roof is trimmed in such a way as to present the appearance of a series of thick layers, resting one upon another like shingles, only each lap being eighteen inches to two feet apart, with thick edges. It was interesting and curious to find in the ancient province of Yamato this peculiar treatment of the slopes of a thatched roof, precisely like certain roofs seen among the houses of the Ainos of Yezo.

In the provinces of Totomi and Suruga a form of ridge was observed, unlike any encountered elsewhere in Japan. The

Fig. 92. — Thatched Roof in Yamato.

ridge-roof was large and sharply angular. Resting upon the thatch, from the ridge-pole half way down to the main roof, were bamboos placed side by side, parallel to the ridge. Upon this layer of bamboos were wide saddles of bark a foot or more in length, with an interspace of nearly two feet between each saddle, these reaching down to the main roof. On each side of the ridge-roof, and running parallel to the ridge, were large bamboo poles resting on the saddles, and bound down firmly with cords. On the sharp crest of the roof rested a long round ridge-pole. This pole was kept in place by wide bamboo slats, bent abruptly into a yoke, in shape not unlike a pair of sugar-tongs, and these spanning the pole were thrust obliquely into the thatch. These were placed in pairs and cross-wise in the interspaces between the bark saddles. On the ends of the ridge there were two bamboo yokes together. The sketch of this roof (fig. 93) will give a much clearer idea of its appearance and structure than any description. This style of roof was unique, and appeared to be very strong and durable.

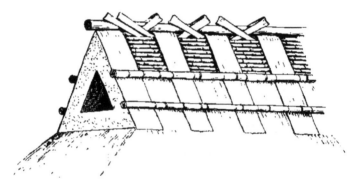

Fig. 93. — Crest of Thatched Roof in Totomi.

In the province of Ise a simple type of roof was seen (fig. 94). The ridge-roof was quite low, sheathed with bark and bound down with a number of bamboos. At the gable were round masses of thatch covered with bark, which formed an ornamental moulding at the verge.[1]

In the province of Osumi, on the eastern side of Kagoshima Gulf, the vertical walls of the buildings are very low; but these support thatched roofs of ponderous proportions. These roofs

---

[1] We have characterized as a ridge-roof that portion which has truncate ends, — in other words, the form of a gable, — and which receives special methods of treatment. The line of demarcation between the long reach of thatch of the roof proper and the ridge-roof is very distinct.

are somewhat steeper than the northern roof, and their ridges are wide and bluntly rounded. The ends of the ridge are finished with a wide matting of bamboo, and this material is used in binding down the ridge itself (fig. 54).

There are doubtless many other forms of thatched roof, but it is believed that the examples given present the leading types.

As one becomes familiar with the picturesqueness and diversity in the Japanese roof and ridge, he wonders why the architects of our own country have not seen fit to extend their taste and ingenuity to the roof, as well as to the sides of the house.

FIG. 94. — CREST OF THATCHED ROOF IN ISE.

There is no reason why the ridge of an ordinary wooden house should invariably be composed of two narrow weather-strips, or why the roof itself should always be stiff, straight, and angular. Certainly our rigorous climate can be no excuse for this, for on the upper St. Johns, and in the northern part of Maine, one sees the wooden houses of the French Canadians having roofs widely projecting, with the eaves gracefully turning upward, presenting a much prettier appearance than does the stiff angular roof of the New England house.

It is indeed a matter of wonder that some one in building a house in this country does not revert to a thatched roof. Our architectural history shows an infinite number of reversions, and if a thatched roof were again brought into vogue, a new charm would be added to our landscape. The thatched roof is picturesque and warm, and makes a good rain-shed. In Japan an

ordinary thatched roof will remain in good condition from fifteen to twenty years; and I have been told that the best kinds
of thatched roof will endure for fifty years, though this seems
incredible. As they get weather-worn they are often patched
and repaired, and finally have to be entirely renewed. Old
roofs become filled with dust, assume a dark color, and get
matted down; plants, weeds, and mosses of various kinds grow
upon them, as well as masses of gray lichen. When properly
constructed they shed water very promptly, and do not get water-
soaked, as one might suppose.

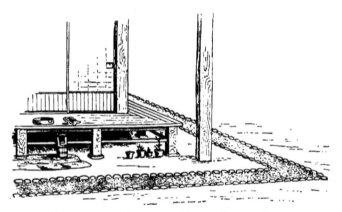

FIG. 95. — PAVED SPACE UNDER EAVES OF THATCHED ROOF.

It is customary in the better class of houses having thatched
roofs to pave the ground with small cobble-stones, for a breadth
of two feet or more immediately below the eaves, to catch the
drip, as in a thatched roof it is difficult to adjust any sort of a
gutter or water-conductor. Fig. 95 illustrates the appearance of
the paved space about a house, the roof of which is shown in
fig. 85.

The translation of the terms applied to many parts of the house
are quite curious and interesting. The word *mune*, signifying the

ridge of the house, has the same meaning as with us; the same word is applied to the back of a sword and to the ridge of a mountain. In Korea the ridge of the thatched roof is braided, or at least the thatch seems to be knotted or braided at this point; and the Korean word for the ridge means literally *back-bone*, from its resemblance to the back-bone of a fish.

In Japan the roof of a house is called *yane*. Now, *yane* literally means *house-root;* but how such a term could be applied to the roof is a mystery. I have questioned many intelligent Japanese in regard to this word, and have never received any satisfactory answer as to the reason of its application to the roof of a house. A Korean friend has suggested that the name might have been applied through association : a tree without a root dies, and a house without a roof decays. He also told me that the Chinese character *ne* meant origin.

In Korea the foundation of a house is called the foot of the house, and the foundation stones are called shoe-stones.

The Japanese word for ceiling is *ten-jō,* — literally, " heaven's well." It is an interesting fact that the root of both words, *ceiling* and *ten-jō,* means " heaven."

CHAPTER III.

INTERIORS.

GENERAL DESCRIPTION. — PLANS. — MATS. — SLIDING SCREENS. — FUSUMA. — HIKITE. — SHŌJI. — TOKONOMA. — CHIGAI-DANA. — TEA-ROOMS. — KURA. — CEILINGS. —WALLS. — RAMMA. — WINDOWS. — PORTABLE SCREENS.

THE interior of a Japanese house is so simple in its construction, and so unlike anything to which we are accustomed in the arrangement of details of interiors in this country, that it is difficult to find terms of comparison in attempting to describe it. Indeed, without the assistance of sketches it would be almost impossible to give a clear idea of the general appearance, and more especially the details, of Japanese house-interiors. We shall therefore mainly rely on the various figures, with such aid as description may render.

The first thing that impresses one on entering a Japanese house is the small size and low stud of the rooms. The ceilings are so low that in many cases one can easily touch them, and in going from one room to another one is apt to strike his head against the *kamoi*, or lintel. He notices also the constructive features everywhere apparent, — in the stout wooden posts, supports, cross-ties, etc. The rectangular shape of the rooms, and the general absence of all jogs and recesses save the *tokonoma* and companion recess in the best room are noticeable features. These recesses vary in depth from two to three feet or more, depending on the size of the room, and are almost invariably in that side of the room which runs at a right angle with the verandah (fig. 96); or if in the second story, at a right

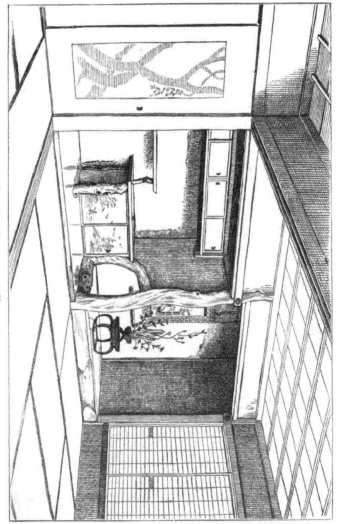

FIG. 96. — GUEST-ROOM IN HACHI-ISHI.

angle with the balcony. The division between the recesses consists of a light partition, partly or wholly closed, which generally separates the recesses into two equal bays. The bay nearest the verandah is called the *tokonoma*. In this recess hangs one or two pictures, usually one; and on its floor, which is slightly raised above the level of the mats of the main floor, stands a vase or some other ornament. The companion bay has usually a little closet or cupboard closed by sliding screens, and one or two shelves above, and also another long shelf near its ceiling, all closed by sliding screens. At the risk of some repetition, more special reference will be made farther on to these peculiar and eminently characteristic features of the Japanese house.

In my remarks on Japanese house-construction, in Chapter I., allusion was made to the movable partitions dividing the rooms, consisting of light frames of wood covered with paper. These are nearly six feet in height, and about three feet in width. The frame-work of a house, as we have already said, is arranged with special reference to the sliding screens, as well as to the number of mats which are to cover the floor. In each corner of the room is a square post, and within eighteen inches or two feet of the ceiling cross-beams run from post to post. These cross-beams have grooves on their under side in which the screens are to run. Not only are most of the partitions between the rooms made up of sliding screens, but a large portion of the exterior partitions as well are composed of these light and adjustable devices. A house may have a suite of three or four rooms in a line, and the outside partitions be made up entirely of these movable screens and the necessary posts to support the roof, — these posts coming in the corners of the rooms and marking the divisions between the rooms. The outer screens are covered with white paper, and when closed, a subdued and diffused light enters the room. They may be quickly removed, leaving the entire front of the house open to the air and sunshine. The screens between the rooms are covered with a thick paper, which may be left plain, or ornamented with sketchy or elaborate drawings.

The almost entire absence of swinging doors is at once noticeable, though now and then one sees them in other portions of the house. The absence of all paint, varnish, oil, or filling, which too often defaces our rooms at home, is at once remarked; and the ridiculous absurdity of covering a good grained wood-surface with paint, and then with brush and comb trying to imitate Nature by scratching in a series of lines, the Japanese are never guilty of. On the contrary, the wood is left in just the condition in which it leaves the cabinet-maker's plane, with a simple surface, smooth but not polished, — though polished surfaces occur, however, which will be referred to in the proper place. Oftentimes in some of the parts the original surface of the wood is left, sometimes with the bark retained. Whenever the Japanese workman can leave a bit of Nature in this way he is delighted to do so. He is sure to avail himself of all curious features in wood: it may be the effect of some fungoid growth which marks a bamboo curiously; or the sinuous tracks produced by the larvæ of some beetle that oftentimes traces the surface of wood, just below the bark, with curious designs; or a knot or burl. His eye never misses these features in finishing a room.

The floors are often roughly made, for the reason that straw mats, two or three inches in thickness, cover them completely. In our remarks on house-construction, allusion has already been made to the dimensions of these mats.

Before proceeding further into the details of the rooms, it will be well to examine the plans of a few dwellings copied directly from the architect's drawings. The first plan given (fig. 97) is that of a house built in Tokio a few years ago, in which the writer has spent many pleasant hours. The main house measures twenty-one by thirty-one feet; the L measures fifteen by twenty-four feet. The solid black squares represent the heavier upright beams which support the roof. The solid black circles represent the support for the L as well as for the verandah roof. The areas marked with close parallel lines indicate the verandah, while the double parallel lines indicate the sliding screens, — the solid black lines showing the permanent partitions. The kitchen, bath-room, and certain platforms are indicated by parallel lines somewhat wider apart than those that indicate the verandah. The lines running obliquely indicate an area where the boards run towards a central gutter slightly depressed below the common level of the floor. Here stands the large earthen water-jar or the wooden bath-tub; and water spilled upon the floor finds its way out of the house by the gutter. The small areas on the outside of the house, shaded in section, represent the closets or cases in which the storm-blinds or wooden shutters, which so effectually close the house at night, are stowed away in the day-time. The house contains a vestibule, a hall, seven rooms, not including the kitchen, and nine closets. These rooms, if named after our nomenclature, would be as follows: study, library, parlor, sitting-room, dining-room, bed-room, servants'-room, and kitchen. As no room contains any article of furniture like a bedstead, — the bed consisting of wadded comforters, being made up temporarily upon the soft mats, — it is obvious that the bedding can be placed in any room in the house. The absence of nearly all furniture gives one an uninterrupted sweep of the floor, so that the entire floor can be covered with sleepers if necessary, — a great convenience certainly when one has to entertain unexpectedly a crowd of guests over-night. Certain closets are used as receptacles for the comforters, where they are stowed away during the day-time.

The absence of all barns, wood-sheds, and other out-houses is particularly noticeable, and as the house has no cellar, one wonders where the fuel is stowed. In certain areas of the kitchen

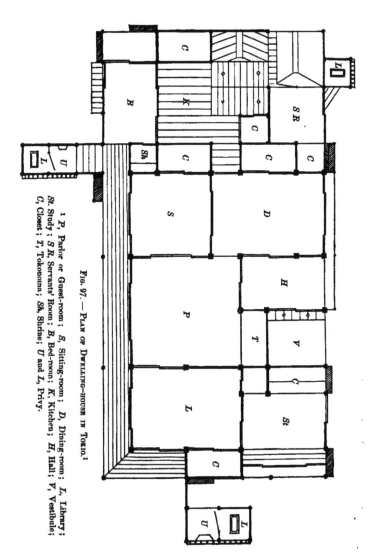

Fig. 97. — Plan of Dwelling-house in Tokio.[1]

[1] P, Parlor or Guest-room; S, Sitting-room; D, Dining-room; L, Library; St, Study; S R, Servants' Room; B, Bed-room; K, Kitchen; H, Hall; V, Vestibule; C, Closet; T, Tokonoma; Sh, Shrine; U and L, Privy.

floor the planks are removable, the edges of special planks being notched to admit the finger, so that they can be lifted up one by one; and beneath them a large space is revealed, in which wood and charcoal are kept. In the vestibule, which has an earth floor, is a narrow area of wood flush with the floor within, and in this also the boards may be lifted up in a similar way, disclosing a space below, wherein the wooden clogs and umbrellas may be stowed out of sight. These arrangements in the hall are seen in the houses of the moderately well-to-do people, but not, so far as I know, in the houses of the wealthy.

In this house the dining-room and library are six-mat rooms, the parlor is an eight-mat room, and the sitting-room a four and one-half mat room; that is, the floor of each room accommodates the number of mats mentioned. The last three named rooms are bordered by the verandah.

The expense of this house complete was about one thousand dollars. The land upon which it stood contained about 10,800 square feet, and was valued at three hundred and thirty dollars. Upon this the Government demanded a tax of five dollars. The house furnished with these mats, requires little else with which to begin house-keeping.

A comfortable house, fit for the habitation of a family of four or five, may be built for a far less sum of money, and the fewness and cheapness of the articles necessary to furnish it surpass belief. In mentioning such a modest house and furnishing, the reader must not imagine that the family are constrained for want of room, or stinted in the necessary furniture; on the contrary, they are enabled to live in the most comfortable manner. Their wants are few, and their tastes are simple and refined. They live without the slightest ostentation; no false display leads them into criminal debt. The monstrous bills for carpets, curtains, furniture, silver, dishes, etc., often entailed by young house-keepers at home in any attempt at house-keeping, — the premonition even of such bills often preventing marriage, — are social miseries that the Japanese happily know but little about.

Simple as the house just given appears to be, there is quite as much variety in the arrangement of their rooms as with us. There are cheap types of houses in Japan, as in our country, where room follows room in a certain sequence; but the slightest attention to these matters will not only show great variety in their plans, but equally great variety in the ornamental finishing of their apartments.

The plan shown in fig. 98 is that of the house represented in figs. 36 and 37. The details are figured as in the previous plan. This house has on the ground-floor seven rooms beside the kitchen, hall, and bath-room. The kitchen and bath-room are indicated, as in the former plan, by their floors being ruled in wide parallel lines, — the lines running obliquely, as in the former case, indicating the bath-room or wash-rooms.

The owner of this house has often welcomed me to its soft mats and quiet atmosphere, and in the enjoyment of them I have often wondered as to the impressions one would get if he could be suddenly transferred from his own home to this unpretentious house, with its quaint and pleasant surroundings. The general nakedness, or rather emptiness, of the apartments would be the first thing noticed; then gradually the perfect harmony of the tinted walls with the wood finish would be observed. The orderly adjusted screens, with their curious free-hand ink-drawings, or conventional designs on the paper of so subdued and intangible a character that special attention must be directed to them to perceive their nature; the clean and comfortable mats everywhere smoothly covering the floor; the natural woods composing the ceiling and the structural finishing of the room everywhere apparent; the customary recesses with their cupboard and shelves, and the room-wide lintel with its elaborate lattice or carving

above,— all these would leave lasting impressions of the exquisite taste and true refinement of the Japanese.

I noticed that a pecu-
liarly agreeable odor of the
wood used in the structure
of this house seemed to fill
the air of the rooms with
a delicate perfume;[1] and

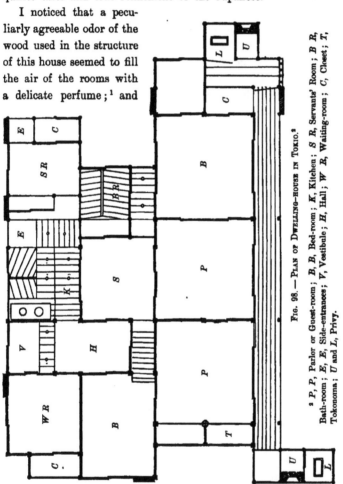

Fig. 98.— Plan of Dwelling-house in Tokio.[2]

[2] *P, P,* Parlor or Guest-room; *B, B,* Bed-room; *K,* Kitchen; *S R,* Servants' Room; *B R,* Bath-room; *E, E,* Side-entrances; *V,* Vestibule; *H,* Hall; *W R,* Waiting-room; *C,* Closet; *T,* Tokonoma; *U* and *L,* Privy.

[1] An odor which at home we recognize as "Japanesy," arising from the wood-boxes in which Japanese articles are packed.

in this connection I was led to think of the rooms I had seen in America encumbered with chairs, bureaus, tables, bedsteads, wash-stands, etc., and of the dusty carpets and suffocating wall-paper, hot with some frantic design, and perforated with a pair of quad-rangular openings, wholly or partially closed against light and air. Recalling this labyrinth of varnished furniture, I could but remem-ber how much work is entailed upon some one properly to attend to such a room ; and enjoying by contrast the fresh air and broad flood of light, limited only by the dimensions of the room, which this Japanese house afforded, I could not recall with any pleasure the stifling apartments with which I had been familiar at home.

If a foreigner is not satisfied with the severe simplicity, and what might at first strike him as a meagreness, in the appointments of a Japanese house, and is nevertheless a man of taste, he is compelled to admit that its paucity of furniture and carpets spares one the misery of certain painful feelings that incongruities always produce. He recalls with satisfaction certain works on household art, in which it is maintained that a table with carved cherubs beneath, against whose absurd con-tours one knocks his legs, is an abomination ; and that carpets which have depicted upon them winged angels, lions, or tigers, — or, worse still, a simpering and reddened maiden being made love to by an equally ruddy shepherd, — are hardly the proper surfaces to tread upon with comfort, though one may take a certain grim delight in wiping his soiled boots upon them. In the Japanese house the traveller is at least not exasperated with such a medley of dreadful things; he is certainly spared the pains that "civilized" styles of appointing and furnishing often produce. Mr. Lowell truthfully remarks on "the waste and aimlessness of our American luxury, which is an abject enslavement to tawdry upholstery."

We are digressing, however. In the plan referred to, an idea of the size of the rooms may be formed by observing the number of mats in each room, and recalling the size of the mats, which is about three feet by six. It will be seen that the rooms are small, much smaller than those of a similar class of American houses, though appearing more roomy from the absence of furniture. The three rooms bordering the verandah and facing the garden are readily thrown into one, and thus a continuous apartment is secured, measuring thirty-six feet in length by twelve in width; and this is uninterrupted, with the exception of one small partition.[1]

In the manner of building, one recognizes the propriety of constructive art as being in better taste; and in a Japanese house one sees this principle carried out to perfection. The ceiling of boards, the corner posts and middle posts and transverse ties are in plain sight. The corner posts which support the roof play their part as a decorative feature, as they pass stoutly upward from the ground beneath. A fringe of rafters rib the lower surface of the wide overhanging eaves, and these in turn rest firmly on an unhewn beam which runs as a girder from one side of the verandah to the other. The house is simply charming in all its appointments, and as a summer-house during the many long hot months it is incomparable. In the raw and rainy days of winter, however, it is not so pleasant, at least to a foreigner, — though I question whether to a Japanese it is more unpleasant than the ordinary houses at home are with us, with some of the apartments hot and stifling, and things cracking with the furnace heat, while other parts are splitting with the cold; with gas from the furnace, and chimneys that often refuse to draw, and an impalpable though tangible soot and coal-dust settling on every object, and many other abomi-

---

[1] In the plan (fig. 97) *P* is an eight-mat room; *D* and *L* are six-mat rooms; *S* is a four and one-half mat room; *B*, *H*, and *St.* are three-mat rooms; *S R*, and *V* are two-mat rooms.

In the plan (fig. 98) *P*, *P*, and *B* are eight-mat rooms; *B* is a six-mat room; *W R*, and *S*, are four and one-half mat rooms; *H*, and *S R*, are three-mat rooms.

nations that are too well known. The Japanese do not suffer
from the cold as we do. Moreover, when in the house they clothe
themselves much more warmly; and for what little artificial
warmth they desire, small receptacles containing charcoal are
provided, over which they warm themselves, at the same time
keeping their feet warm, as a hen does her eggs, by sitting on
them. Their indifference to cold is seen in the fact that in
their winter-parties the rooms will often be entirely open to
the garden, which may be glistening with a fresh snowfall.
Their winters are of course much milder than our Northern
winters. At such seasons, however, an American misses in
Japan the cheerful open fireplace around which the family in
his own country is wont to gather; indeed, with the social
character of our family life a Japanese house to us would be
in winter comfortless to the last degree.

The differences between the houses of the nobles and the
samurai are quite as great as the differences between these
latter houses and the rude shelters of the peasant class. The
differences between the interior finish of the houses of the first
two mentioned classes are perhaps not so marked, as in both
cases clean wood-work, simplicity of style, and purity of finish
are aimed at; but the house of the noble is marked by a
grander entrance, a far greater extent of rooms and passages,
and a modification in the arrangement of certain rooms and
passages not seen in the ordinary house.

The accompanying plan of a Daimio's house (fig. 99) is from a
drawing made by Mr. Miyasaki, a student in the Kaikoshia, a private school of architecture in Tokio, and exhibited with other plans
at the late International Health and Education Exhibition held in
London. Through the kindness of Mr. S. Tejima the Japanese com-
missioner, I have been enabled to examine and study these plans.

The punctilious way in which guests or official callers were
received by the Daimio is indicated by a curious modification

of the floor of one of a suite of rooms, which is raised a few inches above the level of the other floors, forming a sort of dais. These rooms are bordered by a sort of passage-way, or intermediate portion, called the *iri-kawa*, which comes between the room and the verandah. To be more explicit: within the boundary of the principal guest-room there appears to be a suite of smaller rooms marked off by *shōji*; one of these rooms called the *ge-dan* has its floor on a level with the other floors of the house. The other room, called the *jō-dan*, has its floor raised to a height of three or four inches above that of the *ge-dan*, its boundary or border being marked by a polished plank forming a frame, so to speak, for the mats. On that side of the *jō-dan* away from the *ge-dan* is the *tokonoma* and *chigai-dana*. On entering such a room from the verandah one passes through the usual *shōji*, and then across a matted area called the *iri-kawa*, the width of one mat or more; here he comes to another line of sliding screens, which open into the apartments just described. When the Daimio receives the calls from those who come to congratulate him on New Year's day, and other important occasions, he sits in great dignity in the *jō-dan;* his chief minister and other attendants occupy the *iri-kawa*, while the visitors enter the *ge-dan*, and there make their obeisance to the Worshipful Daimio Sama. In the same plan there is another suite of rooms called the *kami-noma* and *tsugi-noma* surrounded by *iri-kawa*, probably used for similar purposes.

In this plan the close parallel lines indicate the verandahs; the thick lines, permanent partitions; and the small black squares, the upright posts. The lines of *shōji* and *fusuma* are shown by the thin lines, which with the thick lines represent the boundaries of the rooms, passage-ways, etc.

A more minute description of the mats may be given at this point. A brief allusion has already been made to them in the remarks on house-construction. These mats, or *tatami*, are made very carefully of straw, matted and bound together with stout

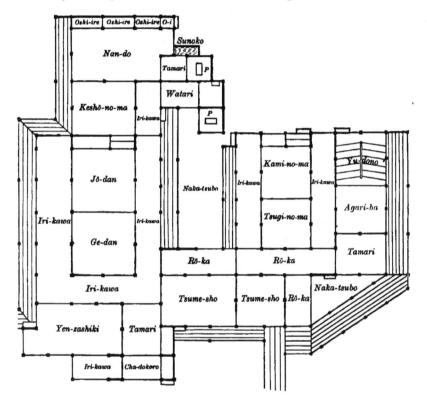

Fig. 99. — Plan of a Portion of a Daimio's Residence.[1]

[1] The following is a brief explanation of the names of the rooms given in plan fig. 99: *Agari-ba* (*Agari*, "to go up;" *ba*, "place"), Platform, or place to stand on in coming out of the Bath. *Cha-dokoro*, Tea-place; *Ge-dan*, Lower Step; *Jō-dan*, Upper Step; *Iri-kawa*, Space between verandah and room; *Kami-no-ma*, Upper place or room; *Tsugi-no-ma*, Next place or room; *Keshō-no-ma*, Dressing-room (*Keshō*, — "adorning the face with powder"). *Nan-do*, Store-room; *Naka-tsubo*, Middle space; *Oshi-ire*, Closet (literally, "push," "put in"); *Rō-ka*, Corridor, Covered way; *Tamari*, Ante-chamber; *Tsume-sho*, Waiting-room for servants; *Yu-dono*, Bath-room; *Yen-zashiki*, End parlor; *Watari*, — "to cross over;" *Sunoko*, Bamboo shelf or platform.

string to the thickness of two inches or more, — the upper surface
being covered with a straw-matting precisely like the Canton
matting we are familiar with, though in the better class of
mats of a little finer quality. The edges are trimmed true
and square, and the two longer sides are bordered on the upper
surface and edge with a strip of black linen an inch or more
in width (fig. 100).

The making of mats is quite a separate trade from that of
making the straw-matting with which they are covered. The
mat-maker may often be seen at work in front of his door,
crouching down to a low frame upon which the mat rests.

Fig. 100. — Mat.

As we have before remarked, the architect invariably plans
his rooms to accommodate a certain number of mats; and since
these mats have a definite size, any indication on the plan of
the number of mats a room is to contain gives at once its dimensions also. The mats are laid in the following numbers, —
two, three, four and one-half, six, eight, ten, twelve, fourteen,
sixteen, and so on. In the two-mat room the mats are laid side
by side. In the three-mat room the mats may be laid side by
side, or two mats in one way and the third mat crosswise
at the end. In the four and one-half mat room the mats are
laid with the half-mat in one corner. The six and eight mat
rooms are the most common-sized rooms; and this gives some

indication of the small size of the ordinary Japanese room and house, — the six-mat room being about nine feet by twelve; the eight-mat room being twelve by twelve; and the ten-mat room being twelve by fifteen. The accompanying sketch (fig. 101) shows the usual arrangements for these mats.

In adjusting mats to the floor, the corners of four mats are never allowed to come together, but are arranged so that the corners of two mats abut against the side of a third. They are supposed to be arranged in the direction of a closely-wound spiral (see dotted line in fig. 101). The edges of the longer sides of the ordinary mats are bound with a narrow strip of black linen, as before remarked. In the houses of the nobles this border strip has figures worked into it in black and white, as may be seen by reference to Japanese illustrated books showing interiors. These mats fit tightly, and the floor upon which they rest, never being in sight, is generally made of rough boards with open joints. The mat, as you step upon it, yields slightly

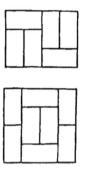

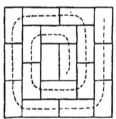

Fig. 101. — Arrangement of Mats in different-sized Rooms.

to the pressure of the foot; and old mats get to be slightly uneven and somewhat hard from continual use. From the nature of this soft-matted floor shoes are never worn upon it, — the Japanese invariably leaving their wooden clogs outside the house, either on the stepping-stones or on the earth-floor at the entrance. The wearing of one's shoes in the house is one of the many coarse and rude ways in which a foreigner is likely to offend these people. The hard heels of a boot or shoe not only leave deep indentations in the upper matting, but oftentimes break through. Happily, however, the act of removing one's shoes on entering the house is one of the very few customs that foreigners recognize,— the necessity of compliance being too obvious to dispute. In spring-time, or during a rain of long duration, the mats become damp and musty; and when a day of sunshine comes they are taken up and stacked, like cards, in front of the house to dry. They are also removed at times and well beaten. Their very nature affords abundant hiding-places for fleas, which are the unmitigated misery of foreigners who travel in Japan; though even this annoyance is generally absent in private houses of the better classes, as is the case with similar pests in our country.

Fig. 102. — Attitude of Woman in Sitting.

Upon these mats the people eat, sleep, and die; they represent the bed, chair, lounge, and sometimes table, combined. In resting upon them the Japanese assume a kneeling position, — the legs turned beneath, and the haunches resting upon the calves of the legs and the inner sides of the heels; the toes being turned in so that the upper and outer part of the instep bears directly on the mats. Fig. 102 represents a woman in the attitude of sitting. In old people one often notices a callosity on that part of the foot which comes in contact with the mat, and but for a knowledge of the customs of the people in this matter might well wonder how such a hardening of the flesh could occur in such an odd place. This position is so painful to a foreigner that it is only with a great deal of practice he can become accustomed to it. Even the Japanese who have been abroad for several years find it excessively difficult and painful to resume this habit. In this attitude the Japanese receive their company. Hand-shaking is unknown. but bows of various degrees of profundity are made by placing the hands together upon the mats and bowing until the head oftentimes touches the hands. In this ceremony the back is kept parallel with the floor, or nearly so.

At meal-times the food is served in lacquer and porcelain dishes on lacquer trays, placed upon the floor in front of the kneeling family; and in this position the repast is taken.

At night a heavily wadded comforter is placed upon the floor; another equally thick is provided for a blanket, a pillow of diminutive proportions for a head-support, — and the bed is made. In the morning these articles are stowed away in a large closet. Further reference will be made to bedding in the proper place.

A good quality of mats can be made for one dollar and a half a-piece; though they sometimes cost three or four dollars, and even a higher price. The poorest mats cost from sixty to eighty cents a-piece. The matting for the entire house represented in plan fig. 97 cost fifty-two dollars and fifty cents.

Reference has already been made to the sliding screens, and as they form so important and distinct a feature in the Japanese house, a more special description of them is necessary. In our American houses a lintel is the horizontal beam placed over the door; this is cased with wood, and has a jamb or recess corresponding to the vertical recesses into which the door shuts. For the sake of clearness, we may imagine a lintel running entirely across the room from one corner to the other, and this is the *kamoi* of the Japanese room. The beam is not cased. On its under surface run two deep and closely parallel grooves, and directly beneath this *kamoi* on the floor a surface of wood shows in which are two exceedingly shallow grooves. This surface is level with the mats; and in these grooves the screens run. The grooves in the *kamoi* are made deep, in order that the screens may be lifted out of the floor-grooves and then dropped from the upper ones, and thus removed. In this way a suite of rooms can be quickly turned into one, by the removal of the screens. The grooves are sufficiently wide apart to permit the screens being pushed by each other. From the adjustable nature of these sliding partitions

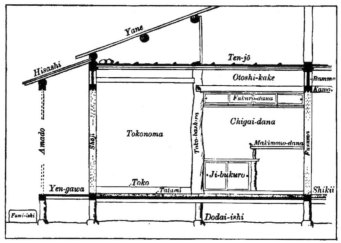

FIG. 103. — SECTION THROUGH VERANDAH AND GUEST-ROOM.

one may have the opening between the rooms of any width he desires.

There are two forms of these sliding screens, — the one kind, called *fusuma*, forming the partitions between rooms; the other kind, called *shōji*, coming on the outer sides of the rooms next to the verandah, and forming the substitutes for windows (fig. 103).

The *fusuma* forming the movable partitions between the rooms are covered on both sides with thick paper; and as it was customary in past times to use Chinese paper for this purpose, these devices are also called *kara-kami*, — " China-paper." The frame is not unlike the frame used for the outside screens, consisting of thin vertical and horizontal strips of wood forming a grating, with the meshes four or five inches in width, and two inches in height. The outside frame or border is usually left plain, as is the case with most of their wood-work. It is not uncommon, however, to see these frames lacquered. The material used for covering them consists of a stout, thick, and durable paper; and this is often richly decorated. Sometimes a continuous scene will stretch like a panorama across the whole side of a room. The old castles contain some celebrated paintings on these *fusuma*, by famous artists. The use of heavy gold-leaf in combination with the paintings produces a decorative effect rich beyond description. In the commoner houses the *fusuma* are often undecorated save by the paper which covers them; and the material for this purpose is infinite in its variety, — some kinds being curiously wrinkled, other kinds seeming to have interwoven in their texture the delicate green threads of some sea-weed; while other kinds still will have the rich brown sheaths of bamboo shoots worked into the paper, producing a quaint and pleasing effect. Often the paper is perfectly plain; and if by chance an artist friend comes to the house, he is asked to leave some little sketch upon these surfaces as a memento of his visit : others perhaps may have already covered portions of the surface with some landscape or spray of flowers. In old inns one has often pointed out to him the work of some famous artist, who probably paid his score in this way.

While the *fusuma* are almost invariably covered with thick and opaque paper, it occurs sometimes that light is required in a back-room; in that case, while the upper and lower third of the *fusuma* retains its usual character, the central third has a *shōji* inserted, — that is, a slight frame-work covered with white paper, through which light enters as in the outside screens. This frame is removable, so that it can be re-covered with paper when required.   This frame-work is often made in ornamental patterns, geometrical or natural designs being common.   In summer another kind of frame may be substituted in the *fusuma*, termed a *yoshi-do*, in which a kind of rush called *yoshi* takes the place of paper; the *yoshi* is arranged in a close grating through which the air has free access and a little light may enter.   The *fusuma* may be entirely composed of *yoshi* and the appropriate frame-work to hold it. One of this kind is represented in fig. 104.   The lower portion consists of a panel of dark cedar, in which are cut or perforated the figures of bats; above this panel are transverse bars of light cedar, and filling up the border of the frame is a close grating of brown reeds or rushes placed vertically; at the top is a wide interspace crossed by a single root of bamboo.   The *yoshi* resembles miniature bamboo, the rods being the size of an ordinary wheat-straw, and having a warm brown tint.   This

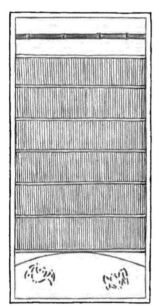

Fig. 104. — Reed-screen.

is employed in many ways in the decoration of interiors, and the use of so fragile and delicate a material in house-finish is one of the many indications of the quiet and gentle manners of the Japanese.

Oftentimes a narrow permanent partition occurs in which is an opening, — the width of one *fusuma*, — which takes the place of our swinging and slamming door.   In this case the *fusuma* is a more solid and durable structure. The one shown in fig. 105 is of the nature of a door, since it guards the opening which leads from the hall to the other apartments of the house. A rich and varied effect is produced by the use and arrangement of light and dark bamboo and heavily-grained wood, the central panels being of dark cedar. In the vestibule one often sees sliding screens consisting of a single panel of richly-grained cedar.

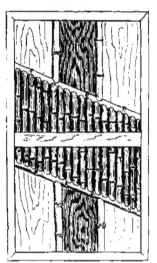

Conveniences for pushing back the *fusuma* are secured in a variety of ways; the usual form consists of an oval or circular plate of thin metal, having a depressed area, inserted in the *fusuma* in about the same position a door-knob would be with us. These are called *hikite*, and often present beautiful examples of metal-work, being elaborately carved and sometimes enamelled. The same caprices and delights in ornamentation seen elsewhere in their work find full play in the designs

FIG. 105. — SLIDING PANEL.

of the *hikite*. Fig. 106 shows one from the house of a noble; its design represents an inkstone and two brushes, — the brushes being silvered and tipped with lacquer, while in the recessed portion is engraved a dragon. Fig. 107 represents one made of copper, in which the leaves and berries are enamelled; the leaves green, and the berries red and white. Figs. 108 and 109 show more pretentious as well as cheaper forms, the designs being stamped and not cut by hand. Sometimes *hikite* are made of porcelain. In the cheaper forms of *fusuma*, the *hikite* consists of a depressed area in the paper formed by a modification of the frame itself. In illustrations of fine interiors one often noti-

FIG. 106. — HIKITE.

ces a form of *hikite* from which hang two short cords of silk tied in certain formal ways, on the ends of which are tassels. From the almost universal presence of these in old illustrated books, one is led to believe that formerly the cord was the usual handle by which the *fusuma* was pulled back and forth, and that these gradually fell into disuse, the recessed plate of metal alone remaining. This form of *hikite* is rarely seen to-day, though a few of the old Daimio's houses still possess it. Fig. 110 represents two forms copied from a book entitled "Tategu Hinagata."

FIG. 107. — HIKITE.

The outside screens, or *shōji*, which take the place of our windows, are those screens

FIG. 108. — HIKITE.

which border the verandah, or come on that side of the room towards the exterior wall of the house. These consist of a light frame-work made of thin bars of wood crossing and matched into each other, leaving small rectangular interspaces. The lower portion of the *shōji*, to the height of a foot from the floor, is usually a wood-panel, as a protection against careless feet as well as to strengthen the frame. The *shōji* are covered on the outside with white paper. The only light the room receives when the *shōji* are closed comes through this paper, and the room is flooded with a soft diffused light which is very agreeable. The *hikite* for pushing the *shōji* back is arranged by one of the rectangular spaces being papered on the opposite side, thus leaving a convenient recess for the fingers.

Sometimes little holes or rents are accidentally made in this paper-covering of the *shōji;* and in the mending of these places the Japanese, ever true in their artistic feeling, repair the damage, not by square bits of paper as we should probably, but by cutting out pretty designs of cherry or plum blossoms and patching the rents with these.

FIG. 109. — HIKITE.

When observing this artistic device I have often wondered how the broken panes of some of our country houses must look to a Japanese, — the repairs being effected by the use of dirty bags stuffed with straw, or more commonly by battered hats jammed into the gaps. Sometimes the frame of a *shōji* gets sprung or thrown out of its true rectangular shape; this is remedied by inserting at intervals in the meshes of the frame-work elastic strips of bamboo, and the constant pressure of these strips in one direction tends to bring the

FIG. 110. — HIKITE WITH CORD.

frame straight again. Fig. 111 illustrates the appearance of this; the curved lines representing the elastic strips.

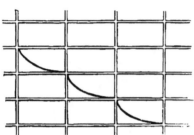

FIG. 111. — STRAIGHTENING SHŌJI FRAME.

There are innumerable designs employed in the *shōji;* and in this, as in many other parts of the interior, the Japanese show an infinite amount of taste and ingenuity. Fig. 112 illustrates one of these ornamental forms. At present in the cities it is common to see a narrow strip of window glass inserted across the *shōji* about two feet from the floor. It seems odd at first sight to see it placed so low, until one recalls the fact that the inmates sit on the mats, and the glass in this position is on a level with their line of vision. As a general rule the designs for the *shōji* are more simple than those employed for certain exterior openings which may be regarded as windows, while those which cover the openings between the rooms are most complex and elaborate. Further reference, however, will be made to these in the proper place.

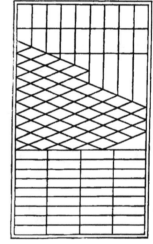

FIG. 112. — SHŌJI WITH ORNAMENTAL FRAME.

It has been necessary to anticipate the special description of the details of a room in so far as a description of the mats and screens were concerned, since a general idea of the interior could not be well understood without clearly understanding the nature of those objects which form inseparable elements of every Japanese room, and which are so unlike anything to which we are accustomed. Having given these features, it may be well to glance at a general view of the few typical rooms before examining farther into the details of their finish.

The room shown in fig. 96 gives a fair idea of the appearance of the guest-room with its two bays or recesses, the *tokonoma* and *chigai-dana,* — one of which, the *tokonoma,* is a clear recess, in which usually hangs a picture; and in the other is a small closet and shelf, and an additional shelf above, closed by sliding doors. The sketch was taken from the adjoining room, the *fusuma* between the two having been removed. The grooves for the *fusuma* may be seen in the floor and in the *kamoi* overhead. The farther recess is called the *tokonoma,* which means literally, " bed-space." This recess, or at least its raised platform, is supposed to have been anciently used for the bed-place.[1]

Let us pause for a moment to consider the peculiar features of this room. The partition separating the two recesses has for its post a stick of timber, from which the bark only has been removed; and this post, or *toko-bashira* as it is called, is almost invariably a stick of wood in its natural state, or with the bark only removed; and if it is gnarled, or tortuous in grain, or if it presents knots or burls, it is all the more desirable. Sometimes the post may be hewn in such a way that in section it has an octagonal form, — the cutting being done in broad scarfs, giving it a peculiar appearance as shown in fig. 113. Sometimes the post may have one or two branches above, which are worked into the structure as an ornamental feature. The ceiling of the *tokonoma* is usually, if not always,

---

[1] See chapter viii. for further considerations regarding the matter.

flush with the ceiling of the room, while that of the *chigai-dana* is much lower.   The floor of the *tokonoma* is higher than that of the *chigai-dana*, and its sill may be rough or finished ; and even when finished squarely, some natural surface may be left through the curvature of the stick from which it has been hewn, and which had been selected for this very peculiarity, — a fea-

ture, by the way, that our carpenters would regard as a blemish.   The floor of the *tokonoma* is in nearly every case a polished plank ; the floor of the *chigai-dana* is also of pol-

FIG. 113.
PORTION OF
TOKO-BASHIRA.

ished wood.   A large and deep *tokonoma* may have a mat, or *tatami*, fitted into the floor ; and this is generally bordered with a white strip, and not with black as in the floor *tatami*. The *tatami* in this place is found in the houses of the Daimios.

Spanning the *tokonoma* above is a finished beam a foot or more below the ceiling, the interspace above being plastered, as are the walls of both recesses.   A similar beam spans the *chigai-dana* at a somewhat lower level. When the cross-beam of the *chigai-dana* connects with the *toko-bashira*,

FIGS. 114, 115, 116, AND 117.
ORNAMENTAL-HEADED NAILS.

as well as in the joining of other horizontal beams with the up-rights, ornamental-headed nails are used.   These are often of elaborately-wrought metal, representing a variety of natural or conventional forms. Figs. 114, 115, 116, and 117 present a few of the cheaper forms used; these being of cast metal, the finer lines only having been cut by hand. These nails, or *kazari-kugi,* are strictly ornamental, having only a spur behind to hold them into the wood.

The partition dividing these two recesses often has an ornamental opening, either in the form of a small window barred with bamboo, or left open; or this opening may be near the floor, with its border made of a curved stick of wood, as in the figure we are now describing.

In the *chigai-dana* there are always one or more shelves ranged in an alternating manner, with usually a continuous shelf above closed by sliding doors. A little closet on the floor in the corner of the recess is also closed by screens, as shown in the figure. The wood-work of this may be quaintly-shaped sticks or highly-polished wood.

This room illustrates very clearly a peculiar feature in Japanese decoration, — that of avoiding, as far as possible, bi-lateral symmetry. Here are two rooms of the same size and shape, the only difference consisting in the farther room having two recesses, while the room nearest has a large closet closed by sliding screens. It will be observed, however, that in the farther room the narrow strips of wood, upon which the boards of the ceiling rest, run parallel to the *tokonoma,* while in the nearest room the strips run at right angles. The mats in the two rooms, while arranged in the usual manner for an eight-mat room, are placed in opposite ways; that is to say, as the mats in front of the *tokonoma* and *chigai-dana* are always parallel to these recesses, the other mats are arranged in accordance with these. In the room coming next, the arrangement of mats, while being the same, have the two mats running parallel to the line dividing the rooms, and of course the other mats in accordance with these. This asymmetry is carried out, of course, in the two recesses, which are unlike in every detail, — their floors as well as the lower borders of their hanging partitions being at different levels.   And in the details of the *chigai-dana* symmetrical arrangement is almost invariably avoided, the little closet on the floor being at one side, while a shelf supported on a single prop runs from the corner of this closet to the other side of the recess; and if another shelf is added, this is arranged in an equally unsymmetrical manner.   In fact everywhere, in mats, ceiling, and other details, a two-sided symmetry is carefully avoided.

How different has been the treatment of similar features in the finish of American rooms!   Everywhere in our apartments, halls, school-houses, inside and out, a monotonous bi-lateral symmetry is elaborated to the minutest particular, even to bracket and notch in pairs.   The fireplace is in the middle of the room, the mantel, and all the work about this opening, duplicated with painful accuracy on each side of a median line; every ornament on the mantel-shelf is in pairs, and these are arranged in the same way; a single object, like a French clock, is adjusted in the dead centre of this shelf, so that each half of the mantel shall get its half of a clock; a pair of andirons below, and portraits of ancestral progenitors on each side above keep up this intolerable monotony; and opposite, two windows with draped curtains parted right and left, and a symmetrical table or cabinet between the two, are in rigid adherence to this senseless scheme. And outside the monotony is still more dreadful, even to the fences, carriage-way and flower-beds; indeed, false windows are introduced in adherence to this inane persistency in traditional methods.   Within ten years some progress has been made among the better class of American houses in breaking away from this false and tiresome idea, and our houses look all the prettier for these changes.   In decoration, as well, we have made great strides in the same direction, thanks to the influence of Japanese methods.

While the general description just given of the *tokonoma* and *chigai-dana* may be regarded as typical of the prevailing features of these recesses, nevertheless their forms and peculiarities are infinitely varied. It is indeed rare to find the arrangement of the shelves and cupboards in the *chigai-dana* alike in any two houses, as will be seen by a study of the figures which are to follow. Usually these two recesses are side by side, and run at right angles with the verandah, the *tokonoma* almost invariably coming next to the verandah. Sometimes, however, these two recesses may stand at right angles to one another, coming in a corner of the room away from the verandah. The *tokonoma* may be seen also without its companion recess, and sometimes it may occupy an entire side of the room, in which case it not infrequently accommodates a set of two or three pictures. When these recesses come side by side, it is usual to have an entire mat in front of each recess. The guest of honor is seated on the mat in front of the *tokonoma*, while the guest next in honor occupies a mat in front of the *chigai-dana*.

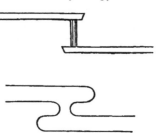

Fig. 118. — Shelves contrasted with Conventional Drawing of Mist, or Clouds.

This recess has a variety of names, according to the form and arrangement of the shelves. It is usually called *chigai-dana*,—the word *chigai* meaning "different," and *dana*, "shelf," as the shelves are arranged alternately. It is also called *usu-kasumi-dana*, which means "thin mist-shelf,"—the shelves in this case being arranged in a way in which they often conventionally represent mist or clouds, as shown in their formal designs of these objects (fig. 118, in which the upper outline shows the form of shelf, and the lower outline the conventional drawing of cloud). When only one shelf is seen it may be called *ichi-yo-dana;* the form of the shelf suggests such names as willow-leaf shelf, fish-shelf, etc. In this recess, as we have seen, are usually shelves and a cupboard; and the arrangements of these are almost as numberless as the houses containing them, — at least it is rare to see two alike. A shelf in the *chigai-dana*, having a rib or raised portion on its free end, is called a *makimono-dana.* On this shelf the long picture-scrolls called *makimono* are placed; the ceremonial ·hat was also placed on one of the shelves. It was customary to place on

FIG. 119. — GUEST-ROOM.

top of the cupboard a lacquer-box, in which was contained an ink-stone, brushes, and paper. This box was usually very rich in its gold lacquer and design. In the houses of the nobles the top of the cupboard was also used to hold a wooden tablet called a *shaku,* — an object carried by the nobles in former times, when in the presence of the Emperor. It was anciently used to make memoranda upon, but in later days is carried only as a form of court etiquette. The sword-rack might also be placed on the cupboard. In honor of distinguished guests the sword-rack was placed in the *tokonoma* in the place of honor; that is, in the middle of its floor, or *toko*, in front of the hanging picture, — though if an incense-burner occupied this position, then the sword-rack was placed at one side. While these recesses were usually finished with wood in its natural state or simply planed, in the houses of the nobles this finish was often richly lacquered.

Resuming our description of interiors, a peculiar form of room is shown in the house of a gentleman of high rank (fig. 119).

Fig. 120. — Guest-room, with Recesses in Corner.

Here the *tokonoma* was much larger than its companion recess, which in this case was next to the verandah. The *chigai-dana* was small and low, and the spaces beneath the shelves were enclosed by sliding screens forming cupboards. The *tokonoma* was large and deep, and its floor was covered by a mat or *tatami;* the flower-vase was at one side.

The depth of the *tokonoma* is generally governed by the size of the room. The appointments of this recess are also always in proportion, — the pictures and flower-vase being of large size in the one just described.

In a spacious hall in Tokio is a *tokonoma* six feet in depth, and very wide. The flower-vases and pictures in this recess were colossal. In an adjoining room to the one last figured the *tokonoma* came in one corner of the room, and the *chigai-dana* was at right angles with it. To the right of the *tokonoma* was a perma-

Fig. 121. — GUEST-ROOM SHOWING CIRCULAR WINDOW.

nent partition, in the centre of which was a circular window closed by *shōji* which parted right and left. The *shōji* may have run within the partition, or rested in a grooved frame on the other side of the wall. Above this circular window and near the ceiling was a long rectangular window, also having *shōji*, which could be open for ventilation. To the left of the *chigai-dana* was a row of deep cupboards enclosed by a set of sliding screens; above was a broad shelf, upon the upper surface of which ran *shōji*, which when opened revealed another room beyond. The frieze of this recess had a perforated design of waves (fig. 120).

Severe and simple as a Japanese room appears to be, it may be seen by this figure how many features for decorative display come

Fig. 122. — Guest-room showing Writing-place.

in. The ornamental openings or windows with their varied lattices, the sliding screens and the cupboards with their rich sketches of landscapes and trees. the natural woods, indeed many of these features might plainly be adopted without modification for our rooms.

In another room (fig. 121) of a gentleman famous for his invention of silk-reeling machinery the *tokonoma*, instead of being open to the verandah, was protected by a permanent

partition filling half the side of the room bordering the verandah. In this partition was a large circular window, having a
graceful bamboo frame-work. This opening was closed on the
outside by a *shōji*, which hung on hooks and could be removed
when required. In this case the honored guest, when seated
in front of the *tokonoma*, is protected from the wind and sun
while the rest of the room may be open. In the place of this

Fig. 123. — Guest-room with wide Tokonoma.

partition there is often seen, in houses of. the better class, a
recess having a low shelf, with cupboards beneath and an ornamental window above. This is the writing-place (fig. 122);
and upon the shelf is placed the ink-stone, water-bottle, brush-
rest and brushes, paper-weight, and other conveniences of a
literary man. Above is often suspended a bell and wooden
hammer, to call the servants when required. A hanging vase
of flowers is often suspended from the partition above. For

want of an original sketch showing this recess I have adapted
one from a Japanese book, entitled "Daiku Tana Hinagata," Vol.
II. Those who have chanced to see the club rooms of the
Koyokuan will recall the elaborate and beautiful panel of geometric work that fills the window of a recess of this nature.

Fig. 124. — SMALL GUEST-ROOM.

In Fig. 123 the *tokonoma* occupies almost the entire side
of the room, the *chigai-dana* being reduced to an angular cupboard placed in the corner and a small hooded partition hanging down from above; the small window near by, with bamboo
lattice, opened into another room beyond. A *tokonoma* of this
kind is available for the display of sets of three or four pictures. This room was in the house of a former Daimio.

In the next figure (fig. 124) we have the sketch of a small
room with the *tokonoma* facing the verandah, and with no companion recess. The little window near the floor opened into
the *tokonoma*, which extended behind the partition as far as

FIG. 125. — GUEST-ROOM OF DWELLING IN TOKIO.

the upright beam. The post which formed one side of the *tokonoma* was a rough and irregular-shaped stick. The treatment of cutting away a larger portion of it, though hardly
constructive, yet added a quaint effect to the room; while the
cross-beam of the *tokonoma*. usually a square and finished

beam, in this case was in a natural state, the bark only being removed.

In fig. 125 is shown a room of the plainest description ; it was severe in its simplicity. Here the *tokonoma*, though on that side of the room running at right angles with the veiandah, was in the corner of the room, while the *chigai-dana* was next to the verandah. The recesses were quite deep, — the *chigai-dana* having a single broad shelf, as broad as the depth

FIG. 126. — GUEST-ROOM IN KIYOMIDZU, KIOTO.

of the recess, this forming the top of a spacious closet beneath. In the partition dividing these two recesses was a long narrow rectangular opening. The little bamboo flower-holder hanging to the post of the *toko-bashira* had, besides a few flowers, two long twigs of willow, which were made to bend gracefully in front of the *tokonoma*. The character of this room indicated that its owner was a lover of the tea-ceremonies.

The next figure (fig. 126) is that of a room in the second story of the house of a famous potter in Kioto. This room

10

was remarkable for the purity of its finish. The *toko-bashira*
consisted of an unusually twisted stick of some kind of hard
wood, the bark having been removed, exposing a surface of
singular smoothness. The hooded partition over the *chigai-dana*
had for its lower border a rich dark-brown bamboo; the ver-

Fig. 127. — Guest-room of Dwelling in Tokio.

tical piece forming the other side of the *chigai-dana* was a black
post hewn in an octagonal shape, with curious irregular cross-
cuts on the faces. The sliding doors closing the shelf in this
recess were covered with gold paper. The *hikite* consisted of
sections of bamboo let in to the surface. The plaster of both
recesses was a rich, warm, umber color. The ceiling consisted

of large square panels of old cedar richly grained. This room was comparatively modern, having been built in 1868.

Fig. 127 represents a room in the second story of a house in Tokio. The recesses were remarkably rich and effective. The entire end of the room formed a recess, having a plaited ceiling; and within this recess were the *tokonoma* and *chigai-dana*, each having its own hooded partition at a different level

FIG. 128. — GUEST-ROOM OF A COUNTRY HOUSE.

and depth, — the vertical partition usually dividing these recesses being represented only by a square beam against the wall. A reference, however, to the figure will convey a clearer idea of these features than any description. The ceiling, which was quite remarkable in its way, will be described later.

The next interior (fig. 128) represents a room in a country house of the poorer class. The recesses were of the plainest description. The *tokonoma* was modified in a curious way by a break in the partition above, and beneath this modification was a shelf wrought out of a black, worm-eaten plank from some old shipwreck. The *chigai-dana* had an angular-shaped shelf in one of its corners, and in the other corner two little shelves supported by a post. The floor of this recess was on a level with the mats, while the floor of the *tokonoma* was only slightly raised above this level.

The figures of interiors thus far given present some idea of the infinite variety of design seen in the two recesses which characterize the best room in the house. The typical form

having been shown in fig. 96, it will be seen how far these bays may vary in form and structure while still possessing the distinguishing features of the *tokonoma* and *chigai-dana*. In the first recess hangs the ever present scroll, upon which may be a picture; or it may present a number of

FIG. 129. — CORNER OF GUEST-ROOM.

Chinese characters which convey some moral precept, or lines from some classical poem. On its floor rests the vase for flowers, a figure in pottery, an incense burner, a fragment of quartz, or other object, these being often supported by a lacquer stand. In the *chigai-dana* convenient shelves and closets are arranged in a variety of ways, to be used for a variety of purposes.

The arrangement of the cross-ties in relation to the *tokonoma* and *shōji* is illustrated in fig. 129, which shows the corner of a room with the upper portion of the *tokonoma* and *shōji* showing. The use made of the ornamental-headed nail is seen where the *kamoi* joins the corner post.

In houses of two stories greater latitude is shown in the arrangement of these recesses. They may come opposite the balcony, and the *chigai-dana* may have in its back wall an opening either circular, crescent-shaped, or of some other form. from which a pleasing view is obtained either of the garden below or some distant range beyond.

Thus far we have examined the room which would parallel our drawing-room or parlor; the other rooms vary from this in being smaller, and having, of course, no recesses such as have been described. By an examination of the plans given in the first part of this chapter, it will be seen how very simple many of the rooms are, — sometimes having a recess for a case of drawers or shelves; a closet, possibly, but nothing else to break the rectangular outline, which may be bounded on all sides by the sliding *fusuma,* or have one or more permanent partitions.

Another class of rooms may here be considered, the details of which are more severely simple even than those of the rooms just described. These apartments are constructed expressly for ceremonial tea-parties. A volume might be filled with a description of the various forms of buildings connected with these observances; and indeed another volume might be filled with the minor details associated with their different schools.

In brief, the party comes about by the host inviting a company of four to attend the tea-ceremony, and in their presence making the tea in a bowl after certain prescribed forms, and offering it to the guests. To be more explicit as to the mode of conducting this ceremony, — the tea is first prepared by grinding it to a fine, almost impalpable. powder. This may be done by a servant before the assemblage of the guests, or may be ordered ground from a tea shop; indeed, the host may grind it himself. This material, always freshly ground for each party, is usually kept in a little earthen jar, having an ivory cover, — the well-known *cha-ire* of the collector. Lacquer-boxes may also be used for this purpose. The principal utensils used in the ceremony consist of a *furo*, or fire-pot, made of pottery (or use may be made of a depression in the floor partially filled with ashes, in which the charcoal may be placed); an iron kettle to boil the water in; a bamboo dipper of the most delicate construction, to dip out the water; a wide-mouthed jar, from which to replenish the water in the kettle; a bowl, in which the tea is made; a bamboo spoon, to dip out the powdered tea; a bamboo stirrer, not unlike certain forms of egg-beaters, by which the tea is briskly stirred after the hot water has been added; a square silk cloth, with which to wipe the jar and spoon properly; a little rest for the tea-kettle cover, made of pottery or bronze or section of bamboo; a shallow vessel, in which the rinsings of the tea-bowl are poured after washing; a brush, consisting of three feathers of the eagle or some other large bird, to dust the edge of the fire-vessel; and finally a shallow basket, in which is not only charcoal to replenish the fire, but a pair of metal rods or *hibashi* to handle the coal, two interrupted metal rings by which the kettle is lifted off the fire, a circular mat upon which the kettle is placed, and a small box containing incense, or bits of wood that give out a peculiar fragrance when burned. With the exception of the fire-vessel and an iron kettle, all these utensils have to be brought in by the host with great formality and in a certain sequence, and placed with great precision upon the mats after the prescribed rules of certain schools. In the making of the tea, the utensils are used in a most exact and formal manner.

To watch the making of the tea, knowing nothing about the ceremony, seems as grotesque a performance as one can well imagine. Many of the forms connected with it seem uselessly absurd; and yet having taken many lessons in the art of tea-making, I found that with few exceptions it was natural and easy; and the guests assembled on such an occasion, though at first sight appearing stiff, are always perfectly at their ease. The proper placing of the utensils, and the sequence in handling them and making the tea are all natural and easy movements, as I have said. The light wiping of the tea-jar, and the washing of the bowl and its wiping with so many peripheral jerks, the dropping of the stirrer against the side of the bowl with a click in rinsing, and a few of the other usual movements are certainly grotesquely formal enough; but I question whether the etiquette of a ceremonious dinner-party at home, with the decorum observed in the proper use of each utensil, does not strike a Japanese as equally odd and incomprehensible when experienced by him for the first time.

This very brief and imperfect allusion has been made in order to explain, that so highly do the Japanese regard this ceremony that little isolated houses are specially constructed for the express purpose of entertaining tea-parties. If no house is allotted for the purpose, then a special room is fitted for it. Many books are devoted to the exposition of the different schools of tea-ceremonies, illustrated with diagrams showing the various ways of placing the utensils, plans of the tea-rooms, and all the details involved in the observances.

The tea-ceremonies have had a profound influence on many Japanese arts. Particularly have they affected the pottery of Japan; for the rigid simplicity, approaching an affected roughness and poverty, which characterizes the tea-room and many of the utensils used in the ceremony, has left its impress upon many forms of pottery. It has also had an influence on even the few rustic and simple adornments allowed in the room, and has held its sway over the gardens, gateways, and fences surrounding the house. Indeed, it has had an effect on the Japanese almost equal to that of Calvinistic doctrines on the early Puritans. The one suppressed the exuberance of an art-loving people, and brought many of their decorative impulses down to a restful purity and simplicity; but in the case of the Puritans and their immediate descendants, who had but little of the art-spirit to spare, their sombre dogmas crushed the little love for art that might have dawned, and rendered intolerably woful and sepulchral the lives and homes of our ancestors; and

FIG. 130. — TEA-ROOM IN NAN-EN-JI TEMPLE, KIOTO.

when some faint groping for art and adornment here and there appeared, it manifested itself only in wretched samplers and hideous tomb-stones, with tearful willow or death-bed scenes done in cold steel. Whittier gives a good picture of such a home, in his poem "Among the Hills": —

> " bookless, pictureless,
> Save the inevitable sampler hung
> Over the fireplace; or a mourning-piece, —
> A green-haired woman, peony-cheeked, beneath
> Impossible willows; the wide-throated hearth
> Bristling with faded pine-boughs, half concealing
> The piled-up rubbish at the chimney's back."

But we are digressing. Having given some idea of the formal character of the tea-ceremonies, it is not to be wondered at that special rooms, and even special buildings, should be designed and built expressly for those observances. We give a few illustrations of the interiors of rooms used for this purpose.

Fig. 130 is that of a room in Nan-en-ji temple, in Kioto, said to have been specially designed, in the early part of the seventeenth

FIG. 131.— TEA-ROOM IN FUJIMI POTTERY, NAGOYA.

century, by Kobori Yenshiu, — a famous master of tea-ceremonies, and a founder of one of its schools. The room was exceedingly small, a four and a half mat room I believe, which is the usual size. The drawing, from necessity of perspective, makes it appear much larger. The ceiling was of rush and bamboo; the walls were roughly plastered with bluish-gray clay; the cross-ties and uprights were of pine, with the bark retained. The room had eight small windows of various sizes, placed at various heights in different parts of the room; and this was in accordance with Yenshiu's taste. Only one recess, the *tokonoma*, is seen in the room, — in which may hang at the time of a party a picture, to be replaced, at a certain period of the ceremony, by a hanging basket of flowers. The *ro*, or fireplace, is a depressed area in the floor, deep enough to hold a considerable amount of ashes, as well as a tripod upon which the kettle rests.

FIG. 132. — TEA-ROOM IN MIYAJIMA.

Fig. 131 represents an odd-looking tea-room, at the Fujimi pottery, in Nagoya, where tea was made and served to us by the potter's daughter. The room was simple enough, yet quite ornate compared with the one first described. The ceiling consisted of a matting of thin wood-strips, bamboo and red pine being used for the cross-ties and uprights. The *tokonoma*, having a bamboo post, is seen at the left of the figure. The *ro*, in this case, was triangular.

In fig. 132 is represented a view of a small tea-room at Miyajima; the chasteness of its finish is but feebly conveyed in the figure. Here the *ro* was circular, and was placed in a wide plank of polished wood. The room was connected with other apartments of the house, and did not constitute a house by itself.

In some houses there is a special place or room adjoining the tea-room, in which the tea-utensils are kept properly arranged, and from which they are brought when tea is made, and to which

Fig. 133. — Kitchen for Tea-utensils.

they are afterwards returned with great formality. Fig. 133 represents one of these rooms in a house in Imado, Tokio. In this room the same simplicity of finish was seen. It was furnished

with shelves, a little closet to contain the utensils, and a depressed area in the floor, having for its bottom a bamboo grating
through which the water ran when emptied into it. Resting upon
this bamboo grating was a huge pottery-vessel for water, and a
common hand-basin of copper. The floor was of polished wood.

FIG. 134. — TEA-ROOM IN IMADO, TOKIO.

At the farther end was the entrance, by means of a low door,
closed by *fusuma*.

In fig. 134 is given the view of a room in a Tokio house
that was extremely ornate in its finish. The owner of the
house had built it some thirty years before, and had intended
carrying out Chinese ideas of design and furnishing. Whether
he had got his ideas from books, or had evolved them from his
inner consciousness, I do not know; certain it is, that although
he had worked into its structure a number of features actually

brought from China, I must say that in my limited observations in that country I saw nothing approaching such an interior or building. The effect of the room was certainly charming, and the most elaborate finish with expensive woods had been employed in its construction. It seemed altogether too ornamental for the

FIG. 135. — CORNER OF TEA-ROOM SHOWN IN FIG. 134.

tea-ceremonies to suit the Japanese taste. The ceiling was particularly unique; for running diagonally across it from one corner to the other was a stout bamboo in two curves, and upon this bamboo was engraved a Chinese poem. The ceiling on one side of the bamboo was finished in large square panels of an elaborately-grained wood; on the other side were small panels of cedar. Exotic woods, palms, bamboo, and red-pine were used for cross-ties and uprights. The panels of the little closet in some cases had beautiful designs painted upon them; other panels were of wood, with the designs inlaid in various colored woods, — the musical instrument, the *biwa*, shown in the sketch, being inlaid in this way. The walls were tinted a sober brown. It was certainly one of the most unique interiors that I saw in Japan. To the right of the *tokonoma* the apartment opened into a small entry which led to a flight of stairs, — for this room was in the second story of the house. The corner of the room, as it appeared from the *tokonoma*, is shown in fig. 135. The long, low window (which also shows in fig. 134) opened on the roof of the entrance below; another narrower and higher window opened on the roof of an L. The little recess which has for a corner-post a crooked stick, — the crook forming one border of an opening in the corner, — was used to hang a picture or a basket of flowers.

The second story of shops are often used as living rooms. Fig. 136 represents a room of this nature in a shop in Kawagoye, in Musashi, nearly three hundred years old. Two long, low windows, opening on the street, were deeply recessed and heavily barred; above these openings were low deep cupboards, closed by long sliding doors. The room was dusty and unused, but I could not help noticing in this old building, as in the old buildings at home, the heavy character of the framework where it appeared in sight.

Reference has been made to the fact that *kura*, or fire-proof buildings, are often fitted up for living-rooms. Fig. 137 (see page 160) represents the lower room of the corner building shown on page 75 (fig. 57). It has already been stated that the walls of such a building are of great thickness, and that one small window and doorway are often the only openings in the room. The walls are consequently cold and damp at certain seasons of the year.

For the fitting up of such a room, to adapt it for a living-place, a light frame-work of bamboo is constructed, which stands away from the walls at a distance of two or three feet; upon this, cloth is stretched like a curtain. The frame-work forms a ceiling as well, so that the rough walls and beams of the floor above are concealed by this device. At one side the cloth is arranged to be looped up like a curtain, so that one may pass outside the drapery.

FIG. 136. — Room in Second Story of Old Building in Kawagoye, Musashi.

The owner of this apartment was an eminent antiquarian, and the walls of the room were lined with shelves and cases which were filled with old books and pictures, rare scrolls, and bric-à-brac. A loft above, to which access was gained by a perilous flight of steps, was filled with ancient relics of all kinds, — stone implements, old pottery, quaint writing-desks, and rare manuscripts. The cloth which formed this supplementary partition was of a light, thin texture; and when the owner went in search of some object on the other side of it, I could trace him by his candle-light as he wandered about behind the curtain. The furniture used in the room, and shown in the sketch, — consisting of book-shelves, table, *hibachi*, and other objects, — were in nearly every case precious antiques.

That the rooms of *kura* were fitted up in this way in past times is evident in the fact that old books not only represent this method in their pictures, but special details of the construction of

Fig. 137. — Room in Kura fitted up as a Library, Tokio.

the framework are given. In an old book in the possession of Mr. K——, published one hundred and eighty years ago, a figure of one of these frames is given, with all the details of its struc-ture, metal sockets, key-bolts, etc., a copy of which may be seen in fig. 138.

In connection with this room, and the manner of looping up the curtains at the side, I got from this scholar the first rational explanation of the meaning of the two narrow bands which hang down from the upper part of the usual form of a Japanese picture, — the *kake-mono*. That these were survivals of useful appendages, — rudimentary organs, so to speak, there could be no doubt. Mr. K—— told me that in former times the pictures, mainly of a religious character, were suspended from a frame. Long bands trailed down behind the picture; and shorter ones, so as not to obscure it, hung down in front. When the picture was rolled up, it was held in position by tying these bands. When the custom came to hang these pictures permanently against the wall, the long bands were finally discarded, while the shorter ones in front survived. In old books there are illustrated methods by which curtain-like screens hanging on frames were tied up

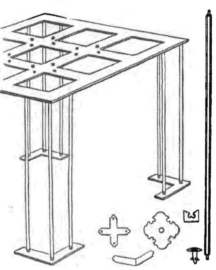

Fig. 138. — Framework for Draping Room in Kura.

in this way, — the long bands being behind, and the short ones showing in front. When the wind blew through the apartment the curtains were tied up; and, curiously enough, the bands on a *kake-mono* are called *fū-tai*, or *kaze obi*, which literally means "wind-bands." This is the explanation given me; but it is quite probable that large pictures hanging against the walls, when disturbed by the wind, were tied up by these bands.

While the *kura* generally stands isolated from the dwelling-house, it is often connected with the house by a light structure of

11

wood, roofed over, and easily demolished in case of a fire. Such an apartment may be used for a kitchen, or porch to a kitchen,

Fig. 139. — Space between Dwelling and Kura, roofed over
and utilized as a Kitchen in Tokio.

or store-room for household utensils. A figure is here given (fig. 139) showing the appearance of a structure of this kind, which is lightly attached to the sides of the *kura*. This apartment was used as a store-room, and in the sketch is shown a wooden case, lanterns, and buckets, and such objects as might accumulate in a shed or store-room at home.

The ponderous doors of the *kura,* which are kept permanently open, have casings of boards held in place by a wooden pin, which passes through an iron staple in the door. This casing is to pro-

FIG. 140. — DOORWAY OF AN OLD KURA IN KIOTO.

tect the door — which, like the walls of the *kura,* is composed of mud and plaster supported by a stout frame — from being scarred and battered; and at the same time it is so arranged that in case of fire it can be instantly removed and the door closed. The light structure forming this porch may quickly burn down, leaving the *kura* intact.

Oftentimes the outside of the *kura* has a board-casing kept in place by long wooden strips, which drop into staples that are firmly attached to the walls of the *kura.* These hooks may be seen in fig. 57, though in the case of this building the wooden casing had never been applied. Casings of this nature are provided the better to preserve the walls from the action of the weather.

In fig. 139 (see page 162) the *kura* had been originally built some fifteen feet from the main house, and subsequently the intervening space had been roofed over as shown in the drawing.

The doors of the *kura* are ponderous structures, and are usually left open for ventilation; a heavily grated sliding-door, however, closes the entrance effectually when the thick doors are left open. Fig. 140 represents the doorway of an old *kura* in Kioto illustrating these fea-

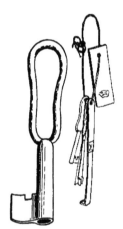

Fig. 141.— Key to Kura, and Bunch of Keys.

Fig. 142. — Padlock to Kura.

tures. In fig. 141 the large key is the one belonging to the inner grated door, while fig. 142 shows the padlock to the outer doors.

The upper room of the *kura* is often utilized as a store-room, taking the place of the country attic; and one may find here bundles of dried herbs, corn, an old spinning-wheel, chests, and indeed just such objects as ultimately find a resting-place in our attics at home.

In this section it would have been more systematic to deal with the *tokonoma* and *chigai-dana* separately; but in the description of interiors, it was difficult to describe them without including under the same consideration these recesses, as they form an integral part of the principal room.

In my remarks on house-construction, reference was made to the ceiling and the way in which it is made and held in place, the form of ceiling there described being the almost universal one throughout the country. The Japanese word for ceiling is *tenjō*, — literally, "heaven's well."

In selecting wood for the ceiling, great care is taken to secure boards in which the grain is perfectly even and regular, with no signs of knots. A wood much prized for the ceiling, as well as for other interior finish, is a kind of cedar dug up from swamps in Hakone, and other places in Japan. It is of a rich, warm gray or brown color; and oftentimes planks of enormous thickness are secured for this purpose. This wood is called *Jin dai sugi*, meaning "cedar of God's age." A wood called *hinoki* is often used for ceilings.

It is rare to see a ceiling differing from the conventional form, consisting of light, thin, square strips as ceiling-beams, upon which rest crosswise thin planks of wood with their edges overlapping. One sees this form of ceiling everywhere, from north to south, in inns, private dwellings, and shops. This form is as universal in Japan as is the ordinary white plaster-ceiling with us. In many other forms of ceiling, however, wood of the most tortuous grain is preferred.

In the little houses made for the tea-parties the ceiling is often of some rustic design, — either a layer of rush resting on bamboo rafters, or thin, wide strips of wood braided or matted like basket-work.

Sometimes the ceiling instead of being flat is arching; that is, the sides run up like a roof, and meet above in a flat panel, or the ceiling may be made up of panels either square or angular.

A very elaborate and beautiful ceiling is seen in fig. 127 (see page 146). The structure is supposed to be in imitation of a country thatched roof. The centre panel consists of a huge plank of cedar, the irregular grain cut out in such a way as to show the lines in high-relief, giving it the appearance of very old wood, in which the softer lines have been worn away. The round sticks which form the frame for the plank, and those bordering the ceiling, as well as those running from the corners of the ceiling to the corners of the plank, are of red pine with the bark unremoved. The radiating rafters are of large yellow bamboo, while the smaller beams running parallel to the sides of the room consist of small dark-brown and polished bamboo; the body of the ceiling is made up of a brown rush, called *hagi*, — this representing the thatch. This ceiling was simply charming; it was clean, pure, and effective; it gave the room a lofty appearance, and was moreover thoroughly constructive. Our architects might well imitate it without the modification of a single feature.

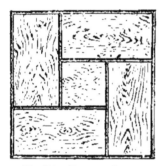

Fig. 143. — Panelled Ceiling.

The ceiling figured on page 156 (fig. 134) consisted of square panels of cedar, arranged on either side of a double curved bamboo, which ran across the ceiling diagonally from one corner of the room to another. Upon the bamboo was engraved a Chinese poem, in beautiful characters. The beauty of this ceiling consisted not only in its general quaint effect, but in the rich woods and good workmanship everywhere displayed in its construction. The same might be said of the ceiling shown in fig. 126 (see page 145); here, indeed, the whole room was like a choice cabinet. Lately, these panelled ceilings have come more into use. Fig. 143 represents a form of ceiling which may be occasionally seen, consisting of large, square planks of *sugi*, with a framework of bamboo or *keyaki* wood.

It seems a little curious that the space enclosed under the roof (a garret in fact) is rarely, if ever, utilized. Here the rats hold high carnival at night; and one finds it difficult to sleep, on account of the racket these pests keep up in racing and fighting upon the thin and resonant boards composing the ceiling. The rats make a thoroughfare of the beam which runs across the end of the house from one corner to the other; and this beam is called the *nedzumi bashira*, — literally, " rat-post."

In my remarks on house-construction I made mention of the plaster walls, and of the various colored sands used in the plaster. There are many ways of treating this surface, by which curious effects are obtained. Little gray and white pebbles are sometimes mixed with the plaster. The shells of a little fresh-water bivalve (*Corbicula*) are pounded into fragments and mixed with the plaster. In the province of Mikawa I saw an iron-gray plaster, in which had been mixed the short fibres of finely-chopped hemp, the fibres glistening in the plaster; the effect was odd and striking. In the province of Omi it was not unusual to see white plastered surfaces smoothly finished, in which iron-dust had been blown evenly upon the surface while the plaster was yet moist, and, oxidizing, had given a warm brownish-yellow tint to the whole.

In papering plaster-walls rice-paste is not used, as the larvæ of certain insects are liable to injure the surface. In lieu of this a kind of seaweed similar to Iceland moss is used, the mucilaginous portion of which forms the cement. This material is used in sizing paper, and also in the pasteboard or stiff paper which is made by sticking a number of sheets together.

Plastered rooms are often papered; and even when the plaster is tinted and the plastered surface is left exposed, it is customary to use a paper called *koshi-bari,* which is spread on the wall to a height of two feet or more in order to protect the clothes from the plaster. This treatment is seen in common rooms.

Simple and unpretending as the interior of a Japanese house appears to be, it is wonderful upon how many places in their apparently naked rooms the ingenuity and art-taste of the cabinet-maker can be expended. Naturally, the variety of design and finish of the *tokonoma* and *chigai-dana* is unlimited save by the size of their areas; for with the sills and upright posts, the shelves and little closets, sliding-doors with their surfaces for the artists' brush, and the variety of woods employed, the artisan has a wide field in which to display his peculiar skill. The ceiling, though showing less variety in its structure, nevertheless presents a good field for decorative work, though any exploits in this direction outside the conventional form become very costly, on account of the large surface to deal with and the expensive cabinet-work required. Next to the *chigai-dana* in decorative importance (excepting of course the ceiling, which, as we have already seen, rarely departs from the almost universal character of thin boards and transverse strips), I am inclined to believe that the *ramma* receives the most attention from the designer, and requires more delicate work from the cabinet-maker. It is true that the areas to cover are small, yet the designs which may be carved or latticed, — geometric designs in fret-work, or perforated designs in panel, — must have a strength and prominence not shown in the other interior finishings of the room.

The *kamoi,* or lintel, as we have seen, is a beam that runs entirely across the side of the room at the height of nearly six feet from the floor (fig. 103). On its under surface are the grooves in which the *fusuma* run; between this beam and the ceiling is a space of two feet or more depending, of course, upon the height of the room. The height of the beam itself from the floor, a nearly constant factor, is always lower than are our doorways, because the average height of the Japanese people is less than ours; and aggravatingly low to many foreigners is this beam, as can be attested by those who have cracked their heads against it in passing from one room to another. The space between the *kamoi* and the ceiling is called the *ramma*, and offers another field for the exercise of that decorative faculty which comes so naturally to the Japanese. This space may be occupied simply by a closed plastered partition, just as in our houses we invariably fill up a similar space which comes over wide folding doors between a suite of rooms. In the Japanese room, however, it is customary to divide this space into two or

Fig. 144. — Ramma in Hakóne Village.

more panels, — usually two; and in this area the designer and wood-worker have ample room to carry out those charming surprises which are to be seen in Japanese interiors.

The designs are of course innumerable, and may consist of diaper-work and geometric designs; or each panel may consist of a single plank of wood with the design wrought out, while the remaining wood is cut away, leaving the dark shadows of the room beyond as a back-ground to the design; or the design may be in the form of a thin panel of cedar, in which patterns of birds, flowers, waves, dragons, or other objects are cut out in perforated work. Fret-work panels are very often used in the decoration of the *ramma*, of designs similar to the panels now imported from Japan; but the figures are worked out in larger patterns.

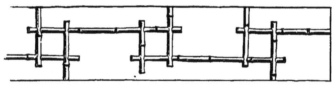

FIG. 145. — BAMBOO RAMMA.

Light and airy as the work seems to be, it must nevertheless be strongly made, as it is rare to see any displaced or broken portions in panels of this nature.

The design represented in fig. 144 is from a *ramma* in an old house in the village of Hakóne. The room was very large, and there were four panels in the *ramma*, which was nearly twenty-four feet long. A light trellis of bamboo is a favorite and common device for this area. Fig. 145 gives a simple

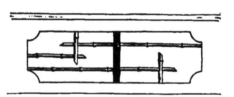

FIG. 146. — PORCELAIN RAMMA IN TOKIO.

form of this nature, which may be often seen. In a house in Tokio we saw a similar design carried out in porcelain (fig. 146), — the central vertical rod having a dark-blue glaze, while the lighter horizontal rods were white in color. It should be understood that in every case the interspaces between the designs, except in the perforated ones, is freely open to the next room. By means of these open *ramma* much better ventilation of the rooms is secured when the *fusuma* is closed. A combination of perforated panels and a grating of bamboo is often seen (fig. 147).

The *ramma* requiring great skill in design and execution are those in which the wood-carver, having his design drawn upon a solid plank, cuts away all the wood about it, leaving the design free; and this is then delicately wrought.

In an old house at Gojio, Yamato, is a *ramma* having a single panel the length of the room. Fig. 148 illustrates this

FIG. 147. — RAMMA OF BAMBOO AND PERFORATED PANEL.

design, which consists of chrysanthemums supported on a bamboo trellis, and was carved out of a single plank, the flowers and delicate tracery of the leaves being wrought with equal care on both sides; in fact, the *ramma* in every case is designed to be seen from both rooms. I have often noticed that in quite old houses the *ramma* was of this description. In an old house at Yatsushiro. in Higo, I saw a very beautiful form of this nature (fig. 149). The *ramma* was divided into two panels, and the design was continuous from one panel to another. It represented a rustic method of conducting water by means of wooden troughs, propped up by branched sticks, and sticks tied together. The representation of long leaves of some aquatic plant, with their edges ragged by partial decay, was remarkably well rendered. The plank out of which the design was wrought must have been less than an inch in thickness, and yet the effect of relief was surprising. A white substance like chalk filled the interstices of the carving, giving the appearance that at one time the whole design had been whitened and the coloring matter had subsequently worn away. The house was quite old, and the work had been done by a local artist.

It is a remarkable fact, and one well worth calling attention to, that in the smaller towns and villages, in regions far apart, there seems to be artistic workmen capable of designing and executing these graceful and artistic carvings, — for such they certainly are. Everywhere throughout the Empire we find good work of all kinds, and evidence that workmen of all crafts have *learned* their trades, — not "served" them, — and are employed at home. In other words, the people everywhere appreciate artistic designs and the proper execution of them; and, consequently, men capable in their various lines find their services in demand wherever they may be. I do not mean to imply by this general statement that good workmen in Japan are not drawn to the larger cities for employment, but rather that the smaller towns and villages everywhere are not destitute of such a class, and that the distribution of such artisans is far more wide and general than with us. And how different such conditions are with us may be seen in the fact that there are hundreds of towns and thousands of villages in our country where the carpenter is just capable of making a shelter from the weather; and if he attempts to beautify it — but we will not awaken the recollection of those startling horrors of petticoat scallops fringing the eaves and every opening, and rendered, if possible, more hideous by the painter.

Throughout the breadth and length of that land of thirty-six million people men capable of artistic work, and people capable of appreciating such work, abound. In our land of fifty-five millions one has to seek the great centres of population for similar work, — for elsewhere the good work and its appreciation are exceptional.

At Nagoya, in the house of a poor man, I saw a simple and ingenious form of *ramma*, in which two thin boards, one

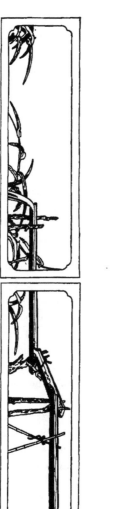

Fig. 149. — Carved-wood Ramma in Town of Yatsushiro, Higo.

Fig. 148. — Carved-wood Ramma in Gujo Village, Yamato.

of light and the other of dark cedar, had been cut in the
form of mountain contours. These were placed in juxtaposition,
and from either side the appearance of two ranges of mountains
was conveyed. Fig. 150 gives a faint idea of the appearance
of this simple *ramma*. There are many suggestions in the decoration and utilization for ventilating rooms through certain
portions of the frieze, which might be adopted with advantage
in the finish of our interiors.

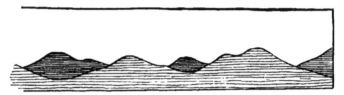

Fig. 150. — Ramma, composed of two Thin Boards, in Nagoya, Owari.

As the room, when closed, receives its light through the *shōji*,
the windows proper — that is, certain openings in permanent
partitions which may be regarded as windows — have in most
cases lost their functional character, and have become modified
into ornamental features merely, many of them being strictly
decorative, having none of the functions of a window whatever.
These openings assume an infinite variety of forms, and appear
in the most surprising places in the room. They may be placed
low down near the floor, or close to the ceiling; indeed, they occur between the rooms when permanent partitions are present,
and similar openings may be seen in the partition which separates
the *tokonoma* from the *chigai-dana*. A window often occurs in a
partition that continues some little distance beyond the outer
edge of the *tokonoma*. This window is usually square, and is
closed by a *shōji*. The upper cross-piece of the *shōji*-frame
projects at each end, so that it may be hung in place on iron
hooks (fig. 151). If the window comes near the *tokonoma* the

shōji is hung on the outside of the room, as its appearance in this way is better from within. If it occurs in a partition near the *chōdzu-bachi,* the *shōji* is hung inside the room. Sometimes the *shōji* rests on grooved cleats or bars, which are fastened above and below the window, and oftentimes it runs inside the partition, — that is, in a partition that is double. The *shōji* in this case is often made in two portions, and parts to the right or left. The frame-work of the *shōji* forming

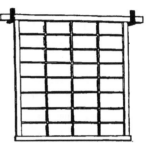

Fig. 151. — Shōji for Window.

the windows is often a marvel of exquisite taste. The designs are often geometric figures, as in fig. 152; though other designs

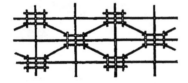

Fig. 152. — Shōji-frame for Window.

are seen, as in fig. 153, representing a mountain. These designs, being made of very thin strips of white pine, it would seem that in such examples portions of the frame-work must have been fastened to the paper to keep them in place, for there is no means of sustaining such a frame in position without some such method.

At Nagoya, in an old house, I saw a remarkable partition of dark cedar, in which a circular window, five feet in diameter, was occupied by a panel of thin cedar, in which was a perforated design of waves; the drawing was of the most graceful description. The curious, formal, curled tongues of water, like young sprouting ferns, the long graceful sweep of the waves, and the circular drops suspended above the breaking crests presented a charming effect, as the light coming through from the outside illuminated these various openings.

When these windows occur in the second story they are arranged to overlook some pleasant garden or distant landscape;

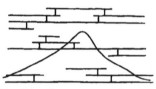

FIG. 153. — SHOJI-FRAME FOR WINDOW.

for this purpose the window is usually circular, though it may be in the shape of the crescent moon, or fan-shaped; indeed, there seems to be no end to designs for these apertures. Openings of this nature between rooms may or may not have *shōji*, but they always have a lattice-work of bamboo, or some other material, arranged in certain ornamental ways. The outside windows not only have the *shōji*, but may have an ornamental lattice-work as well. In fig. 121 the large circular window next the *tokonoma* had a lattice-work of bamboo arranged in an exceedingly graceful design.

Great attention is devoted to the window which comes in the recess used for writing purposes. The frame of this window may be lacquered, and the lattice-work and *shōji*

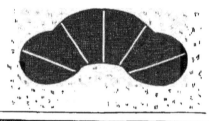
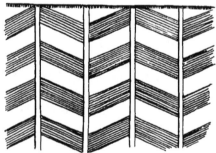

FIG. 154. — WINDOW.

are often marvels of the cabinet-maker's art. Windows of curious construction are often placed in some passage-way or space at the end of the verandah leading to the lavatory, when one exists. The accompanying figure (fig. 154) shows a window of this nature, seen from the outside; the bars were of iron, and below the opening the wood-finish consisted of alternate panels of cedar-bark and light wood.

There are hundreds of forms of these windows, or *mado*, as they are called. The few to which allusion has been made serve to give one some idea of the almost entirely ornamental character of these openings. It is worthy of note that each form has its appropriate name, and books are specially prepared, giving many designs of windows and their modes of construction.

In the chapter on Gardens a few descriptions and sketches are given of other forms of windows belonging to summer-houses.

The open character of the Japanese house has caused the development of a variety of forms of portable screens, bamboo shades, curtains, and the like, upon which much ingenuity of construction and an infinite amount of artistic talent has been expended. The *biyŏ-bu*, or folding screens, are too well known to require more than a passing allusion. These consist of a number of panels or folds covered on both sides with stout paper. A narrow border of wood forms an outer frame, and this may be plain or lacquered. The end folds have the corners as well as other portions of its frame decorated with wrought metal pieces. Just within the frame runs a border of brocade of varying width, and on its inner edge a narrow strip of brocade; within this comes the panel or portion to receive the artist's efforts. Each fold or panel may have a separate picture upon it; or, as is most usually the case, a continuous landscape or composition covers the entire side of the, screen. Many of the great artists of Japan have embodied some of their best works on screens of this kind, and the prices at which some of these are held are fabulous.

12

The rich and heavily-gilded screens now so rare to obtain are marvels of decorative painting. While the front of the screen may have a broad landscape, the back may be simply a plain gold surface, or have some sketchy touches of bamboo, pine, etc., in

FIG. 155. — BIYŌ-BU, OR FOLDING SCREEN.

black. I have been told that the gold-leaf was so thick on many of the old screens, that the sacrilege has often been committed of destroying them for the gold contained on their surfaces.

The six-panelled gold-screen is, beyond all question, the richest object of household use for decorative purposes ever devised. There certainly is no other device in which so many decorative arts are called into play. The rich lacquered frame, the wrought metallic mountings, the border of gold brocade, and the great expanse for the artist's brush (for when both sides of a six-fold screen is decorated, an area is obtained nearly five feet in height and twenty-four feet in length) give great variety for richness of adornment. The rich, dead gold-leaf with which it is gilded softens the reflections, and gives a warm, radiant tone to the light. Its adjustable nature permits it to display its painting in every light. We refer now, of course, to the genuine old gold-screens which came in sets of two. One possessing a set of these screens may consider himself particularly fortunate. The one figured (fig. 155) has depicted upon it a winter scene painted by Kano Tsunenobu, and is nearly one hundred and seventy years old; the companion of this has represented upon it a summer scene, by the same artist. On the reverse sides are painted with bright and vigorous touches the bamboo and pine. Fig. 156 shows one corner of the screen-frame with its metal mounting. These screens may have two folds, or three, or even six, as in this case. A set of screens when not in use are enclosed in silk bags, and then placed in a long, narrow wooden box (fig. 157). This box, like other articles of household use, such as bureaus and chests of drawers, has long hanging iron handles,

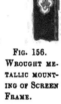

FIG. 156.
WROUGHT ME-
TALLIC MOUNT-
ING OF SCREEN
FRAME.

which when turned upwards project above the level of the top, forming convenient loops through which a stick may be passed, — and thus in case of fire may be easily transported upon the shoulders of men.

When the screen is unfolded and placed on the floor, various devices are provided to prevent the end panels being swayed by the wind. These devices may be in the shape of some metal figure which acts as a check, or a heavy weight of pottery made in the shape shown in fig. 158, the end of the screen fitting into the slot in the weight.

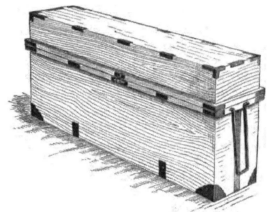

FIG. 157. — SCREEN-BOX.

On certain festival days, it is customary for the people bordering the wider thoroughfares to throw open their houses and display their screens; and in Kioto, at such times, one may

FIG. 158. — FOOT-WEIGHT FOR SCREEN.

walk along the streets and behold a wonderful exhibition of these beautiful objects.

A screen peculiar to Kioto, and probably farther south, is seen, in which panels of rush and bamboo split in delicate bars are inserted in each leaf of the screen. Such a screen when spread admits a certain amount of light as well as air, and may be used in summer.

A low screen of two folds, called a *furosaki biyō-bu* is placed in front of the *furo,* or fire-vessel, used for boiling water for tea. The purpose of this is to screen the *furo* from the wind and prevent the ashes from being blown about the room.

Sometimes these screens are made in a rigid form of wood, with the wings at right angles, the panels being of rush; and in the corner of the screen a little shelf is fixed, upon which the tea-utensils may be placed. Such an one is

FIG. 159. — FUROSAKI BIYŎ-BU.

here figured (fig. 159); there are many designs for this kind of screen.

In the old-fashioned *genka,* or hall-way, there stands a solid screen of wood with heavy frame, supported by two transverse feet. This screen is called a *tsui-tate,* and is an article of furniture belonging to the hall. It is often richly decorated with gold lacquer, and is usually much lower in height than the ordinary screen. In old Japanese picture-books this form is often represented. Diminutive models of the *tsui-tate* (fig. 160) are made in pottery or porce-

FIG. 160. — MODEL OF TSUI-TATE IN POTTERY.

lain, and these are for the purpose of standing in front of the ink-stone to prevent the mats from being spattered when the ink is rubbed. In another form of *tsui-tate* a stand is made having uprights placed in such a way that a screen covered with stout paper or a panel may be placed upon the stand and held in a vertical position by these uprights, as shown in fig. 161.

When the *shōji* are removed, and the room thrown wide open to the light and air, curtains composed of strips of bamboo or rush are used as sun-screens; these are generally hung up just below the edge of the supplementary roof or *hisashi*, or may be suspended just outside the room. They can be rolled up and tied, or dropped to any desired length. These

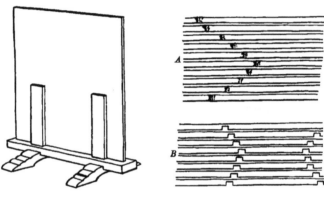

FIG. 161. — TSUI-TATE.   FIG. 162. — BAMBOO CURTAINS.

curtains may be either plain or have traced upon them delicate designs of vines or gourds, or conventional patterns. These designs are produced either by the joints on the bamboo being adjusted to carry out a zigzag or other design, as shown in fig. 162 (*A*), or else the thin strips of bamboo may have square notches cut out from their lower edges as in fig. 162 (*B*). In this case the shade of the room within gives the necessary back-ground tó bring out the design as shown in fig. 163. These devices are called *noren;* if made of bamboo, they are called *sudare.*

In illustrated books there is often seen figured a screen such as is shown in fig. 164. This consists of a lacquered stand, from which spring two upright rods, which in turn support a transverse bar not unlike some forms of towel-racks ; dependent from this is a curtain of cloth, which is long enough to sweep the floor. I have never seen this object, though it is probably in use in the houses of the Daimios.

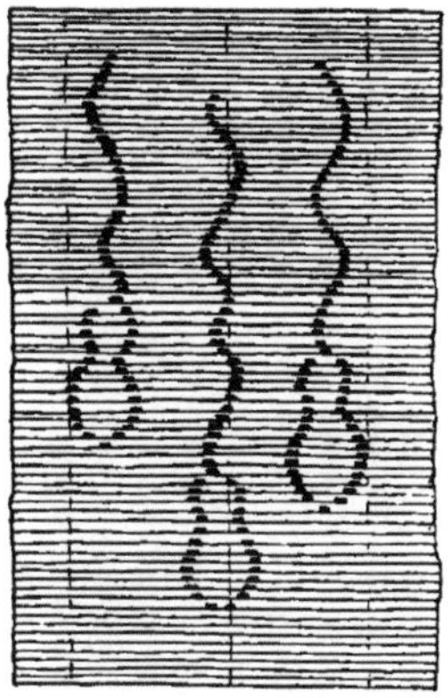

FIG. 163. — BAMBOO CURTAIN.

FIG. 164. — CURTAIN-SCREEN.

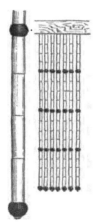

A screen or curtain is often seen in doorways and passage-ways, consisting of a fringe of cords, upon which has been strung like beads short sections of bamboo, with black seeds at intervals. A portion of one of these fringed curtains is illustrated in fig. 165. Such a curtain has the advantage not only of being a good screen, but the inmates may pass through it, so to speak, without the necessity of lifting it. There are many forms of this curtain to be seen, and at present the Japanese are exporting a variety of delicate ones made of glass beads and sections of rushes.

Cloth curtains are used at the entrance to the kitchen, and also to screen closet-like recesses. The cloth is cut at intervals, leaving

FIG. 165. — FRINGED CURTAIN.

a series of long flaps.   This curtain is not readily swayed by
the wind, and can easily be passed through as one enters the
room (fig. 166).   In front of the Japanese shop one may see
a similar form of curtain slit at intervals, so that it may not
be affected by ordinary winds.

There are doubtless many other forms of screens and curtains
not here enumerated, but most of those described present the
common forms usually observed.

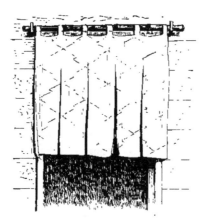

FIG. 166. — SLASHED CURTAIN.

CHAPTER IV.

INTERIORS (*Continued*).

THE kitchen, as an apartment, varies quite as much in Japan as it does in our country, and varies in the same way; that is to say, in the country, in houses of the better class, both in Japan and the United States, the kitchen is large and oftentimes spacious, well lighted and airy, in which not only the preparation of food and the washing of dishes go on, but in which also the meals are served. The kitchen of the common city house in both countries is oftentimes a dark narrow room, ill-lighted, and altogether devoid of comfort for the cook. Among this class of houses the kitchen is the least defined of Japanese rooms; it lacks that tidiness and definition so characteristic of the other rooms. It is often a narrow porch or shed with pent roof, rarely, if ever, possessing a ceiling ; its exposed rafters are blackened by the smoke, which finds egress through a scuttle, through which often comes the only light that illuminates the dim interior. In the city house the kitchen often comes on that side of the house next the street, for the reason that the garden being in the rear of the house the best rooms face that area ; being on the street too, the kitchen is convenient for the vender of fish and vegetables, and for all the kitchen traffic, which too often with us results in the strewing of our

little grass-plots with the wrapping paper of the butcher's bundles and other pleasing reminiscences of the day's dinner.   In the
country the kitchen is generally at the end of the house usually
opening into some porch-like expansion, where the tubs, buckets,
etc., and the winter's supply of wood finds convenient storage.

Fig. 167. — Kitchen in old Farmhouse at Kabutoyama.

In public inns and large country houses, and also in many
of the larger city tea-houses, the customary raised floor is divided
by a narrow area, which has for its floor the hard trodden earth ;
and this area forms an avenue from the road to the heart of
the house, and even through the house to the garden beyond.
This enables one to pass to the centre of the house without
the necessity of removing one's shoes.   Porters and servants
bring the guest's baggage and deposit it directly upon the mats ;

and in the inns more privacy is secured by the *kago* being
brought to the centre of the house, where the visitor may alight
at the threshold of the very room he is to occupy. A plank or
other adjustable platform is used to bridge this avenue, so that
occupants may go from one portion of the house to another in
their bare or stockinged feet.

If this area is in a public inn, the office, common room, and
kitchen border one side of this thoroughfare. In the common
room the baby-tend-
ing, sewing, and the
various duties of the
family go on under
the heavily-raftered
and thatched roof,
which blackened by
the smoke from the
kitchen fire, and fes-
tooned with equally
blackened cobwebs,
presents a weird ap-

Fig. 168. — Kitchen Range.

pearance when lighted up by the ruddy glow from the hearth.
We speak now of the northern country houses, particularly where
the fireplace, as in the Aino house, is in the middle of the
floor. In country houses of the better class the kitchen is large
and roomy; the well is always conveniently near, and often
under the same roof. An enormous quantity of water is used
in the kitchen of a Japanese house; and if the well is outside,
then a trough is arranged beside the well, into which the water
is poured, and from this trough a bamboo spout conveys the
water into a big water-tank within the kitchen. In the vicinity
of the well it is always wet and sloppy; the vegetables, rice,
dishes, and nearly every utensil and article of food seems to
come under this deluge of water.

Fig. 167 (page 186) gives a sketch of an old kitchen at Kabutoyama in the western part of the province of Musashi. This kitchen is nearly three hundred years old, and is the type of a kitchen of a wealthy and independent Japanese farmer. The great wooden curbed well is seen in front, with a pulley above in which the rope runs. Near by is a trough from which a bamboo spout leads to some trough in another portion of the house. The *kamado*, or cooking-range, is seen to the left, and beyond is a room partly closed by *fusuma*. Directly beyond the well two girls may be seen in the act of preparing dinner, which consists in arranging the dishes on little raised lacquered trays, which are to be carried in when dinner is ready. Near the range are little portable affairs made of soft stone and used as braziers. The raised floor is composed of broad planks; kitchens invariably have wooden floors, which are oftentimes very smooth and polished.

The usual form of kitchen range is represented in fig. 168; this is made of broken tiles and mud or clay compacted together and neatly plastered and blackened on the outside. In this range there are two recesses for fire, which open directly in front; and this structure rests upon a stout wooden frame having a place for ashes in front, and a space beneath in which the wood and charcoal are kept. Sometimes this range, retaining the same form, is made of copper; within this water is kept, and little openings permit the wine-bottle to be immersed in order to heat it, as the *sake* is drunk hot without the admixture of hot water.

In another kitchen in a house in Imado, Tokio, a hood of sheet-iron was arranged to convey the smoke outside the building. This is probably a modern device (fig. 169).

In fig. 170 a sketch is given of a kitchen in Tokio in which the range was a closed affair made of stone, with a funnel at the end as in our stoves. I was told by the owner of this house that

FIG. 169. — KITCHEN RANGE, WITH SMOKE-CONDUCTOR.

this kind of a stove had been in use in his family for three generations, at least. In this kitchen an area level with the

ground is seen, in which stands the sink containing an inverted
rice-kettle.   Beside the sink stands a huge water-jar, with water-
bucket and water-dipper conveniently near; above is a shelf upon
which are numerous buckets and tubs.   On one of the posts hangs
the usual bamboo rack for skewers, wooden spoons, spatulas, etc.,
and below it is a case for the meat and fish knives.   On a bam-

FIG. 170. — KITCHEN IN CITY HOUSE.

boo pole a few towels hang, and also two large fishes' heads from
which a thin soup is to be made.   On a post near the mouth
of the stove hangs a coarse wire sieve with which to sift the
ashes for the little bits of unburnt charcoal, which are always
frugally saved, and near by is a covered vessel to hold these cin-
ders.   The customary stone brazier for heating water for the tea
stands near the stove.

Fig. 171 represents more clearly the form of this brazier, which is called a *shichirin*. It is a convenient and economical device for the cooking of small messes or boiling water, charcoal being used for the purpose. Instead of bellows, a fan is used for kindling or quickening a fire. A short bamboo tube is also used through which the cook's lungs act as a bellows in performing a like service.

Fig. 172 gives a clearer view of the bamboo rack and the knife-case below, with which almost every kitchen is supplied. Often in public inns the kitchen opens on the street, where the cook may be seen conspicuously at work. In our country the chop-houses oftentimes have the grilling and stewing ostentatiously displayed in the same way, as an appetizing inducement to attract guests.

Fig. 171. — BRAZIERS.

Fig. 174 gives a view of a common arrangement for the kitchen in the north of Japan, and in the country everywhere. Here the fireplace is in the centre of the room. A kettle is suspended over the fire by a chain, and other kettles are huddled around it to be heated. Overhead a rack hangs, from which fish and meat are suspended, and thus the smoke which ascends from the fire is utilized in curing them. Sometimes a large cushion ·of straw is suspended above the smoke, and little fish skewered with pointed sticks are thrust into this bunch of straw like pins in a pin-cushion.

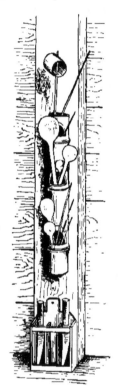

FIG. 172. — BAMBOO RACK AND KNIFE-CASE.

In fig. 175 a more elaborate affair is shown from which to suspend the tea-kettle. This is a complex mechanism with a curious joint, so that it may be hoisted or lowered at will.

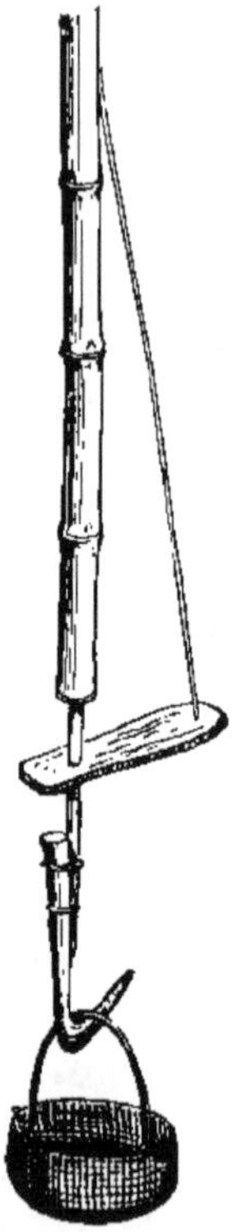

In the hut of the peasant a simple affair is seen (fig. 173) made out of bamboo, which answers the same purpose. This is called a *ji-zai*, which means "at one's will." In the front of fig. 175 a square copper box is noticed, having two round openings. This box is filled with water, which becomes heated by the fire, and is for the purpose of warming the *sake*, or wine. The tongs are stuck into the ashes in one corner.

FIG. 173. — JI-ZAI.

These consist of a long pair of iron chop-sticks held together at one end by a large ring, so that one leg of the tongs, so to speak, may not get misplaced. No inconsiderable skill is required to pick up hot coals with this kitchen implement, as in unaccustomed or awkward hands the ring prevents the points from coming together.

It may be proper to mention here an arrangement for holding a pot over the fire, seen in a boat coming down the Kitakami River, and which is probably used in the north of Japan, though I have never seen it in the house. It consisted of an upright stick having a groove through the centre. In this groove fitted a jointed stick resting horizontally, and arranged in such a way that it could be adjusted at any height. Fig. 176 (page 195) will illustrate the manner of its working better than any description can.

The floor of most rooms, being permanently covered with the mats already described in previous chapters, has no special attention bestowed upon it; at all events, the floor is often of rough boards

Fig. 174. — Fireplace in Country House.

laid in such a way that irregular spaces occur between them. When the house has a proper hall or vestibule, the floor is composed of wide planks; and the smooth, ivory-like, polished condition in which such floors are often kept is surprising. In

13

country houses it is not unusual to see polished-wood floors in portions of the front rooms, and as one rides along the

Fig. 175. — The best Fireplace.

road he may often see the reflection of the garden beyond in their polished surfaces. In country inns the floor in the front of the house is often of plank. Matted floors are, however, universal from the extreme north to the extreme south of the Empire.

In houses of traders bordering the street the matted floor properly terminates a few feet within the sill, the space between

FIG. 176. — AN ADJUSTABLE DEVICE FOR SUPPORTING A KETTLE.

being of earth. The floor being raised, the space between the edge of the floor and the earth is generally filled with plain panels of wood, though sometimes designs of flowers or conventional figures are cut in the panel. These panels are often arranged so that they can be removed, revealing a space under the floor in which shoes, umbrellas, etc., can be stowed away.

One of the surprising features that strikes a foreigner as he becomes acquainted with the Japanese house is the entire absence of so many things that with us clutter the closets, or make squirrel-nests of the attic,—I speak now of the common house. The reason of this is that the people have never developed the miserly spirit of hoarding truck and rubbish with the idea that some day it may come into use: this spirit when developed into a mania converts a man's attic and shed into a junk-shop. The few necessary articles kept by the Japanese are stowed away in boxes, cupboards, or interspaces beneath the floors.

The kitchens in every case have wood floors, as do the halls, verandahs, and all passage-ways. The ground beneath the floor is, in the houses of the better class, prepared with gravel and mortar mixed with clay, or macadamized.

A variety of closets is found in

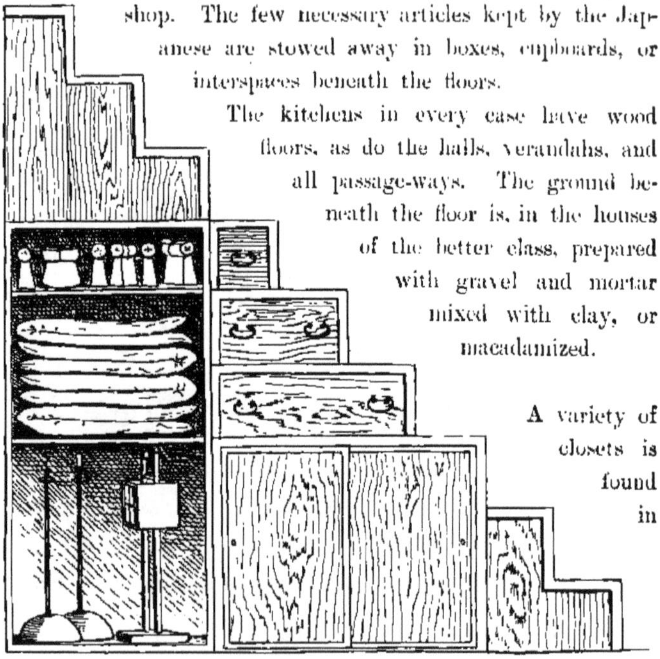

Fig. 177. — Kitchen Closet, Drawers, Cupboard, and Stairs combined.

the Japanese house. The larger closets, closed by sliding screens, or *fusuma*, are used for clothing and bedding. The *tansu* — a chest of drawers not unlike our bureau — is often placed within the closet, which is also a receptacle for chests and trunks. The ordinary high closet is not so often seen; and where in our

houses it is deemed a necessity to have each chamber provided
with a closet, in the Japanese house bed-chambers rarely contain
such conveniences. There are low cupboards or closets in certain recesses, the upper part or top of which forms a deep
open shelf. In the kitchen, dressers and similar conveniences
are used for the dishes. In the province of Omi it is common
to see a case of shelves with cupboard beneath; upon the shelves
the larger dishes are displayed. In the kitchen there is often
combined with the flight of stairs a closet; and this closet usually has a door swinging on hinges. In this closet are often
kept the bed-clothes, pillows, candle-sticks, and night-lamps.
Fig. 177 illustrates the appearance of this closet. In the hall-
way, also, a closet is sometimes seen in which to stow away the
geta, or wooden clogs. A closet of this nature is described
farther on.

As most of the houses are of one story, and the area between
the ceiling and the roof never utilized, as with us, stairways are
not common; when they do occur they are primitive in their
construction. A stairway incorporated into the structure of a
building and closed below I have never seen in Japan; nor is
there any approach to the broad, low steps and landings or spiral staircases such as we are familiar with in American houses.
If the house be of two stories the staircase assumes the form of
a rather precipitous step-ladder; that is, it has two side-pieces, or
strings, in which the steps, consisting of thick plank, are mortised. This ladder is so steeply inclined that one has to step
sideways in ascending, otherwise his knee would strike the step
above. Rarely is there any convenience to hold on by: if present,
however, this consists of a strip of wood fastened to the wall,
or a rope is secured in the same way. The front of the step is
open, — that is, there is no riser; but if the back of the steps
face an open room, then slats of wood are nailed on behind.

In a beautiful house recently erected in one of the imperial gardens is a remarkably pure and simple staircase and rail (fig. 178).

In the inns and large farm-houses the step-ladder form is often seen, and this is removable if occasion calls for it. Another kind, common to the same class of houses, has the appearance of a number of square boxes piled one upon another, like a set of different-sized blocks. This is a compact structure, however, though in reality consisting of a number of compartments which may be separated. There are many forms of this kind of staircase. The one shown in fig. 177 has the first two steps closed; then comes a low cupboard with sliding doors at the side, its upper corner forming another step. Upon the cupboard rest three more

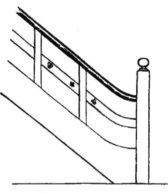

FIG. 178. — STAIR-RAIL.

steps, each of which has a drawer which pulls out at the side. Next to this comes a high closet, supporting on its top two or three more steps. This closet usually has a swinging door, — a feature rarely seen elsewhere within the Japanese house proper. This closet contains on its floor the night-lamp, or *andon,* and tall candlesticks, and above are stowed away the bedding and pillows; or it may be used for trays and dishes. The steps are not so steep as in the ladder form, have no baluster or rail, and are remarkably solid. It may be well to say here that the wood composing the staircase, as well as certain floors, is highly finished, often with a surface like polished ivory. I have frequently examined the wood for evidences of wax or polish applied to its surface, but found none. Inquiry brought out the curious information that the water from the bath is often used to moisten the cloth with which the wood is wiped; and evidently the sebaceous secretions of the skin had much to do with the beautiful polish often attained. When a house possesses a *genka*, or hall, the steps, two or three in number, are as broad as the hall, and generally the steps are somewhat higher than our steps. These steps are in every case permanently built into the structure of the floor. In the steps which lead from the verandah to the ground the usual form is in the shape of square or irregular blocks of stone or wood; if of wood, the step may be a transverse section of some

Fig. 179. — Steps to Verandah.

huge tree, or a massive plank. Other forms of steps may consist simply of two side-pieces, with the steps made of plank and mortised in (fig. 179); or a more compact structure may be made with a very low hand-rail. These forms are all adjustable; that is, they may be placed at any part of the verandah.

There is no feature of social life in Japan which has been more ignorantly, and in some cases wilfully, animadverted upon than the custom of public bathing; nevertheless, I dare to say that there is no feature in Japanese life to be more heartily commended than this same system of public bathing. But by this assertion I do not mean to suggest that we shall forthwith proceed to establish baths after the Japanese style, and

take them after the Japanese fashion.   The Japanese, as well
as other Eastern people, have for centuries been accustomed to
see nakedness, without its provoking among them the slightest
attention, or in any way suggesting immodesty.   With us,
on the contrary, the effect has been different ; and the dire
result is seen in the almost utter extinction in our country of
the classical drama, and the substitution therefor of ballet-
dancing and burlesques, — of anything in fact that shall present
to the vulgar gaze of thousands the female form in scanty
apparel.[1]   A Turkish woman looks upon her Christian sister as
not only immodest and vulgar, but absolutely immoral, because
she unblushingly parades the public street with a naked face ;
but the Christian woman knows that the established customs
of her country sanction such an exposure as entirely proper.
A girl who in our country would deem it immodest to appear
among the members of her own family in a *robe de chambre,*
and yet under the glare of a bright gas-light, in the midst of
scores of strangers, appears with low *corsage,* is committing
an act which to a Turkish woman would appear inexplicable.
To a Japanese, the sight of our dazzling ball-rooms, with girls
in *décolleté* dresses, clasped in the arms of their partners and
whirling to the sound of exciting music, must seem the wildest
debauch imaginable ; for in Japan the sexes, except among the
lower classes, never intermingle.   No free and happy picnics,
sleigh-rides, boat-sails, and evening parties among the girls and

---

[1] A correspondent in the " Pall Mall Gazette," in protesting against the attempt to
impose European clothing on those people who are accustomed to go without any, says :
" In many parts of India there is a profound suspicion of the irreligiousness of clothing.
The fakir is distressed even by the regulation rag upon which the Government modestly
insists, and a fully dressed fakir would be scouted.   The late Brahmo minister, Chesub
Chunder Sen, expressed the belief that India would never accept a Christ in hat and
boots.   The missionary should remember that clothes-morality is climatic, and that if a
certain degree of covering of the body has gradually become in the Northwest associated
with morality and piety, the traditions of tropical countries may have equally connected
elaborate dress rather with the sensualities of Solomon in his glory than with the purity
of the lily as clothed by Nature."

boys are known there ; no hand-shake, no friendly kiss. If the Japanese visitor in this country is a narrow-minded and witless scribbler, he will probably startle his friends at home with accounts of the grossly immoral character of Christians. Unfamiliar as he is with the corner loafer eying every girl that walks by, or with that class which throng our walks with the sole purpose of staring at the girls, who are there for the purpose of being stared at, what must he think of our people when he visits our summer resorts at the seaside and sees a young girl — nay, swarms of them — tripping over the sand under a bright sun, bare-legged, clad only in a single wrapper, which when wet clings to her form and renders her an object of contemplation to a battalion of young men who fringe the beach !

In Japan, among the lower classes, the sexes bathe together, but with a modesty and propriety that are inconceivable to a foreigner until he has witnessed it. Though naked, there is no indecent exposure of the person. While in the bath they are absorbed in their work, and though chatting and laughing seem utterly unmindful of each other. The grossest libels have been written about the Japanese in reference to their custom of public bathing ; and I hazard the statement, without fear of contradiction, that an intelligent Japanese, seeing many of our customs for the first time, without knowing the conditions under which they had grown up, would find infinitely more to condemn as immodest, than an intelligent foreigner would find in seeing for the first time certain Japanese customs, with the same ignorance at the outset as to what such customs implied.

If cleanliness is next to godliness, then verily the Japanese are a godly race.[1] The simple statement, without qualification, that numbers of Japanese in their public baths bathe in the same

---

[1] Rein says: "The cleanliness of the Japanese is one of his most commendable qualities. It is apparent in his body, in his house, in his workshop, and no less in the great carefulness and exemplary exactness with which he looks after his fields."

water would seem a filthy habit. Certainly if such a statement were really true in regard to our own lower classes, it would be a most filthy habit. When it is understood, however, that the Japanese working classes — such as the carpenters, masons, and others — often bathe two or three times a day, and must of necessity enter the bath in a state of cleanliness such as our workmen rarely if ever attain, the statement loses some of its force. When it is further added that these people do not wash in the baths, but boil or soak in them for a while, and then upon a platform, with an extra bucket of water and a towel, wash and dry themselves, the filthy character of this performance assumes quite another aspect. A Japanese familiar with his airy and barn-like theatres, his public readings under an open tent-like structure, or gatherings in a room in which one or all sides may·be open to the air even in mid-winter, would look upon the usual public gatherings of our people in lecture-halls, school-rooms, and other closed apartments, wherein the air often becomes so foul that people faint and struggle to the door to get a breath of fresh air, — a Japanese, I say, would justly look upon such practices as filthy to the last degree. And what *would* he say to one of our great political meetings, for example, where a vast unwashed herd of perspiring and excited people actually bathe their delicate membranous lungs in the combined breath of hundreds!

The public baths, however, do not concern us, — though it may be well to contrast our country with Japan in this respect, where in the latter country every village and every town, and in the city nearly every square, possesses public baths where for the price of a cent or two one may find conveniences for a hot bath; while in our country public baths are only found in the larger cities, and few of these even can boast of such a luxury. As for the private houses in our country where bathing is customary, an inquiry shows that few possess the convenience of a bath-tub.

Among the masses of our people a Saturday-night wash may or may not be enforced; when it is, this performance usually takes place in the kitchen, with hot water furnished from the kettle.

But in Japan nearly every house among the higher and middle classes possesses the most ample arrangements for hot baths; and even among the poorer classes, in the country as well as in the city, this convenience is not wanting, with the added convenience of public baths everywhere attainable if desired.

FIG. 180. — BATH-TUB WITH SIDE OVEN.

There are many forms of bathing-tubs, all of them being large and deep. Means for applying the heat direct, which is of course the most economical, is attained in various ways. In the common form (fig. 180), a small chamber of copper is introduced at one end near the bottom of the tub, — the mouth having a frame of stone, or of clay or plaster. In this chamber a fire is built, and the water can be brought, if necessary, to the boiling-point. Within the tub a few transverse bars prevent the bather from coming in contact with the hot chamber in which the fire is burning. In another form, a copper funnel or tube passes directly through the bottom of the bathing-tub (fig. 181). The bottom of this tube has a grating of wire; charcoal is then placed in the tube, and its combustion rapidly heats the water. A pan is placed below

FIG. 181. — BATH-TUB WITH INSIDE FLUE.

the tube to catch the coal and ashes that fall through. In a more elaborate form (fig. 182), the bath-tub is in two sections, separated by the partition of the room.   These two sections are connected by a num-

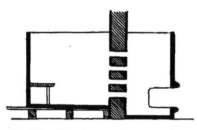

FIG. 182. — BATH-TUB IN SECTION, WITH OVEN OUTSIDE THE ROOM.

ber of bamboo tubes or flues, so that the water may circulate freely. The section outside contains the fire-box, in which the fire is built; by this arrangement the bather escapes the discomfort of the smoke from the fire.

A very excellent form of bathing-tub is shown in fig. 183, in which, outside the tub, is a chamber not unlike a small wooden barrel closed at both ends; through this barrel runs a copper tube, in which a fire of charcoal is built.   The barrel is connected with the bath-tub by a large bamboo tube, having a little square door within, which the bather may close if the water becomes too hot.   In many cases a hood is arranged in such a way that the smoke from the

FIG. 183. — BATH-TUB WITH OUTSIDE HEATING-CHAMBER.

fire is carried off. These tubs stand on a large wooden floor, the planks of which incline to a central gutter.   Here the bather scrubs himself with a separate bucket of water, after having literally parboiled himself in water the temperature of which is so great that it is impossible for a foreigner to endure it.

A very common form of bath in the country consists of a large and shallow iron kettle, upon the top of which is secured a wooden extension, so as to give sufficient depth to the water within (fig. 184). The fire is built beneath the kettle, — the bather having a rack of wood which he sinks beneath him, and upon which he stands to protect his feet from burning. This tub is called a *Goyemon buro*, named after Ishikawa Goyemon, — a famous robber of Taiko's time, who was treated to a bath in boiling oil.

There are doubtless other forms of bath-tubs with conveniences for heating the water, but the forms here given comprise the principal kinds. There is no reason why similar conveniences might not be adopted in

Fig. 184. — BATH-TUB, WITH IRON BASE.

our country in cases where aqueducts or city supply is not available. There are many forms of foot-tubs and large wooden tubs with high backs, in which hot water is poured ; but there is no necessity of describing them here.

While in a Japanese house, as we have seen, the most ample conveniences exist for taking a hot or cold bath, the minor conveniences for washing the face and hands are not always so apparent. In such attempts one is more often reminded of a primitive country house at home, where one either goes down to the kitchen, and amid a clutter of pails and pans manages to wash himself, or else takes a tin basin and goes out to the well, — and this on a fresh cool morning is by far the more agreeable. In the country a Japanese may be seen in the yard or by the roadside washing his face in a bucket or shallow tub; and at inns, and even in private houses, one is given a copper basin, and a bucket of water being brought he uses a portion of the verandah as a wash-stand. That conveniences for this purpose do exist to some extent may be seen from the accompaning sketches.

The one shown in fig. 185 may sometimes be found in country inns at the north. This consists of a shallow trough

Fig. 185. — Lavatory in Country Inn.

resting on the floor at the end of the verandah or passage-way. In the trough is a stout water-bucket with cover, and a copper wash-basin.

The convenience shown in fig. 186 was in a private house in Tokio. Here the trough was above the level of the floor, in a recessed portion of a passage-way which ran behind a suite of rooms. The wood-work about it was made with great care. The sliding window-frames, covered with stout white paper, admitted sufficient light; while the rich brown pottery-jar, the clean wooden dipper, copper basin, and quaint towel-rack were all attractive features from their very neatness and simplicity.

It may seem odd for one to get enthusiastic over so simple an affair as a trough and a few honest contrivances for washing the hands and face; nevertheless such a plain and sensible arrangement is a relief, in contrast to certain guest-chambers at home, where one wishing to go through the rather vigorous performance of dashing into the water with his elbows outstretched, finds these free movements curtailed to the last degree by a regiment of senseless toilet articles in the shape of

Fig. 186. — LAVATORY IN PRIVATE HOUSE.

attenuated bottles, mugs, soap-dishes with rattling covers, and diminutive top-heavy pitchers crowded about his wash-basin, and all resting on a slab of white marble. Things are inevitably broken if they are brought down too hard upon such a bottom. After such recollections, one admires the Japanese sink, with its durable flat-bottomed basin, capacious pottery-jar for water, and ample space to thrash about in without fear of spattering the wall-paper or smashing a lot of useless toilet articles in the act.

The form last described is the usual one seen in private houses. Conveniences of this nature that are brought to the level of the floor, while giving the Japanese who are used to them no trouble, are found to be exceedingly awkward for a foreigner, who is obliged to go through his toilet in a stooping posture.

Often the toilet places are rendered exceedingly attractive by the ornamental wood-work used in their construction.

Fig. 187 is a drawing from a design in a Japanese book, entitled "Yaye Gaki no Den." I have modified the drawing to conform more to our methods of perspective. This was placed at the end of the verandah, and on a level with the floor. A

FIG. 187.—LAVATORY COPIED FROM JAPANESE BOOK.

low partition formed a screen at one side; within the recess thus made was a low shelf for the pottery water-jar. The floor of the sink consisted of bamboo rods placed close together, through which the spilled water found its way by proper channels to the ground without. A paper-lantern hung against the wall, and dipper and towel-rack were conveniently at hand. Other forms might be given, but enough has been shown to illustrate how well these conveniences are arranged for that important daily operation of washing the face and hands. Further conveniences for simply washing the hands are offered in the *chōdzu-bachi*, description and figures of which will be given under that head.

The towel-rack merits some attention from its exceedingly simple structure. There are many forms, most of them rustic

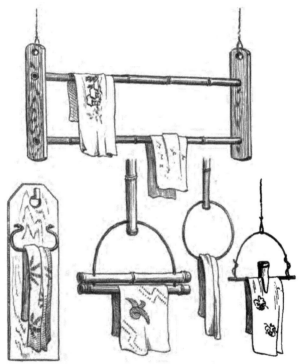

FIGS. 188-192. — FORMS OF TOWEL-RACKS.

in design and made to be suspended. The following figures (figs. 188-192) illustrate some of the forms in common use. The simplest kind is in the shape of a ring of bamboo suspended by a larger bamboo, to the end of which it is attached.

14

Another form, and a very common one, is a yoke of bamboo, the lower ends of which are firmly secured to a larger bamboo, confining at the same time a piece of bamboo which slides freely up and down on the yoke, and by its own weight resting on the towel which may be thrown across the lower bamboo. Another form consists of a loop of bamboo suspended to the side of a board which is hung against the wall.

The towels are pretty objects, being of cotton or linen, and usually have printed upon them sketchy designs in two shades of blue.

After living in Japan for a time one realizes how few are the essentials necessary for personal comfort. He further realizes that his personal comfort is enhanced by the absence of many things deemed indispensable at home. In regard to the bed and its arrangements, the Japanese have reduced this affair to its simplest expression. The whole floor, the whole house indeed, is a bed, and one can fling himself down on the soft mats, in the draught or out of it, upstairs or down, and find a smooth, firm, and level surface upon which to sleep, — no creaking springs, hard bunches or awkward hollows awaiting him, but a bed-surface as wide as the room itself, and comfortable to the last degree. To be more explicit, the bed is made upon the mats; there is no bedstead, or frame, or circumscribed area of any kind upon or within which the bed is placed.[1] The bed-clothes consisting of lightly or heavily wadded comforters are spread upon the floor, one or more forming the bed, and another one acting as a covering. The common ones are wadded with cotton; the best ones are made of silk, and are stuffed with floss silk. In private houses one often gets a bed consisting of a number of these silk comforters, — and a most

[1] From the name *tokonoma*, which means "bed-place," literally "bed of floor," it is supposed that in ancient times the bed was made or placed in this recess.

delightful bed they make. In summer the foreigner finds these wadded affairs altogether too hot and stuffy; and at all times he misses the clean sheets which at home intervene between the bed-clothes and his person, — though a clean night-dress is provided if desired, and this answers as a substitute for the sheets. In the day-time these comforters are folded up and stowed away in some closet.

The usual form of pillow, or *makura*, consists of a light closed wooden box, with a bottom either flat or slightly convex. On the top of this box is secured a small cylindrically-shaped

FIG. 193. — FORMS OF PILLOW IN COMMON USE.

cushion stuffed with buckwheat hulls. This cushion is tied to the box, and the same string that holds it in place also secures the pillow-case, which is simply a sheet of soft paper folded several times, as shown in the figures here given (fig. 193).

There are many other forms of pillow, either in the shape of a hard cushion or of a square oblong box, the ends being of wood, and the rest of basket-work. Porcelain pillows are also seen, but rarely. There are also many forms of portable ones, some of which fold and stow away in small compass, and others which are in the shape of a box, within which are drawers and spaces for paper-lantern, matches, mirror, comb, and various articles of the toilet. These are generally used by travellers. The Japanese, with a pillow of this kind, can literally take up his bed and walk; for if he has a head-rest or pillow containing these conveniences, he can get along very well. Pillows in all cases are arranged to support the head naturally, when the shoulder rests on the floor, as in the following figure (fig. 194). To a foreigner, until he becomes accustomed to it, the Japanese pillow seems exceedingly awkward, and his first experience with it results in a stiff neck the next morning; and at intervals during the night he has the sensation that he is falling out of bed, for any freedom of movement of the head results in its downfall from the pillow.

Getting used to it, however, one recognizes that this pillow has its good points; the neck is kept free for the air to circulate beneath, and the head is kept cool. This peculiar form of pillow was a necessity for the Japanese so long as the

FIG. 194. — SHOWING POSITION OF HEAD IN RESTING ON PILLOW.

hair was done up in the rigid *queue,* and is still a necessity for women with their methods of hair-dressing; but with the general abandonment of the *queue* on the part of the men, a few of them are resorting to head-rests more like our pillows, though much smaller and harder, and on the whole I believe many find this substitute more comfortable.

This simple form of bed entails much less work on the chamber-maid than do our arrangements. In a large inn one girl will do the chamber-work for the entire house. In fact this work is ridiculously simple. The *futons,* or comforters, are rapidly folded up and stowed away, or hung over the balcony rail to air. She gathers up a huge pile of the light pillow-boxes in her arms, and carries them to the room below; here she unties the strings which hold the cushions in place, substitutes clean sheets of folded paper for the soiled ones, — and the work of bed-making is done. With a duster, consisting of strips of tough paper tied to the end of a slender bamboo, the rooms are dusted and made ready for the next arrivals. As matters pertaining to the toilet are performed in other portions of the house, the rooms are placed in order in an incredibly short time.

In a crowded inn each guest may occupy the dimensions of one mat; and the entire floor is occupied in this way. In winter a thickly-wadded comforter is provided, which is made in the form of a huge garment having capacious sleeves.

Many rooms have a square hole in the floor in which, when needed, a fire of charcoal may be kindled; this is called a *ro.* Above the *ro* a square frame of wood is adjusted, and the

Fig. 195. — Heating Arrangement in Floor.

bed-clothes being placed over this frame are thoroughly heated, so that one may go to bed in the warmest of nests. In the day-time one may gather a portion of the bed-clothes about him, and keep warm by the little coal-fire burning beneath Fig. 195 is an illustration of this opening in the floor, with frame-work above to keep the bedclothes from falling on the fire below. A little wooden box is used for the purpose of holding an earthen receptacle for coals, and this is taken to bed as a substitute for the hot stone or brick which is often used at home for a similar purpose. From the inflammable nature of the bedding, many fires must originate from carelessness in the use of this luxury.

In this connection it may be well to add that oftentimes little square thin cushions are provided for guests to sit upon; and one often sees a light round cushion which is used as an elbow-rest when one is reclining (fig. 196).

FIG. 196. — ELBOW-REST.

Mosquito nettings, or *kaya*, are to be found in all houses, even the poorest people being supplied with them. The usual form of netting is made in the shape of a square box, nearly as large as the room; and this, when placed in position, is suspended at the four corners by cords which are tied to pegs in the four corners of the room. A smaller netting for infants is made on a frame-work of bamboo like a cage, and this may be placed over the infant wherever it may drop to sleep on the mats.

An inseparable accompaniment of every Japanese home, from the most exalted to the very humblest, is the *hibachi*. This object consists of a vessel partially filled with fine ashes, containing when in use a few bits of burning charcoal. This vessel may be of bronze, iron, porcelain, earthenware, or even of wood lined with copper, or a wooden box containing an earthen vessel. The most usual form of *hibachi* consists of a square wooden box lined with copper, between which and the wood is a layer of clay or plaster (fig. 200). A very cheap and common form is a wooden box in which is a cylindrical jar of black unglazed earthenware (fig. 197).

A pair of iron rods generally held together at one end by a large ring answers as tongs, being used after the manner of chop-sticks. These are either stuck in the ashes, or when the wooden box contains the fire-vessel separately there may be secured in the corner of this box a bamboo tube in which the tongs are kept.

In bronze *hibachi* there are handles or rings on the sides for convenience of moving. In the square-box *hibachi* cleats are nailed on opposite sides to answer as handles; or, as is more usually the case, narrow holes are cut through the sides of

FIG. 197. — COMMON HIBACHI.

the box to accommodate the fingers, as shown in the previous figure (197).

Much art and skill are displayed in the bronze and iron *hibachi*, and forms such as might be found in an ordinary house in Japan would be regarded as gems in collections of bric-à-brac at home. Even the wooden *hibachi* are often ob-

FIG. 198. — HIBACHI.

jects of exquisite taste. We recall an old one made of the richest grained wood, in which were drawers at one end to hold pipes and tobacco, and around the base of the box ran a deep band of black lacquer inlaid with ornaments of pearl, the design representing in various positions the iron bits of a horse. So various and oftentimes inexplicable are the surprises in their designs, that one might almost imagine the decorator to have opened while blindfolded a dictionary of objects, and to have taken the first word he saw as the theme for his subject.

A very favorite form of wooden *hibachi* is shown in fig. 198. This consists of a single piece of oak or other hard wood turned in a cylindrical form, the grain being brought into relief by special treatment, and the inside lined with copper. An old one richly colored and polished by age is much esteemed.

The *hibachi* may be quite a large affair, and subserve the duties of a stove as well. An iron ring having three legs,

or a grid spanning the box, is provided on which the tea-kettle is supported, or even fishes broiled. The *hibachi* is a sort of portable fireplace, around which the family gather to gossip, drink tea, or warm their hands. The one represented

FIG. 199. — HIBACHI.

in fig. 199 shows a little child warming itself, while wrapped in a thick night-garment. One will often observe a Japanese absent-mindedly stirring the coals or ashes with the tongs, just as we are fond of doing at home.

A sentiment prompts many families to keep the *hibachi* fire burning continually; and I was told that in one family in Tokio the fire had been kept alive continuously for over two hundred years.

In a winter party the *hibachi* are previously arranged by the servants, one being allotted to each guest; and the place where each is to sit on the matted floor is often indicated by a little square cloth-cushion. Fig. 200 illustrates the arrangement of *hibachi* for company.

Whenever you call on a friend, winter or summer, his very first act of hospitality is to place the *hibachi* before you. Even

FIG 200. -- HIBACHI ARRANGED FOR COMPANY.

in shops the *hibachi* is present, or is brought in and placed on the mats when a visitor enters.

A smaller form of *hibachi*, called a *tabako-bon* (fig. 201), is also usually brought to a visitor. It is a convenience used by smokers, and is commonly in the form of a square wooden box containing a small earthen vessel for holding hot coals, and a seg- ment of bamboo either with or without a cover. This last is a hand cuspidore, and great refine- ment is shown in using it. either by averting the head or screening the mouth with the hand. The

FIG. 201. — TABAKO-BON.

cuspidore, or spittoon, as commonly used by us. seems vulgar in comparison with that of the Japanese. Sometimes the *tabako-bon* is made out of the burl of an oak in which a natural de- pression occurs (fig. 202). This form is often seen in Japanese picture-books. Another form is shown in fig. 203. There are many and various designs for this convenience, some of them being very odd. To replenish the *hibachi* with hot coals there is provided a shallow iron bowl called a *dai-jū-nō* (fig. 204).

FIG. 202. — TABAKO-BON.

Upon the bottom of this bowl is riveted a bent strip of iron, which in turn is secured to a stand of wood. The bowl has an iron socket, into which is fitted a wooden handle. In this vessel burning coals are brought by the servant.

When the *hibachi* is properly arranged, it is customary to heap the ashes in a pyramidal pile about the coals and mark a series of radiating lines upon it. The charcoal to replenish the fire is generally kept in a basket, though sometimes a deep wooden box with a handle is used. The baskets used for this purpose are always tasty affairs, having often a rich brown color from age. In the basket is a pair of old brass or copper rods with which to handle the coal. A single stick of coal buried vertically in the ashes is burned for several hours. The charcoal-vender has a curious way of utilizing the small and pulverized fragments of the

FIG. 203. — TABAKO-BON.

charcoal, by mixing the powder with some kind of sea-weed, and then forming the mass into round balls the size of a large orange. In making these balls he goes through a motion precisely like that seen in making snow-balls. These are afterwards dried in the sun, and seem to burn very well. In riding

along the streets one often sees trays filled with these black balls
exposed to the sun.

Before kerosene oil was introduced into Japan the means of
illumination were of the most meagre description. One can hardly
realize the difficulty a student must have experienced in studying
his Chinese Classics by the feeble light emitted from tiny wicks,
or the dim and unsteady
flame of a vegetable-wax
candle, — a light rendered
all the more feeble when
filtered through a paper
lantern. It is related that
in former times devout
students of the Chinese
Classics were accustomed
at night to read a single
character at a time by
the dim illumination of a

Fig. 204. — Pan for holding burning
Charcoal.

glowing coal at the end of an incense-stick held close to the page !
Of the many things which the Japanese have adopted and
promptly utilized from Western nations, I know of nothing which
has been so great a boon to all the people as kerosene oil. The
Western practice of medicine is rapidly displacing the empir-
ical Chinese practice, and this when accomplished will be, beyond all question, the greatest boon. There are many outlying
districts, however, as well as thousands of inhabitants of the
cities, still under the sway of Chinese methods, and the beneficent
effects of the rational treatment of disease has not yet been widely
felt ; but everywhere throughout the Empire the bright light of
kerosene has lengthened the day for all.

Japanese candles are made of a vegetable wax, having a wick
consisting of a roll of paper, not unlike the ordinary paper lamp-

lighter. This wick, being hollow, is fitted to a sharp spur of iron about an inch long, in the candlestick (in England the pricket candlestick went out of use a few centuries ago; in Japan it is still retained). At the top of the candle the wick projects in a firm, hard point. When a candle has burned low, it is removed from the candlestick and placed on the end of the new candle, which is then adjusted on the sharp spur. By this simple device all the candle is utilized in combustion.

A superior kind of candle, made in the province of Aidsu, is beautifully painted in bright colors, with designs of flowers and other ornamental subjects.

Candles are depended upon to illuminate the rooms, as well as to light the hand-lanterns which are carried about the streets, and those which are used for the house, — these last consist-

ing of a square or hexagonal frame, covered with paper and attached to the end of a short handle.

A common form of Japanese candlestick, called *te-shoku*, is represented in fig. 205. It is a rude affair made of iron, sup-

FIG. 205. — IRON CANDLESTICK.

ported on three legs, and has a wide disk to prevent the melted wax from dropping on the mats, and a ring about the candle to prevent its falling over. It is easily picked up from the floor by its longer arm.

Another common form of candlestick consists of a hemispherical base of brass, ten or fifteen inches in diameter, from which a rod of the same metal runs up to the height of two feet or more, on the end of which is the usual cup and spur. Candlesticks of this description are seen in fig. 177 (page 196).

The snuffer is usually in the form of a blunt pair of tweezers, with which the burnt wick is removed; the servants, however,

often take the *hibachi*, or tongs, and, removing the wick, thrust
it into the ashes of the *hibachi*.

Candlesticks of rustic design, manufactured of curious woods,
are made at Nikko and other famous resorts, more as mementos
to carry away than as implements intended for actual use.

The Japanese lamp is usually in the form of a shallow saucer,
in which vegetable oil is burned. The wick, consisting of long
slender rods of pith, is held down
by a little ring of iron, to which
a spur is attached for a handle.
The unburned portion of the wick
projects beyond the saucer, and

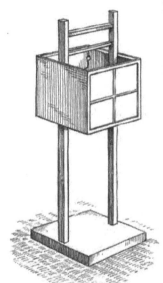

Fɪɢ. 206. — Lᴀᴍᴘ.   Fɪɢ. 207. — Lᴀᴍᴘ.

as it burns away at one end is moved along. The saucer rests
in a disk or ring of iron, which is suspended within a frame
covered with paper. A common form of this lamp, or *andon*,
is shown in fig. 206. It consists of a square frame of wood
covered with paper, open above and below, and having one side

in the shape of a movable lid, which can be raised when the lamp needs tending. This frame is secured to two uprights, which spring from a wooden stand in which may be a drawer containing extra wicks and a pair of snuffers. These uprights extend above the lantern, and have a cross-piece by which the

lantern is lifted, and another cross-bar just below from which the lamp hangs. The light from this night-lamp is feeble and uncertain, and by it one can barely see his way about the room.

There are many kinds of *andon*, some being very ingenious. One form is cylindrical, being composed of two frames, one within the other, — the outer frame revolving in a groove in the stand. One half of each lantern is covered with paper, so that by turning the outer

FIG. 208. — LAMP AND LACQUERED STAND.

frame the openings are brought together, and thus access is gained to the lamp. Another form of *andon* (fig. 207) opens in a different way, with a little shelf in one corner to hold the saucer of oil.

Still another form (fig. 208) is copied from an old colored picture-book; this consists of an elaborate lacquered stand mounted in metal, with a lamp supported on the top.

In the passage-ways, and at the head of stairways, lamps are often fixed to the wall. In Osaka I saw a curious one, which is represented in fig. 209. The frame was hung by hinges to a board which was affixed to the wall (the hinges being above), and rested against the board like a cover, and was lifted up when the lamp needed attention. In an *andon* in Osaka, I saw a good bit of iron-work (fig. 210) made to suspend the lamp.

FIG. 209. — WALL-LAMP.

FIG. 210. — LAMP.

Lamps made of pottery are rarely seen. Fig. 211 is a sketch of an old lamp of Oribe ware from the author's collection. An inclined portion within supports the wick, and the cover is notched in front and behind to allow the passage of the wick. Another form from the same collection, made in the province of Iga, is shown in fig. 212. In this lamp the wick must have been made from some fibre; a hole in the wick-tube is seen through which the wick can be moved along. The handle of the lamp has a slot in it, so that it may be hung against the wall. It is possible that these two lamps, or at least the last one, are for the *kami-dana*, — a shelf which supports the household shrine.

FIG. 211. — POTTERY LAMP.

In connection with lamps made of pottery, it may be well to add that now and then one meets with a pottery candlestick. That shown in fig. 213 rep·resents one from the author's collection, made of Owari pottery.

Near the *chōdzu-bachi,* hanging from the edge of the verandah roof above, is usually seen an iron lantern, generally a quaint old rusty affair suspended by a chain, and, when lighted, admitting through the perforations in its side the faintest possible glimmer. In figs. 240 and 253 (pages 255 and 267) lanterns of this description may be seen.

Fig. 212. — Pottery Lamp.

Street-lanterns are often affixed to short slender posts at the gateway or doorway of a dwelling. The usual form of this frame and lantern is represented in fig. 214. It is not over five feet in height, and seems to be a frail affair to expose on a public street. The very frailty and lightness of such objects, however, often exposed as they are with entire safety on busy thoroughfares, are striking indications of the gentle manners of the Japanese. One is led to wonder how long such a delicate street-lamp would remain intact in our streets, with those mobs thronging by that seem to be solely a product of our civilization. These, and a thousand similar points of contrast, set a thoughtful man reflecting on the manners and customs of the two great civilizations.

Fig. 213. — Pottery Candle-stick.

In nearly every house one sees perched up on a shelf called the *kami-dana* a curious little architectural affair, which on more special examination proves to be a model of a Shin-tō shrine, or a principal feature of a

Shin-tō altar, — a circular mirror. On the shelf in front of this are a few lamps (or a single lamp) and trays, containing at times food-offerings. If the shrine is in the shape of a box, then accompanying it are various little brass stands, slips of wood with characters written upon them, and in short a miniature representation, apparently, of the paraphernalia used in a large temple. The shelf is high up on the wall near the ceiling; and in old houses this region is black with the accumulations of smoke from the little lamp which is lighted every night, and which may have burned there for a century. These are the Shin-tō shrines.

The Buddhist household shrines, having a figure of Buddha or of one of his disciples, or perhaps of some other god, are much more ornate, and rest on the floor, — at least so I was informed. My informant also told me that the majority of the people worship at the shrines of both great beliefs, and that all Buddhists, unless very strict, have Shin-tō shrines in their houses. Indeed, Buddhists and even Buddhist priests

FIG. 214. — FIXED STREET-LANTERN.

have been known to go into the Roman Catholic cathedral at Osaka, and bow in reverence before the altar and other emblems of an alien religion. The tolerance and charity evinced in such acts is something pathetic, when one recalls the mutually hostile attitude of the two great branches of the Christian Church!

Flowers and incense-burning usually accompany the Buddhist household shrine, while before Shin-tō shrines incense is not burned. Buddhist shrines have placed before them lamps of brass, or hanging lamps, while in front of the Shin-tō shrine

15

candles of vegetable wax are burned.   In unglazed, hand-made
pottery called *kawarake* oil is burned, which is also used for
food-offerings.   For offerings of wine, oval bottles of peculiar
shape, with long narrow necks, are used; these are called *uiki-
dokkuri*, — *miki* being the name of the wine offered to the gods,
and *tokkuri* the name of a *sake* bottle.   In front of these shrines
one may often see the inmates of the house bow their heads,
clap their hands, and then, rubbing the palms together in an
imploring gesture, pray with much earnestness.   So far as I
have observed, every house has this domestic altar.   In shops,

FIG. 215. — HOUSEHOLD SHRINE.

too, one often sees the shrine; and
in the larger and more wealthy
shops the shrine is often a very
expensive affair.   In a famous silk-
shop in Tokio is a large model of
a Shin-tō temple suspended by iron
rods from the beams above.   In
front of it hang two big metal lanterns. It struck me that this display of piety was rather ostentatious,
and paralleled similar displays sometimes seen at home; in this sup-
position, however, I may be doing
an injustice.   Among the intelligent
classes the household shrine seems to be provided for the female
members of the family only, the men having outgrown these
superstitions; and it was interesting to observe that in Japan,
as elsewhere, the women — being as a rule less informed — made
up the majority of those attending public worship.

The sketch here given of a Buddhist household shrine (fig.
215) was seen in a house of the most squalid character.   The
various vessels were filled with boiled rice, with loaves of *mochi*
made of a special kind of rice, and a number of unripe peaches.

On the lower shelf, in the right-hand corner, is seen a sweet potato and a radish propped up on four legs, looking like toy deer or beasts of some kind. Whether this indicated the work of children or represented the horses upon which the gods could take a ride, was not ascertained.

A household shrine to which the children pay voluntary and natural devotion is the birds' nests built within the house. It is a common thing, not only in the country but in large cities like Tokio, for a species of swallow, hardly to be distinguished from the European species, to build its nest in the house, — not in an out-of-the-way place, but in the room where the family may be most actively engaged, or in the shop fronting the street, with all its busy traffic going on. The very common occurrence of these birds' nests in houses is another of the many evidences of the gentle ways of this people, and of the kindness shown by them to animals.

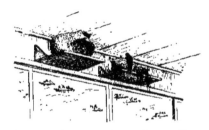

FIG. 216. — SWALLOWS' NESTS IN PRIVATE HOUSE.

When a bird builds its nest in the house, a little shelf is promptly secured beneath it, so that the mats below shall not be soiled. The presence of the bird in the house is regarded as a good omen, and the children take great pleasure in watching the construction of the nest and the final rearing of the young birds. I noticed that many of the nests built within the house were much more elaborately made than those built in more exposed positions. From the symmetrical way in which many of these were constructed, one might almost imagine the birds had become imbued with some of the art instincts of the people. Fig. 216 illustrates the appearance of a group of these birds' nests in a house.

It would be an affectation of false delicacy were no allusion to be made to the privy, which in the Japanese house often receives a share of the artistic workman's attention. From its position in the house, and especially in the public house. it is often a source of great discomfort. In the better class of private houses in Japan, however, there is less annoyance and infinitely less danger from this source than is experienced in many houses of the wealthy in our great cities. In the country the privy is usually a little box-like affair removed from the house, the entrance closed half way up by a swing-

ing door. In the city house of the better class it is at one corner of the house. usually at the end of the verandah, and sometimes there are two at diagonal corners, as a reference to the plans will show.

FIG. 217. — INTERIOR OF PRIVY.

A curious superstition among many is attached to the position of the privy in its relation to the house, — a trace possibly of the Chinese *Fung-shui*. The privy generally has two compartments, — the first one having a wooden or porcelain urinal; the latter form being called *asagaowa,* as it is supposed, to resemble the flower of the morning glory, — the word literally meaning "morning face" (fig. 219). The wooden ones are often filled with branches of spruce, which are frequently replenished. The inner compart-

FIG. 218. — PRIVY OF INN IN HACHI-ISHI VILLAGE, NIKKO.

ment has a rectangular opening cut in the floor, and in the
better class of privies this is provided with a cover having a

long wooden handle. The wood-work about this opening is sometimes lacquered. Straw sandals or wooden clogs are often provided to be worn in this place.

The interior of these apartments is usually simple, though sometimes presenting marvels of cabinet-work. Much skill and taste are often displayed in the approaches and exterior finish of these places.

Fig. 217 shows the interior of a common form of privy. Fig. 218 illustrates the appearance of one in an inn at

FIG. 219. — PRIVY CONNECTED WITH A
MERCHANT'S HOUSE IN ASAKUSA.

Hachi-ishi, near Nikko. The planking in the front of the sketch shows the verandah; from this, at right angles, runs a narrow platform, having for its border the natural trunk of a tree; the corner of a little cupboard is seen at the left; the ceiling is composed of matting made of thin strips of wood, and below is a dado of bamboo. The opening to the first apartment is framed by a twisted grape-vine, while other sticks in their natural condition make up the frame-work. Beyond the arched opening is another one closed by a swinging door; and this is usually the only place in the house where one finds a hinged door, except, perhaps, on the tall closet under the kitchen stairs. The roof is covered thickly with the diminutive shingles already alluded to. Outside a little screen fence is built, a few plants neatly trained below, — and a typical privy of the better class is shown. The wooden trough standing on four legs and holding a bucket of water and a wash-basin is evidently an addition for the convenience of foreign guests. The *chōdzu-bachi* with towel rack suspended above, as already described, is the universal accompaniment of this place.

As one studies this sketch, made at an inn in a country village, let him in all justice recall similar conveniences in many of the country villages of Christendom!

In Fig. 219 is shown the privy of a merchant in Asakusa, Tokio. The door was a beautiful example of cabinet-work,

FIG. 220. — INTERIOR OF A PRIVY IN ASAKUSA.

with designs inlaid with wood of different colors. The interior of this place (fig. 220) was also beautifully finished and scrupulously clean.

The receptacle in the privy consists of a half of an oil barrel, or a large earthen vessel, sunk in the ground, with convenient access to it from the outside. This is emptied every few days by men who have their regular routes; and as an illustration of the value of this material for agricultural purposes, I was told that in Hiroshima in the renting of the poorer tenement houses, if three persons occupied a room together the sewage paid the rent of one, and if five occupied the same room no rent was charged! Indeed, the immense value and importance of this material is so great to the Japanese farmer, who depends entirely upon it for the enrichment of his soil, that in the country personal conveniences for travellers are always arranged by the side of the road, in the shape of buckets or half-barrels sunk in the ground.

Judging by our standards of modesty in regard to these matters there would appear to be no evidence of delicacy among the Japanese respecting them; or, to be more just, perhaps I should say that there is among them no affectation of false modesty, — a feeling which seems to have developed among the English-speaking people more exclusively, and among some of them to such ridiculous heights of absurdity as often to be fraught with grave consequences. But among the Japanese it would seem as if the publicity given by them to the collecting of this important fertilizer had dulled all sensitiveness on their part, if it ever existed, concerning this matter.[1] Indeed, privacy in this matter would be impossible when it is considered that in cities — as in Tokio, for example — of nearly a million of inhabitants this material is carried off daily to the farms outside, the vessels in which it is conveyed being long cylindrical buckets borne by men and horses. If sensitive persons are offended by these conditions, they must admit that

---

[1] In this connection it may be interesting to mention the various names applied to the privy by the Japanese, with a free translation of the same as given me by Mr. A. S. Mihara: *Setsu-in,* " snow-hide;" *Chōdzu-ba,* " place to wash hands " (the *chōdzu-bachi,* a convenience for washing the hands, being always near the privy); *Benjo* and *Yō-ba,* " place for business ;" *Ko-ka,* " back-frame." *Habakari* is a very common name for this place; the word *Yen-riyo,* though not applied to this place, has the same meaning, — it implies reserve.

These words with their meanings certainly indicate a great degree of refinement and delicacy in the terms applied to the privy.

the secret of sewage disposal has been effectually solved by the Japanese for centuries, so that nothing goes to waste. And of equal importance, too, is it that of that class of diseases which scourge our communities as a result of our ineffectual efforts in disposing of sewage, the Japanese happily know but little. In that country there are no deep vaults with long accumulations contaminating the ground, or underground pipes conducting sewage to shallow bays and inlets, there to fester and vitiate the air and spread sickness and death.

On the other hand it must be admitted that their water supply is very seriously affected by this sewage being washed into rivers and wells from the rice-fields where it is deposited; and the scourge of cholera, which almost yearly spreads its desolating shadow over many of their southern towns, is due to the almost universal cultivation of the land by irrigation methods; and the consequent distribution of sewage through these surface avenues renders it impossible to protect the water supply from contamination.

CHAPTER V.

ENTRANCES AND APPROACHES.

VESTIBULE AND HALL. — VERANDAH AND BALCONY. — AMADO. — TO-BUKURO. -- CHODZU-
BACHI. — GATEWAYS. — FENCES.

IN the study of the house-architecture of Japan, as compared
with that of America, it is curious to observe the relative
degree of importance given to similar features by the two peoples.
With us the commonest house in the city or country will have a
definite front-door, and almost always one with some embellishments, in the shape of heavy panels, ornate brackets and braces
supporting some sort of a covering above, and steps approaching it equally pretentious; in the ordinary Japanese house, on
the contrary, this entrance is, as we shall see, often, though not
always, of the most indefinite character. With us, again, the
hall or front-entry stairs may be seen immediately on entering the
house, — and this portion has some display in the baluster and
gracefully curving rail, and in the better class of houses receives
special attention from the architect; in Japan, however, if the
house be of two stories the stairway is never in sight, and is
rarely more than a stout and precipitous step-ladder. On the
other hand, the ridge of the roof, which in Japan almost invariably forms the most picturesque feature of the house exterior,
is with us nothing more than the line of junction of the plainest
rain-shed; though in great edifices feeble attempts have been
made to decorate this lofty and conspicuous line by an inverted
cast-iron design, which is not only absolutely useless as a structural feature, but, so far as the design is concerned, might be

equally appropriate for the edge of a tawdry valentine, or the ornamental fringe which comes in a Malaga raisin-box.

Accustomed as we are, then, to a front-door with steps and rail and a certain pretentious architectural display, it is difficult to conceive of a house without some such distinctive characters to its portal. In the ordinary Japanese house, however, we often look in vain for such indications. In the common class of their houses, and even in those of more importance, the entrance is often vaguely defined; one may enter the house by way of the garden and make his salutations on the verandah, or he may pass into the house by an ill-defined boundary near the kitchen, — a sort of back-door on the front side. In other houses this entrance is by means of a small matted area, which differs in no respect from the other rooms save that the outer edge of its raised floor is some distance within the eaves, and between this and the sill the floor is mother earth. One or two steps, consisting of single planks running the width of the room, lead from the earth to the floor. The roof at this point may be a gable, as more specially marking the entrance. These indefinite entrances, however, belong only to the houses of what may be called the middle and lower classes, though even in houses of the middle classes well-marked entrances, and even entrances of some pretensions, are not uncommon. Some may be inclined to doubt the statement that in the ordinary houses the entrance is often more or less vaguely defined. As a curious proof of this, however, I have in my possession Japanese architects' plans of two houses, consisting of a number of rooms, and representing dwellings far above the ordinary type; and though I have consulted a number of Japanese friends in regard to these plans, none of them have been able to tell me where the main entrance is, or ought to be!

In a better class of houses the entrance is in the form of a wide projecting porch, with special gable roof, having elaborately carved wood-work about its front, the opening being as wide as the porch itself. The floor consists of wide planks running at right angles with the sill, which is grooved to accommodate the *amado*, or storm-doors. From this floor one reaches the floor beyond by means of one or two steps, — the edge of

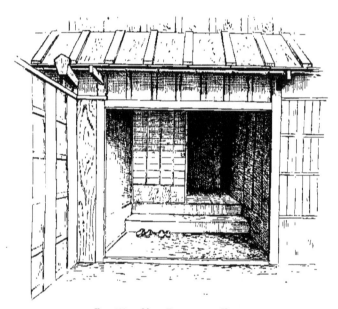

Fig. 221. — MAIN ENTRANCE TO HOUSE.

the floor near the steps being grooved to accommodate the *shōji*. The back partition of this hall is a permanent one. On either side sliding screens lead to the rooms within. A dado of wood runs about the sides of the vestibule, while the wall above is plastered. A low screen, called a *tsui-tate*, is usually the sole ornament of the hall; and in olden times there hung on the wall behind the *tsui-tate* curious long-handled weapons, which now are seen only as museum specimens. This screen has no folds; the frame is thick and lacquered, and the transverse feet are ponderous and also lacquered.

In some houses the floor of the hall, as well as that of the vestibule, is composed of plank; and the polish of the steps

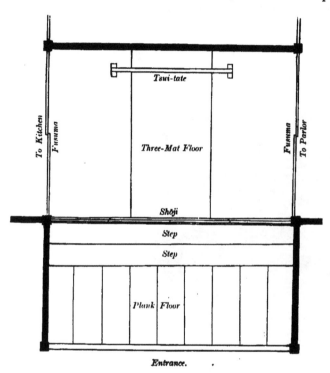

Fig. 222. – Plan of Vestibule and Hall.

and floor is of such exquisite ivory smoothness that the decorated screen and *fusuma* are reflected as from a shaded and quiet expanse of water. Even here no special display is made beyond the porch-like projection and gable roof of the external boundaries of this entrance.

It would seem as if the fitting architecture of this important portal had been transferred to the gateway,—ponderous hinged-doors, bolts, bars, and all; for in the gateways a conspicuous, though oftentimes fictitious, solidity is shown in the canopy of beams and tiles, supported by equally massive posts.

FIG. 223. — SHOE-CLOSET.

In fig. 221 is shown a view of the entrance to the house figured on pages 54 and 55. It is the house of a *samurai*, and is a fair example of the entrance to the house of a gentleman in ordinary circumstances. On the left of the entrance is a plastered partition separating the hall from the kitchen.

On the right is a small room separated from the vestibule by *shōji,* not *fusuma.* This may be considered a waiting-room, where parties on business are shown; a servant usually waits here to attend callers. Directly beyond, one enters a suite of rooms which border the garden at the back of the house. At the immediate entrance is a sill; over this sill one steps upon the earth floor.

The sill is grooved to accommodate the *amado,* which are put in place when the house is closed for the night. When a house has a definite entrance like this, there are usually conveniences for stowing away travelling gear, — such as umbrellas, lanterns, and wooden clogs. For example, in ordinary houses, for the sake of economy in space, a portion of the raised floor of the vestibule consists of movable planks, which may be lifted up, revealing a space beneath sufficiently ample to accommodate these articles.

The plan here given (fig. 222) shows a hall often seen in the better class of houses. The area between the entrance and the *shōji* projects as a porch from the side of the house, the three-matted area coming within the house proper. The lettering on the plan clearly explains the various parts.

In a narrow hall in an old house near Uyeno, in Tokio, I got the accompanying sketch of a shoe-closet (fig. 223). The briefest examination of the various clogs it contained revealed the same idiosyncrasies of walking as with us, — some were down at the heel, others were worn at the sides. There were clogs of many sizes and kinds, — common clogs of the school-children, with the dried mud of the street still clinging to them, and the best clogs with lacquered sides and finely-matted soles. At one side hung a set of shoe-cords ready for emergency.

In another house, just within the vestibule, I noticed a shelf-rack above the *fusuma,* designed for holding the family lanterns (fig. 224). It may as well be stated here, — a fact which is probably well known to most of our readers, — that the Japanese almost invariably carry lighted lanterns when they walk out at night.   Upon the outside of these lanterns is painted the crest, or *mon*, of the family, or the name of the house : a man with an eye to business may advertise it on his lantern by some quaint

FIG. 224. — LANTERN-SHELF IN HALL.

design.   So persistent is this habit of carrying lanterns, that on bright moonlight nights the lantern is brought into requisition ; and nothing strikes a foreigner as so ludicrous as the sight of a number of firemen on the top of a burning building, holding lighted lanterns in their hands!   The lanterns fold up into a small compass ; and on the lantern-shelf which we have shown were a number of thick pasteboard boxes in which were stowed away the lanterns. On each box was painted a design corresponding to the design of the lantern within. In this case the name of the family, or the crest, was indicated.

In this vestibule the *fusuma*, instead of being covered with thick paper, consisted of panels of dark cedar. The effect was very rich.

In the houses of the Dai-mios the entrance is always grandly marked by a special roof, and by a massive struct-ure of carved beams supporting it,—brilliantly colored often-times, and the surroundings in keeping with the dignity of this important region.

The doorways of shops and inns, when they definitely oc-cur, are large square openings stoutly but neatly barred,—and permanently too, a portion of it being made to roll back. The sill of such an opening is

FIG. 225. — GRATED ENTRANCE, WITH SLIDING DOOR.

some little distance from the ground, and one on entering steps over this sill to an earth floor within, called the *do-ma.* Here the wooden clogs are left as he steps upon the raised floor. Fig. 225 illustrates the appearance of this doorway.

The verandah is an essential part of the Japanese house. The word itself is of Oriental origin, and it is difficult to imagine an Oriental house of any pretensions without a verandah of some kind. In the Japanese house it is almost a continuation of the floor of the room, being but slightly below its level. The verandah is something more than a luxury; it is a necessity arising from the

16

peculiar construction of the house. The *shōji*, with their delicate frames and white paper-coverings, which take the place of our glass windows in admitting light to the room, are from their very nature easily injured by the rain; the edge of the room therefore, where these run, must come a few feet within the eaves of the roof, or of any additional rain-shed which may be built above the *shōji*. At this line, therefore, the matted floor ceases, and a plank floor of varying width continues beyond, upon the outer edge of which is a single groove to accommodate another set of screens made of wood. These are called the *amado*, literally "rain-door," and at night and during driving storms they are closed. At times, however, the rain may beat in between the *amado*; but though wetting the verandah, it rarely reaches the *shōji*.

In ordinary houses the verandah has no outer rail, though in the houses of the nobility a rail is often present. The width of the verandah varies in proportion to the size of the house. In some of the temples the verandah floor may be ten feet or more in width, and thickly lacquered, as in some of the Nikko temples. In common houses this area may be three or four feet in width. A reference to the plans (figs. 97 and 98; pages 113, 116), and also to the vertical section (fig. 103; page 126), will give a clear idea of this platform and its relation to the house. There are various ways of treating this feature; it is always supported on wooden posts, rough or hewn, which, like the uprights of the house, rest on single stones partly buried in the ground. The space between the edge of the verandah and the ground is almost invariably left open, as will be seen by reference to figs. 37, 48, 49, 50, and 95 (pages 55, 66, 68, 70, 106), though in Kioto houses it is sometimes filled up by simple boarding or panelling; and here and there are one or more panels which run back and forth in grooves, so that one can go beneath the house if necessary. The planks composing

the floor of the verandah may be narrow or wide; usually however they are quite narrow, and run parallel with the edge of the
verandah, though in some cases they are wide planks running
at right angles. When this platform turns a corner, the ends
of the planks may be mitred (as in fig. 226, *A*), or square (as in
fig. 226, *B*), in which latter case the ends project beyond each
other alternately. Sometimes the floor is made up of narrow
strips of thick plank with the edges deeply chamfered or rounded
(fig. 226, *C*). In this style a considerable space is left between
the planks. The effect of this treatment is looked upon as
rustic and picturesque, but is certainly not so pleasant to walk
upon. In such a form of verandah the *amado* runs in a groove
in close proximity to the *shōji*.

The verandah varies considerably in its height from the ground;
more often it is so low that one
sitting on its edge may rest his feet
comfortably on the ground. In
this case a single wide block, either
of stone or wood, forms the step.
When the verandah is at a greater
height from the ground, permanent or adjustable steps, two or
three in number, are placed in
position. A common form of ve-
randah-step is shown in fig. 179
(page 199). A very good type of
verandah sketched from an old
house in Kioto is shown in fig.
227. The manner in which the

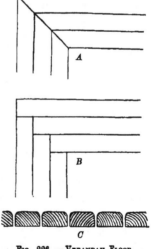

Fig. 226. — Verandah Floor.

uprights support the broad over-hanging eaves, the appearance
of the supplementary roof called *hisashi*, the *shōji* as they are
seen, some closed and some open, disclosing the rooms within,

and other details which will presently be described, are well shown in this figure.

Rooms in the second story also open upon a balcony, the platform of which is generally much narrower than the one below. This balcony has of necessity a rail or balustrade; and here much good artistic work is displayed in design and finish, with simple and economical devices, apparent as in so

FIG. 227. — VERANDAH OF AN OLD KIOTO HOUSE.

many other features of the house. This structure, with a firm hand-rail above, has the interspaces between the posts which support it filled with many quaint and curious devices, either of lattice, bamboo, or panels with perforated designs. Generally a narrow bar runs from post to post close to the platform, so that any object dropped may not roll out; between the end posts of the rail this piece is often removable, to allow dust and dirt to be more easily swept away. (In fig. 228 the piece marked *A* is removable).

Fig. 229 represents a panel from a balustrade in Matsu-shima. In this the design of bamboo was cut through, producing a very light and pretty effect. Fig. 230 shows another panel from a balustrade in Fujisawa; a perforated design of dragons in various attitudes ornamented each panel, which was held in place by a frame composed of round sticks of the red pine.

FIG. 228. — BALCONY RAIL.

It seems surprising that our architects do not oftener employ this method of perforation in their ornamental work, — the designs can be so clearly and sharply cut, while the dark shade of the room or space beyond gives a depth of color to the design, which is at the same time permanent. With the Japanese this method of ornamentation is a favorite one both for outside and inside finish, and they have shown great ingenuity and originality in the infinite variety of designs for this mode of treatment. Nothing seems too difficult for them to attempt, — flying birds, swimming fishes, dashing waves and the rising sun, flowers and butterflies; indeed, the whole range of pictorial design has offered no difficulties to them. In their process of figuring cloths and crape, stencil-plates of thick paper are employed, and in the printing of wall-paper the same methods are resorted to.

FIG. 229. — BALCONY RAIL AND PERFORATED PANELS.

In a balcony rail (fig. 231) a most delicate device was made by using for a middle rail a small bamboo, directly beneath which was another rail composed of a longitudinal section of the middle of a large bamboo; such a section included the transverse partitions of the bamboo as well. This process is often resorted to in the construction of the frame-work of delicate *shōji*, but it is rare to see it used in a balustrade. The

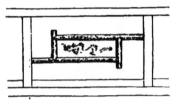

FIG. 230. — BALCONY RAIL.

effect is exceedingly refined and delicate; and one realizes that in a country where such fragile tracery is incorporated in such an exposed structure, there must be an absence of the rough, boisterous children with whom we are familiar, and who in a short time would be as disastrous to a Japanese house as a violent earthquake and typhoon combined. One further realizes that in that country men must keep their feet where they properly belong.

The balustrade is often made very solid and substantial, as may be seen in fig. 232, sketched from the house of a cele-

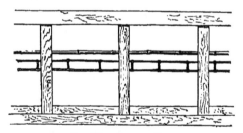

FIG. 231. — BALCONY RAIL.

brated potter in Kioto. The posts had metal tops, and at intervals along the upper rail metal plates were fixed.

Transient guests are often received on the verandah; to which place the *hibachi, tabako-bon,* and tea and cake are

brought. In summer evenings it is much cooler here than on
the matted floor within, and with the garden in view forms a
pleasant place for recreation. Flower-pots are sometimes placed
along its edge; children play upon it; and in a long suite of
rooms it forms a convenient thoroughfare from one apartment
to another. It is often the only means of reaching a room at
one end of the house, unless by passing through other rooms,

Fɪɢ. 232. — Bᴀʟᴄᴏɴʏ Rᴀɪʟ.

as in many cases there are no interior passage-ways, or corri-
dors, as with us. It is needless to say that the verandah is
kept scrupulously clean, and its wooden floor is often polished.[1]

The *amado*, or rain-doors, by which the verandah is closed
at night and during stormy weather, are in the form of light
wooden screens about the size of the *shōji*. These are made

---

[1] The ordinary form of verandah is called *yen*, or *yen-gawa*. In Kishiu it is called
simply *yen*, while in Tokio it is called *yen-gawa*. A low platform is called an *ochi-yen ;*
a platform that can be raised or lowered is called an *age-yen*. When the platform has no
groove for the rain-doors on the outer edge, it is called a *nuri-yen,* — *nuri* meaning wet,
the rain in this case beating in and wetting the verandah. A little platform made of
bamboo, which may be used as a shelf for plants, is called *sunoko*.

of thin boards held together by a light frame-work having a few transverse bars. The *amado* run in a single groove on the outer edge of the verandah; at night the house is effectually closed by these shutters, and during hot summer nights the apartments become almost stifling. In many houses, however, provision is made for ventilation in the shape of long, narrow openings just above the *amado*. Panels are made to fit into these openings, so that in winter the cold to some extent may be kept out. On unusually stormy days and during the prevalence of a typhoon, the house closed in this way is dark and gloomy enough.

These shutters are the noisy features of a Japanese house. Within are no slamming doors or rattling latches; one admires the quiet and noiseless way in which the *fusuma* are gently pushed back and forth; and the soft mats yielding to the pressure of still softer feet, as the inmates like cats step lightly about, are soothing conditions to overstrained nerves, and one cannot help contrasting them with the clatter of heavy boots on our wood floors, or the clouds of filthy dust kicked out of our carpets in any rough play of children. All these miseries are happily avoided in a Japanese house. Truth compels me to say, however, that in the morning you are roughly awakened by the servants pushing back into their appropriate recesses these outer wooden screens; and this act is usually noisy enough. In public houses this performance takes the place of clanging bell or tympanum-bursting gong (a Chinese instrument of torture which our people seem to take peculiar delight in); for not only the rattling bang of these resonant shutters, but the bright glare of daylight where before you had been immersed in darkness, assails you with a sudden and painful shock.

The Japanese have a number of curious devices by which to lock or bolt these shutters. So far as I know, the only night-lock the house possesses is attached to them. So feeble are these devices that they would hardly withstand the attack of a tooth-pick in the hands of a sneak-thief. To a Japanese our houses must appear like veritable prisons with locks, bolts, and auto-matic catches at every opening, — the front door with such mysterious devices that it is quite as impregnable from within as from without. What a land of thieves he must think himself in when he finds door-mats, door-scrapers, fountain-dippers, thermometers, etc., chained, screwed, or bolted to the

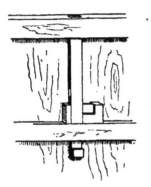 

Fig. 233. — Rain-door Lock unbolted.   Fig. 234. — Rain-door Lock bolted.

house! The simplest device for locking a sliding door, or *amado*, is by means of a ring fastened to the post by the side of which the *amado* comes. In the frame of the *amado* is a little loop of iron; the ring is pushed over the loop, and a wooden pin holds it in place. Another form of lock con-sists of an upright bolt of wood that passes through the upper frame of the *amado* as well as through a transverse bar just below. This bolt being pushed up is held in place by another piece of wood, which slides along in such a way as to pre-vent the bolt from dropping back. A reference, however, to the sketches (figs. 233, 234) will better explain the working of this ingenious device. Sometimes a simple wooden pin is used to hold the last *amado* in place. All these various devices are on the last *amado;* as when this is locked, all the others are secured.

In old houses round-headed iron knobs (fig 235) will be noticed on the outer edge of the groove in which the *amado* run. These are placed at intervals corresponding to the number of *amado,* and are to prevent the *amado* from being lifted

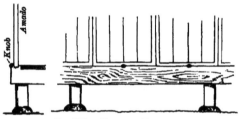

FIG. 235. — KNOB FOR RAIN-DOOR.

out of the groove from the outside and thus removed. This device is rarely seen nowadays.

In the second story the *to-bukuro* may be on a side of the house which runs at right angles with the balcony. As the *amado* are pushed along one after the other, it is necessary to turn them around the corner of the balcony, outside the corner post. To prevent them from slipping off the corner as they turn the post, a little iron roller is secured to the corner of the balcony; the *amado* is pushed by it part way, and then swung around into the other groove. A reference to the sketch (fig. 236) shows the position of this roller, and two forms of it. It will be noticed that there is no groove at this point, so that the *amado* may be turned without lifting them.

In the *amado* which close the entrance to the house, the end one contains a little square door called a *kuguri-do;* this may slide back and forth, or may swing upon hinges. It is used as an entrance after the house is closed for the night. It is also called an earthquake-door, as through it the inmates may easily and quickly find egress, at times of sudden emergency, without the necessity of removing the *amado*.

Not only the verandah but the entrance to the house, as well as the windows when they occur, are closed at night by *amado*. In the day-time these shutters are stowed away in closets called *to-buku-ro*. These closets are placed at one side of the opening or place to be closed, and just outside the groove in which the shutters are to run. They have only the width of one shutter, but are deep enough to accommodate the number that is required to close any

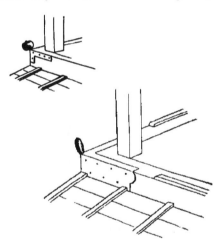

FIG. 236. — CORNER-ROLLER FOR RAIN-DOOR.

one entrance. By reference to the plans (figs. 97 and 98; pages 113, 116) the position of these closets may be seen; and in the views of the houses already given, notably in figs. 35, 38, 49 and 50 (pages 53, 56, 68, and 70), they may be seen at the ends of the verandahs, balconies, entrances, and windows.

In an ordinary house the *to-bukuro* is made of thin boards, and has the appearance of a shallow box secured to the side of the house. In large inns the front of the *to-bukuro* is often composed of a single richly-grained plank. The closet has a notch on the side, so that the hand may grasp the edge of each *amado* in turn, as it is drawn toward the groove in which it runs. A servant will stand at the *to-bukuro* and rapidly remove the *amado* one after the other, pushing them along the groove like a train of cars.

Fig. 237.—Verandah showing Swinging Closet for Rain-doors, and also Chōdzu-bachi.

The *to-bukuro* is almost always a fixture on the side of the house; sometimes, however, it has to come on the verandah in such a position that if it were permanent it would obstruct the light. In such a case it is arranged on pivots, so that after the *amado* are stowed away for the day, it may be swung at right angles away from the verandah, and against the side of some porch or addition. This form of swinging *to-bukuro* is presented in the above sketch (fig. 237).

A curious evidence of the cleanly habits of the Japanese is seen in the *chōdzu-bachi*, a receptacle for water at the end of the verandah near the latrine. This convenience is solely for the purpose of washing the hands. This receptacle, if of bronze or pottery, rests on a stand or post of some kind, which rises from the ground near the edge of the verandah. Its importance is shown by the ornamental features often displayed in its structure and surroundings. In its simplest form it consists of a wooden bucket suspended by a bamboo which hangs from the eaves of the verandah roof above. To this bamboo hangs the dipper also (fig. 238). A towel-rack usually hangs near by. A more common form of *chōdzu-bachi* consists of a vessel of bronze, pottery, or porcelain, supported by a post fixed firmly in the ground, around the base of which is strewn a number of beach-worn pebbles, intermingled with larger stones; so that in washing the hands (which is always done by dipping the water from the vessel and pouring it on the hands) the water spilled finds its way through the pebbles, and thus an unsightly puddle of water is avoided. In simple forms of *chōdzu-bachi*, such as the one shown in fig. 49 (page 68), the pebbles are enclosed in a frame of tiles fixed in the ground edgewise, this frame being sometimes triangular and sometimes circular in form.

For a support to these vessels the quaintest devices come into play: it may be the trunk of a tree, from one side of which a branch springs, covered with leaves and blossoms; or it may be the end of a carved post from some old building, as shown in fig. 237. A favorite support consists of a rudder-post from some old shipwreck, as shown in fig. 239, at a gentleman's house in the suburbs of Tokio. Usually the vessel is of bronze; and one often notices rare old forms used for this purpose, covered with a rich patina. Oftentimes water is conducted by a bamboo pipe, to fall in a continuous stream among the pebbles.

FIG. 238.
CHŌDZU-BACHI.

Many forms of *chōdzu-bachi* are in the shape of ponderous thick blocks of stone, with a depression on the top to hold the water. Of the stone forms there is an infinite variety: it may be a rough-hewn stone, or a square post, or an arch of stone, with a depression for water at the crown of the arch; indeed, the oddest conceits are shown in the designs for this purpose. The usual form, however, is cylindrical (fig. 240); the stone may be wrought in the shape of an urn (fig. 241). Whatever the form, however, they are generally monoliths.

Usually the stone *chōdzu-bachi* has a little wooden frame-work with roof resting on the top, to keep dead leaves from falling into the water. Large irregular-shaped stones, having depressions in them for water, may be seen near the entrance of the little buildings used for the ceremonial tea-parties; in this case the stone rests directly upon the ground.

While in most cases the *chōdzu-bachi* is but slightly removed from the edge of the verandah, so that one may easily reach it

FIG. 239. — CHŌDZU-BACHI.

with the dipper which always rests upon the top of the vessel, in more elaborate surroundings a little platform called *hisashi-yen* is built out from the edge of the verandah. This platform has a floor of bamboo rods, or circular or hexagonal bars of wood. A hand-rail often borders this platform, and a quaint old iron lantern usually hangs from above, to light the *chōdzu-bachi* at night. Fig. 240 represents the appearance of this platform with the *chōdzu-bachi*, at the house of a celebrated Kiyomidzu potter in Kioto; and in the illustration of an old verandah at Kioto (fig. 227, page 244) is shown a Japanese in the act of washing his hands.

Taste and ingenuity are shown here, as elsewhere, in making this corner refined and artistic. Rare woods and expensive rockwork enter into its composition; beautiful flowers, climbing vines, and dwarf-pines are clustered about it; and books are specially prepared to illustrate the many ways in which this convenience may be dealt with.

The general neatness and cleanliness of the people are well shown by the almost universal presence of the *chōdzu-bachi*, not only in the houses and inns, but in the public offices in the busiest parts of the city, — the railway station, to which hundreds throng, being no exception.

While little or no attempt at architectural display is made on that side of the house that comes next the street, the gateway, on the contrary, receives a good deal of attention, and many of

Fig. 240. — Chōdzu-bachi.

these entrances are quite remarkable for their design and structure. These, like the fences, vary greatly as to their lightness or solidity. The gateways bordering the street are often of the most solid description, — well barred within, having a roof above them, and when painted black, as they often are, looking grim enough. Whether solid or light, however, the gateways are usually picturesque. Rustic effects are frequently seen, even in the gateways of the city houses; though often frail in appearance, it is rare to see one in ruins, or even in a dilapidated condition. Many of them are made of light thin material, though the upright posts are stout timbers well braced behind by supplementary posts, with strong cross-beams above. Often quaint old ship-planks or rugged and twisted branches form the frame-work for the most delicate panelling of braided strips or perforated designs, with flattened strips of dark bamboo forming the centre ribs of a series of panels. All these contrasts of strong and frail, rough and delicate in design, material, and exe-

FIG. 241. — CHŌDZU-BACHI AND HISASHI-YEN.

cution, are the surprises which give such a charm to Japanese work of this nature.

There are many different types of gateways. In the city, one type is seen in the long row of buildings which form part of a *yashiki* inclosure; these are solid and ponderous structures. A gateway of a similar kind is seen in the thick high walls of tile, mud, and plaster which surround a *yashiki*. Another type is seen, in which the gateway is flanked on either side by tall, light, wooden or close bamboo fences; and still another, which is found in the garden fences, and is often of the lightest description.

Of the first kind forming the entrance to the *yashiki*, the buildings of which have not been considered in this work, a rough sketch is given in fig. 242. This is a gateway belonging to a small *yashiki* not far from Kudan in Tokio, which opens into a long low building solid and heavy in construction. The larger gateway has on either side a narrow opening for ordinary passage. A heavily-barred and protected window on one side is provided for the gatekeeper, from which he can see any one that passes in or out; the narrow though deep moat in front is bridged by stone. The gateway, though solid, appears far more solid than it is; the gates are apparently studded with heavy round-headed bolts, which as we have seen are often of pretentious solidity, being made of the thinnest sheet-metal and lightly attached. The broad metal straps, sockets, and bindings of the various beams are of the same sheet-copper. Gateways of this nature are often painted black or bright red, and in the olden times were wonderfully decorated with color and metal work.

Fig. 242. — Gateway in Yashiki Building.

Of another group are the ordinary gateways of the better class of city houses. Fig. 243 is a typical one of this description.

17

The sketch shows the appearance of the gateway from within, and illustrates the way in which the upright posts are strengthened by additional posts and braces. The double gates are held together by a strong wooden bar, after the manner of similar gateways at home. In gateways of this description there is usually a small sliding door, its lower edge a foot from the ground, just high enough for a person to crawl through in a stooping attitude. For an alien resident to get in or out of this opening

FIG. 243. — GATEWAY OF CITY HOUSE FROM WITHIN.

without tripping, or knocking off his hat, requires considerable skill and practice. When this little grated door is slid back it is sometimes arranged to jangle a bell, or to rattle a number of pieces of iron hung by a string, as a warning to the servant within. Sometimes this supplementary opening has a swinging instead of a sliding door; in this case a curious rattle is arranged by tying a number of short segments of bamboo to a piece of board which is hung to the gate: these rattle quite loudly whenever the gate is moved. Fig. 244 illustrates the appearance of this primitive yet ingenious gate-knocker.

A number of curious ways are devised to lock the little sliding door in the gateway, one of which is here figured (fig. 243.) To the left of the drawing a portion of the door is shown.

A piece hanging from a panel in the gate is held against the edge of the door by a sliding bolt, which, when pushed back, drops into place, allowing the door to slide by. It is, however, difficult to make this clear by description; a reference to fig. 245 will illustrate it. Not only do the larger gates have these smaller openings, but in the street-entrance of shops and inns the door which closes the entrance has a little door either hinged or on rollers. This is called the earthquake door, as through this in times of sudden danger the inmates escape, the larger doors or rain-shutters being liable to get bound or jammed in the swaying of the building.

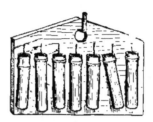

FIG. 244. — GATE–RATTLE.

FIG. 245. — BOLT FOR LITTLE SLIDING DOOR IN GATEWAY.

The gateway shown in fig. 246 was sketched on the road which borders the Shinobadzu pond in Uyeno Park, Tokio. It represents a simple form of gateway in the high wooden fence which encloses the house and garden from the street. The double gates consist of single thin planks; above, a decoration is cut out of the narrow panel; a light coping held in place by two brackets crowns the whole, and a simple yet attractive gateway is accomplished. In this figure the durable way in which a fence is constructed is well shown. The stout wooden sills supported by flat stones, which in turn rest on the stone wall, may here be seen; and the interspace showing between the lower edge of the boards and the sill is a common feature of fence-structure.

FIG. 246. — GATEWAY TO CITY RESIDENCE.

A barred opening in the fence next the gate permits one to communicate with the inmates from without.

A more elaborate gateway on the same street is shown in fig. 247. In this gateway one of the panels slides in a groove behind the other panel, which is fixed. These panels are filled with a braiding of thin strips of cedar. Above these low panels is a stout net-work of wood.

The round gate-posts are held together above by a round beam as well as by a wide and thin plank, in which is cut in perforated pattern a graceful design. The roof of the gate is made of wide thin boards, supported by transverse pieces passing through the upright posts and keyed into place. The doorplate, consisting of a thin board upon which the name of the occupant is painted, is nailed to the post.

Fig. 248 represents a gateway on the road leading from Shiba to Shinagawa, near Tokio. It was remarkable for the beauty of its proportions and the purity of its design. The two upright posts consisted- of the natural trunks of trees stripped of their bark, showing the prominences left by the removal of their branches. The transverse piece crowning the whole had been specially selected to give an upward curve to its ends, such as one sees in the upper transverse beam of a *tori-i*.[1] It had been cut on three of its faces, one answering to its lower face, and the other two to bring it in line with the gate; and these surfaces gave a picturesque effect by intersecting the irregularities of the trunk, producing a waved and irregular section. Directly below this beam was a black worm-eaten plank from some old shipwreck, and immediately below this was another transverse tie in the shape of a huge green bamboo. The gate itself was composed of light narrow strips

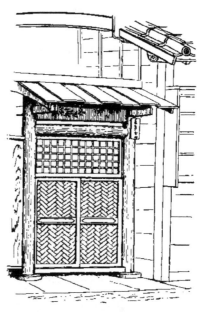

Fig. 247. — GATEWAY TO CITY RESIDENCE.

placed half an inch apart, between which could be seen four transverse bars within. A small square area in one corner was framed in for the little supplementary entrance. The gate was flanked on each side by wings composed of boards, and capped with a heavy wooden rail; and these wings joined the neatest of bamboo fences, which rested on a stone foundation, which in turn formed the inner wall of the street gutter. Heavy

[1] A gate-like structure seen in front of all shrines and temples.

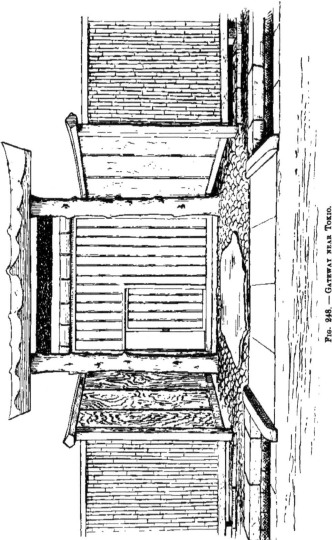

Fig. 248. — Gateway near Tokio.

slabs of dressed stone made a bridge across the gutter, and in front of the gateway was an irregular-shaped flag-stone, showing untouched its natural cleavage from the ledge; on each side and about this slab the ground was paved with round beach-worn cobble-stones. This gateway was exceedingly attractive; and there is no reason why just such an entrance, with perhaps the exception of the bamboo, might not be adopted for many of our own summer residences.

Fig. 249. — GATEWAY.

Another gateway not so pretty, but showing one of the many grotesque ideas of the Japanese, is shown in fig. 249. Here the upper transverse beam is a huge and crooked log of wood,—an old log which had been dragged from the forest just as it fell in ruins from some tree. This peculiar way of arching a gateway with a tortuous stick is quite commonly seen.

Fig. 250 represents a typical form of gateway often observed in the suburbs of Tokio and farther south. Its roof is quite large and complex, yet not heavy. The gate has a wide over-hanging roof of bark; the ridge consists of large bamboos placed longitudinally in two sets, each set being kept apart from each other as well as from the roof by thick saddles of bark resting across the ridge, the whole mass tied together and to the roof by a black-fibred root, the ends of these cords being twisted above into an ornamental plume. Smaller bamboos are placed at intervals nearly to the eaves of the roof. The rafters below were of different sizes and shapes in section, being round and square. The sketch will more fully explain the structure.

Figs. 251 and 252 are rustic gateways in one of the large Imperial gardens in Tokio. In one, two rough logs form the

FIG. 250. — RUSTIC GATEWAY.

posts, the fence being composed of large bamboos in sets of three, alternating on either side of the rails to which they are tied. This was a portal simply. The other had smooth round gate-posts with a light wooden gate with braided panel, and the fence of each side was composed of rush. These gateways and fences were introduced as pleasing effects in the garden.

In the village of Miyajima the deer come down from the woods and wander through the streets. To prevent them from entering the houses and gardens, the passages are guarded by the lightest of latticed gates, against which hangs a weight suspended from above by a cord or long bamboo. The weight answers a double purpose by keeping the gate closed, and also when opened by a caller, by banging loudly against it, thus attracting the attention of a servant.

Large folding gates are often fastened by a transverse bar not unlike the way in which gates are fastened in our country. For light-folding gates an iron ring fastened to one gate by a staple is arranged to slip over a knob or nail on the other gate. In the *yashiki*, one often sees gates that show evidences of disuse, and learns that in former times such gates were only used on rare occasions by special guests of great importance.

There is an infinite variety of forms of garden gates; many of them consisting of the lightest wicker-work, and made solely for picturesque effects. Others, though for the same purpose,

FIG. 251. — RUSTIC GATEWAY.

are more substantial. Fig. 253 represents a quaint garden gate leading into another garden beyond. Frail and unsubstantial as this gate appeared, it was nearly forty years old. The house to the right beyond the gate is for the tea-ceremonies, and the huge fish seen hanging up at the left is made of wood, and gives out a resonant sound when struck; it is the bell, in fact, to call the party from the guest-room to the tea-room beyond at the proper time. The owner of this place is a teacher and master of the *Cha-no-yu*, and a famous expert in old writings.

The variety in design and structure of fences seems almost inexhaustible. Many of them are solid and durable structures, others of the lightest possible description, — the one made with solid frame and heavy stakes, the other of wisps of rush and sticks of bamboo; and between these two is an infinite variety of intermediate forms. A great diversity of material enters into the structure of these fences, — heavy timbers, light boards, sticks

FIG. 252. — RUSTIC GARDEN GATE.

of red-pine, bamboo, reed. twigs, and fagots. Bundles of rush, and indeed almost every kind of plant that can be bound into bundles or sustain its own weight are brought into requisition in the composition of these boundary partitions.

The fences have special names, either derived from their form or the substances from which they are made; thus, a little ornamental fence that juts out from the side of a house or wall is called a *sode-gaki*, — *sode* meaning "sleeve," and *kaki* "fence," the form of the fence having a fanciful resemblance to the curious long sleeve of a Japanese dress. A fence made out of bamboo is called a *ma-gaki*; while a fence made out of the perfumed wood from which the toothpicks are made is called a *kuro-moji-gaki*, and so on.

There are many different groups of Japanese fences. Under one group may be mentioned all those enclosing the ground upon

Fig. 253. — Garden Gateway.

which the house stands. In the city these are often quite tall, usually built of boards, and supported on solid frames resting on a foundation of stone. In the country such fences are hardly more than trellises of bamboo, and these of the lightest description. Many of the fences are strictly ornamental, consisting either of light trellises bounding certain areas, or forming little screens jutting from the side of the house, or from the side of more durable fences or walls. Of these the designs are endless.

Let us examine more in detail some of the principal Japanese types of fences. A simple board-fence consists, as with us, of an upper and lower cross-tie, to which the boards are nailed. A useful modification of the ordinary board-fence consists in having the

FIG. 254.—ORDINARY WOODEN FENCE.

upper and lower rails of thick board, three or four inches wide, and nailed sideways to the fence-posts. The fence-boards are nailed to these rails alternately on one side and on the other. A pretty effect is produced by the interrupted appearance of the rails, and a useful purpose also is subserved by lessening the pressure of the wind which so often blows with great violence, since by securing the boards in this way interspaces occur between the boards the width of the rails. Fig. 254 illustrates a portion of this kind of fence, with its appearance in section as seen from above. This feature in board fences might be imitated with advantage in our country.

Heavy stake fences are made by mortising each stake, which consists of a stout square piece, and running the rail through the mortises thus made, and then pinning each stake in position. In many fences of this

FIG. 255.—STAKE FENCE.

kind there are two rails near together, while the lower ends of the stakes are secured to a foundation-piece, or sill, which is raised an inch or two from the ground by stone props at intervals. By this treatment the sill is preserved both from the ravages of insects and the dampness of the ground. Fig. 255

gives the appearance of this kind of fence. Such fences are made more secure by driving into the ground additional posts at a distance of two feet or more, and binding them together by rails, as shown in the gateway (fig. 243, page 258).

A very serviceable kind of fence is made of bamboo, which is interwoven in the rails of, the fence, as shown in fig. 256. The bamboo stakes are held in place by their elasticity. It will be observed that the post supporting this fence, and also showing the side of a gateway, is marked in a curious fashion. This post is a stout stick of wood in its natu-ral state, the bark only being removed. The design, in a rich brown color, is in this case in the form of diamond-shaped spaces, though spiral lines, like those on a barber's pole, are often seen. This design is burned in, and the wood being carbonized is consequently insoluble as well as unchangeable in color. I was curious to know how such a design was burned in this formal pattern, and learned that a long stout rope, or band of straw soaked in water, was first wound around the post in a wide spiral,

Fig. 256.— Bamboo Fence.

in two directions, leaving diamond-shaped interspaces. A bed of hot coals being prepared, the post was exposed to this heat, and the wood not protected by the wet straw-band became charred. This simple yet ingenious way of getting plain dec-orations, in a rich brown and lasting color, is one that might be utilized in a variety of ways by American architects.

Fences built between house-lots, and consequently bordering the gardens, are made in a variety of decorative ways. A very strong and durable fence is shown in fig. 257, sketched in Hakóne village. The posts in this case were natural trunks of trees, and braces of the same material, fastened by stout wooden pins, were secured to one side. The rail consisted of similar tree-

FIG. 257. — FENCE IN HAKÓNE VILLAGE.

trunks partially hewn, while the fence partition consisted of small bamboo interwoven in the cross-ties.

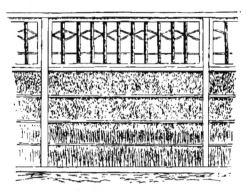

FIG. 258. — RUSTIC GARDEN-FENCE.

Another fence of a more ornamental character (fig. 258) is from a sketch made in Tokio. In this the lower part was filled with a mass of twigs, held in place by slender cross-pieces; and the upper panels consisted of sticks of the red-pine with a slender vine interwoven, making a simple trellis.

In the *sode-gaki*, or sleeve-fence, the greatest ingenuity in design and fabrication is shown; their variety seems endless. I have a Japanese work especially devoted to this kind of fence, in which are hundreds of different designs, — square tops, curving tops, circular or concave edges, panels cut out, and an infinite variety shown in the minor details. This kind of fence is always built out from the side of the house, or from a more permanent fence or wall. It is

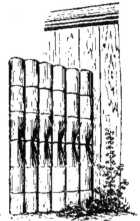

Fig. 259. — Sode-gaki.

rarely over four or five feet in length, and is strictly ornamental, though often useful in screening some feature of the house that is desired to be concealed.

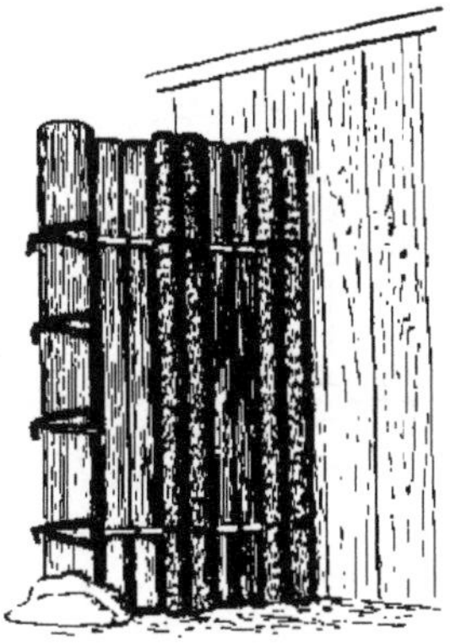

Fig. 259 represents a fence in which cylindrical bundles of rush are bound together by a black-fibred root, and held together by bamboo pieces. Little bundles of fagots are tied to each columns as an odd feature of decoration. In fig. 260 cylindrical bundles of rush and twigs are affixed in pairs on each side of

Fig. 260. — Sode-gaki.

bamboo ties, which run from the outer post to the wooden fence from which the *sode-gaki* springs.   In still another form (fig. 261) the upper portion consists of a bundle of stout reeds tied

by broad bands of the black fibre so often used in such work.   From this apparently hangs a broad mass of brown rush, spreading as it reaches the ground.   Such fences might be added to our gardens, as the materials — such as reeds, rush, twigs, etc. — are easily obtained in this country.   In the stout wooden fences it is not an uncommon sight to see openings the size of a small window protected by a projecting grating of wood (fig. 262).

Besides the fences, a few of which only have been figured, there are stout, durable walls built up with tile and plaster, or mud intermixed.   These structures rest on a foundation of stone, are two or three feet wide at their base, and rise to a height of eight feet or more, at which altitude they may not be over two feet in width, and are crowned with a coping of tiles like a miniature roof-top.   The interior of these walls is filled with a rubble of clay and broken tiles, while the outside ex-

Fig. 262. — Barred Opening in Fence.

hibits an orderly arrangement of tiles in successive layers.

The large enclosures, or *yashikis*, are generally surrounded by walls of this nature.

CHAPTER VI.

GARDENS.

THE Japanese garden, like the house, presents features that never enter into similar places in America. With us it is either modelled after certain French styles, or it is simply beds of flowers in patches or formal plats, or narrow beds bordering the paths; and even these attempts are generally made on large areas only. The smaller gardens seen around our ordinary dwellings are with few exceptions a tangle of bushes, or wretched attempts to crowd as many different kinds of flowers as possible into a given area; and when winter comes, there is nothing left but a harvest of dead stalks and a lot of hideously-designed trellises painted green.

It is no wonder, then, that as our people have gradually become awakened within recent years to some idea of fitness and harmony of color, the conventional flower-bed has been hopelessly abandoned, and now green grass grows over the graves of most of these futile attempts to defy Nature. The grass substitute has at least the merit of not being offensive to the eye, and of requiring but little care save that of the strenuous pushing of the mechanical grass-cutter. This substitute is, however, a confession of inability and ignorance, — as much as if a decorator, after having struggled in vain with his fresco designs upon some ceiling, should give up in disgust and paint the entire surface one color.

15

The secret in a Japanese garden is that they do not attempt too much. That reserve and sense of propriety which characterizes this people in all their decorative and other artistic work is here seen to perfection. Furthermore, in the midst of so much that is evanescent they see the necessity of providing enduring points of interest in the way of little ponds and bridges, odd-shaped stone lanterns and inscribed rocks, summer-houses and rustic fences, quaint paths of stone and pebble, and always a number of evergreen trees and shrubs. We, indeed, have feebly groped that way with our cement vases, jig-saw pavilions green with poisonous compound, and cast-iron fountains of such design that one no longer wonders at the increase of insanity in our midst. One of every hundred of the fountains that our people dote upon is in the form of two little cast-iron children standing in a cast-iron basin, holding over their heads a sheet-iron umbrella, from the point of which squirts a stream of water, — a perennial shower for them alone, while the grass and all about may be sear and yellow with the summer's drought!

The Japanese have brought their garden arts to such perfection that a plot of ground ten feet square is capable of being exquisitely beautified by their methods. Plots of ground that in this country are too often encumbered with coal-ashes, tea-grounds, tin cans, and the garbage-barrel, in Japan are rendered charming to the eye by the simplest means. With cleanliness, simplicity, a few little evergreen shrubs, one or two little clusters of flowers, a rustic fence projecting from the side of the house, a quaintly shaped flower-pot or two, containing a few choice plants, — the simplest form of garden is attained. So much do the Japanese admire gardens, and garden effects, that their smallest strips of ground are utilized for this purpose. In the crowded city, among the poorest houses, one often sees, in the corner of a little earth-area that comes between the sill and the raised floor, a miniature garden made in some shallow box, or even on the ground itself. In gardens of any pretensions, a little pond or sheet of water of irregular outline is an indispensable feature. If a brook can be turned to run through the garden, one of the great charms is attained; and a diminutive water-fall gives all that can be desired. With the aid of fragments of rock and rounded boulders, the picturesque features of a brook can be brought out; little rustic bridges of stone and wood span it, and even the smallest pond will have a bridge of some kind thrown across. A few small hummocks and a little mountain six or eight feet high, over or about which the path runs, are nearly always present.

In gardens of larger size these little mountains are sometimes twenty, thirty, and even forty feet in height, and are built up from the level ground with great labor and expense. On top of these a little rustic lookout with thatched roof is made, from which if a view of Fuji can be got the acme is indeed reached. In still larger gardens, — that is, gardens measuring several hundred feet each way, — the ponds and bridges, small hills and meandering paths, with shrubs trimmed in round balls of various sizes, and grotesquely-shaped pines with long tortuous branches running near the ground, are all combined in such a way by the skilful landscape gardener that the area seems, without exaggeration of statement, ten times as vast.

Irregular and grotesquely shaped stones and huge slabs of rock form an important feature of all gardens; indeed, it is as difficult to imagine a Japanese garden without a number of picturesque and oddly-shaped stones as it is to imagine an American garden without flowers. In Tokio, for example, there being near the city no proper rocks of this kind for garden decoration, rocks and stones are often transported forty or fifty miles for this purpose alone. There are stone-yards in which one may see and purchase rocks such as one might use in building a rough cellar-wall at home, and also sea-worn rocks of various shapes and colors, — among them red-colored stones, that fetch a hundred dollars and more, brought from Sado, an island on the northwest coast of Japan. So much do the Japanese admire stones and rocks for garden decoration, that in their various works on the subject of garden-making the proper arrange-

FIG. 263. — GARDEN TABLET.

ment of stones is described and figured with painstaking minuteness. In the figures to be given of Japanese gardens, reproduced from a work entitled "Chikusan Teizoden," written in the early part of the last century, the arrangement of rocks in the various garden designs will be observed.

Tablets of rock, not unlike a certain type of gravestone, and showing the rough cleavage of the rock from the parent ledge, are often erected in gardens. Upon the face of the rock some appropriate inscription is engraved. The accompanying sketch (fig. 263) is a tablet of this sort, from a famous tea-garden at Omori, celebrated for its plum-blossoms. The legend, freely translated, runs as follows: "The sight of the plum-blossom causes the ink to flow in the writing-room," — meaning that one is inspired to compose poetry under the influence of these surroundings. This tablet was raised on a slight mound, with steps leading to it and quaint pines and shrubs surrounding it. The sketch gives only a suggestion of its appearance.

The stone lanterns (*ishi-dōrō*) are one of the most common yet important accompaniments of garden decoration. Indeed, it is rare to see a garden, even of small size, without one or more of these curious objects. They are usually wrought out of soft volcanic rock, and ordinary ones may be bought for a few dollars. They resemble stout stone-posts of

various contours, round, square, hexagonal, or octagonal; or the upper part may be hexagonal, while the shaft support-ing it may be a round

FIG. 264.
ISHI–DŌRŌ IN TOKIO.

pillar; or they may be of irregular form, built

FIG. 265. — ISHI-
DŌRŌ IN MIYAJIMA.

of water-worn rock. The upper portion is hollowed out, leav-ing various openings cut in ornamental shape; and in this cavity a lamp or candle is placed on special occasions. They are generally made in two or three sections.

There are at least three distinct types, — short and broad ones with tops shaped like a mushroom, these generally standing on three or four legs; tall, slender ones; and a third form composed of a number of sections piled up to a considerable height, looking like a pagoda, which, for all I know, they may be made to imitate.

FIG. 266. — ISHI–DŌRŌ IN SHIRAKO,
MUSASHI.

These stone lanterns are called *ishi-dōrō*. A legend states that in ancient times there was a pond on a certain mountain, in the vicinity of which robbers repeatedly came out and at-tacked travellers. In consequence of this, a god called Iruhiko caused to be built stone lanterns to illuminate the roads, — stone being a more enduring material.   In a temple built by

Prince Shotoko, in the second year of Suiko (594 A. D.), the first *ishi-dōrō* is said to have been erected, and the legend states that it was removed from the region above named to this temple.[1]

A few sketches are here given illustrating some of the forms of *ishi-dōrō* observed.   The one shown in fig. 265 was sketched on the temple grounds of Miyajima, on the inland sea.   I was informed by the priest there that this stone lantern was over seven hundred years old. Its base was buried, and the whole affair showed evidences of great age in the worn

FIG. 267. — ISHI-DŌRŌ IN UTSUNOMIYA.

appearance of its various parts.   Figs. 264 and 266 represent forms from Tokio and Shirako, and fig. 267 an elaborately wrought one from Utsunomiya.

FIG. 268. — STONE FOOT-BRIDGE.

The little bridges of stone and wood are extremely good examples of rustic-work, and might be copied with advantage in our country.   The ingenious device of displacing the stones laterally (fig. 268), or of combining the bridge with stepping-stones, as seen in some of them, is decidedly unique.

[1] This legend is from a work entitled " Chikusan Teizoden."

Fig. 269 illustrates a stone bridge in one of the large gardens of Tokio. The span of this bridge was ten or twelve feet, and yet the bridge itself was composed of a single slab of stone. Fig. 270 shows a little brook in a private garden in Tokio.

FIG. 269. — STONE FOOT-BRIDGE.

Here the foot-bridge consists of an unwrought slab of rock. The *ishi-dōrō* showing in the same sketch consists of a number of naturally-worn stones, except the lantern portion, which has been cut out.

FIG. 270. — GARDEN BROOK AND FOOT-BRIDGE.

The summer-houses are simple and picturesque; sometimes they have a seat and a *do-ma*, or earth floor; others will have a board or a matted floor. These houses are generally open, the square thatched roof being supported on four corner-posts; others again will have two sides closed by permanent partitions, in one of which an ornamental opening or window occurs. We cannot understand what so intelligent an observer as Rein means, when he makes the statement that the Japanese garden contains no summer-house, — for it is rare to see a garden of any magnitude without one, and impossible to refer to any Japanese book on the subject in which these little rustic shelters and resting-places are not figured.

The training of vines and trees about the summer-house window is often delightfully conceived. We recall the circular window of 'one that presented a most beautiful appearance. Three sides of the summer-house were closed by permanent plaster partitions, tinted a rich brown color, with a very broad-eaved thatched roof throwing its dark shade on the matted floor. In the partition opposite the open side was a perfectly circular window five feet in diameter. There was no frame or moulding to this opening, simply the plastering finished squarely at the border ; dark-brown bamboos of various thicknesses, secured across this opening horizontally, formed the frame-work ; running vertically, and secured to the bamboo, was a close grating of brown rush. Over and around this window — it being on the sunny side — there had been carefully trained outside a vine with rich green leaves, so that the window was more or less shaded by it. The effect of the sunlight falling upon the vine was exquisite beyond description. When two or three leaves interposed between the sun's rays, the color was a rich dark green ; where here and there, over the whole mass, a single leaf only interrupted the light, there were bright green flashes, like emerald gems ; at points the dazzling sunlight glinted like sparks. In a few places the vine and leaves had been coaxed through the grating of rushes, and these were consequently in deep shadow. I did not attempt to sketch it, as no drawing could possibly convey an idea of the exceeding richness and charm of the effect, with the cool and shaded room within, the dark-brown lattice of bamboo and rush, the capacious round opening, and, above all, the effect of the various rich greens,— which was greatly heightened as the wind tremulously shifted the leafy screens without, and thus changed the arrangement of the emerald colors within.

My attention was first attracted to it by noticing a number of Japanese peering at it through an open fence, and admiring in rapt delight this charm-ing conception. Such a room and window might easily be arranged in our gardens, as we have a number of vines with light, translucent leaves capable of being utilized in this way.

Fig. 271 gives a view of a summer-house in a private garden in Tokio. Four rough posts and a few cross-ties formed the frame; it had a raised floor, the edge of which formed a seat, and two plas-tered partitions at right an-gles, in one of which was cut

FIG. 271. — SUMMER-HOUSE IN PRIVATE GAR-DEN, TOKIO.

a circular window, and in the other a long, narrow opening above; and crowning the whole was a heavily-thatched roof, its peak capped by an inverted earthen basin. Whether the basin was made expressly for this purpose or not, its warm red color added a pleasing effect to the gray of the thatch. In front and about it stones and rocks were arranged in pleasing disorder, while a number of exotic flowers and quaintly trimmed shrubs added their charms, and a little brook found its way across the path leading to it.

Fig. 272 is the sketch of a summer-house in one of the imperial gardens in Tokio. The frame, as in the one last figured, consisted of round sticks with the bark retained; this was capped with a thatched roof, surmounted by a ridge of thatch and bamboo. A very pretty feature was shown in the trellises, which sprung diagonally from each post, — the frame of these trellises consisting of tree-branches selected for their irregular forms. The lattice was made of bamboo and rush, and each trellis had a different design. The seat within was of porcelain; and about

the slight mound on which the summer-house stood were curiously-trimmed shrubs and dwarfed pines.

The openings or windows in these summer-houses are often remarkable for their curious designs. The following sketches (figs. 273, 274) give a faint idea of the appearance of these rustic openings, — one representing a gourd,

Fig 272. — Summer-house in Imperial Garden, Tokio.

its frame being made of grape-vine; the other suggesting a mountain, the lattice being made of bamboo.

For border hedges, trees of large size are often trained to form a second barrier above the squarely-trimmed shrubs that come next the path. A jinko-tree is trained so that it spreads like a fan, in one direction, to a width of thirty feet or more, while it may not be over two feet in thickness. An infinite amount of patient work is required in tying all the big branches and little twigs to bamboo supports in order to bring trees into such strange forms.

In the garden of Fukiage, in Tokio, some very marvellous effects of landscape-gardening are seen. At a distance you notice high ground, a hill in fact, perhaps fifty or sixty feet in height; approaching it from a plain of rich green grass you cross a little lake, bridged at one point by a single slab of rock; then up a ravine, down which a veritable mountain brook is tumbling, and through a rock foundation so natural, that, until a series of faults and dislocations, synclinals and anticlinals, in rapid succession arouse your geological memories with a rude shock, you cannot believe that all this colossal mass of material has been

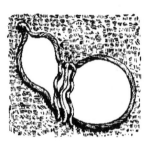

FIG. 273. — RUSTIC OPENING IN SUMMER-HOUSE, KOBE.

transported here by man, from distances to be measured by leagues; and that a few hundred years ago a low plain existed where now are rocky ravines and dark dells, with heavy forest

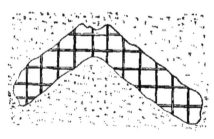

FIG. 274. — RUSTIC OPENING IN SUMMER-HOUSE, OKAZAKI.

trees throwing their cool shadows over all. You wend your way by a picturesque forest-path to the summit of the hill, which is crowned by a rustic summer - house with wide verandah, from which a beautiful view of Fuji is got. Looking back towards the park, you expect to see the ravine below, but, to your amazement, an absolutely flat plain of shrubbery, resembling a closely-cropped tea plantation, level to the top of the hill and extending to a considerable distance, greets your

eye. Have you lost the points of the compass? Walking out
in the direction of this level growth of shrubbery, a new surprise awaits you; for peering through the bushes, you look down
the slopes of the steep hill you had ascended. The forest-trees
which thickly cover the slopes of the hill had been trimmed
above to an absolute level; and this treatment had gone on
for so many years that the tops formed a dense mass having
the appearance, from the summer-house, of a continuous stretch
of low shrubs springing from a level ground.

I have spoken of the love the Japanese have for gardens
and garden effects, the smallest areas of ground being utilized
for this purpose. As an illustration of this, I recall an experience in a cheap inn, where I was forced to take a meal or
go hungry till late at night. The immediate surroundings indicated poverty, the house itself being poorly furnished, the
mats hard and uneven, and the attendants very cheaply dressed.
In the room where our meal was served there was a circular
window, through which could be seen a curious stone lantern
and a pine-tree, the branches of which stretched across the
opening, while beyond a fine view of some high mountains was
to be had. From where we sat on the mats there were all the
evidences of a fine garden outside; and wondering how so poor
a house could sustain so fine a garden, I went to the window
to investigate. What was my surprise to find that the extent
of ground from which the lantern and pine-tree sprung was
just three feet in width! Then came a low board-fence, and
beyond this stretched the rice-fields of a neighboring farmer.
At home such a narrow strip of land would in all likelihood
have been the receptacle for broken glass and tin cans, and
a thoroughfare for erratic cats; here, however, everything was
clean and neat, — and this narrow plot of ground, good for
no other purpose, had been utilized solely for the benefit of the
room within.

Reference has been made to the ponds and brooks as desirable features in garden-making. Where water is not obtainable for the purpose, or possibly for the ingenuity of the idea, the Japanese sometimes make a deceptive pond, which is absolutely destitute of water; so perfectly, however, are the various features of the pond carried out, that the effect of water is produced by the illusion of association. The pond is laid out in an irregular outline, around the border of which plant-pots buried out of sight contain the iris and a number of plants which naturally abound near wet shores. The bottom of the pond is lined with little gray pebbles, and a rustic bridge leads to a little island in the centre. The appearance of this dry pond from the verandah is most deceptive.

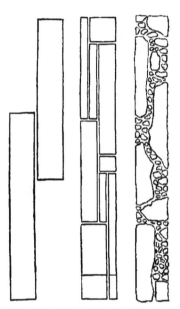

Fig. 275. — Various Forms of Garden Paths.

The real ponds contain either lotus or other aquatic plants, or they may be given up to turtles or gold-fish, and are oftentimes very elaborately laid out with rustic, wooden, or stone bridges. Little promontories with stone lanterns standing at their ends like miniature light-houses, rustic arbors or seats, trellises above supporting a luxuriant growth of wistaria, and tortuous pines with long branches reaching out over the water, are a few of the many features which add so much to that peculiar charm so characteristic of Japanese gardens.

The pathways of stone are of many kinds. Sometimes the slabs of stone may be finished squarely, and then each may be arranged in line across the path, or adjusted in such a way from one side to the other that a zigzag path is made; in other cases the path may consist of long slabs squarely trimmed, or of large irregular slabs interrupted with little stones, all compacted into the hard earth. Fig. 275, copied from " Chikusan Teizoden," shows some of these arrangements; and an idea of the way in which the stone paths are laid out is well illustrated in figs. 283 and 284 (pp. 291, 292), copied from the same work. The entrance from the street is seen at the left. The stone path leads through a courtyard to a second gate, and from thence to the *genka*, or entrance to the house.

Flowers, shrubs, and dwarf trees in pots and tubs are commonly used in the vicinity of the verandah, and also about

the garden for decorative features; and here tasteful and rustic effects are sought for in the design and material of the larger wooden receptacles. Fig. 276 represents a shallow trough made from a fragment of an

Fig. 276. — Wooden Trough for Plants.

old shipwreck, blackened by age, and mounted on a dark woodstand. In this trough are two stones, a bronze crab, and a few aquatic plants. Another wooden flower-pot of large size (fig. 277) is made from the planks of an old vessel, the wood perforated by Teredo, and the grain deeply worn out by age. Its form permits it to be carried by two men.

Among the most extraordinary objects connected with gardens are the dwarf plum-trees. Before the evidence of life appears in the blooming, one would certainly believe that a collection of dwarf plum-trees were simply fragments of old blackened and distorted branches or roots, — as if fragments of dead wood had been selected for the purpose of grotesque display! Indeed, nothing more hopeless for flowers or life could

be imagined than the appearance of these irregular, flattened, and even perforated sticks and stumps. They are kept in the house on the sunny side, and while the snow is yet on the ground, send out long, delicate drooping twigs, which are soon strung with a wealth of the most beautiful rosy-

FIG. 277. — PLANT-POT OF OLD PLANK.

tinted blossoms it is possible to conceive; and, curiously enough, not a trace of a green leaf appears during all this luxuriant blossoming.

Fig. 278 is an attempt to show the appearance of one of these phenomenal plum-trees. It was over forty years old, and stood about three feet high. By what horticultural sorcery life had been kept in this blackened stump, only a Japanese gardener knows. And such a vitality! Not a few feeble twigs and blossoms as an expiring effort, but a delicious growth of the most vigorous and dainty flowers. The pines are equally remarkable in their way. It is very curious to see a sturdy old pine-tree, masculine and gruff in its gnarled branches and tortuous trunk, perhaps forty or fifty years old, and yet not over two feet in height, and growing in a flower-pot; or a thick chunk of pine standing upright in a flower-pot, and sending out vigorous branches covered with leaves (fig. 279), and others trained in ways that seem incredible.

In a large garden in Tokio I saw one of these trees that spread out in a symmetrical convex disk with a diameter of twenty feet or more, yet standing

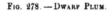

FIG. 278. — DWARF PLUM.   FIG. 279. — DWARF PINE.

not over two feet in height (fig. 280); still another one, in which the branches had been trained to assume the appearance of flattened disks (fig. 281). It would seem as if the artistic and picturesque taste of the gardener followed the shrubs even

FIG. 280. — CURIOUSLY TRAINED PINE-TREE.

to their winter shrouds of straw; for when they are enwrapped for the winter's cold and snow, the objects even in this guise look quaint and attractive, besides being most thoroughly protected, as may be seen by fig. 282 on page 290.

In this brief sketch of Japanese gardens only the more sa-
lient features have been touched upon, and these only in the most
general way. It would have been more proper to have included
the ornamental fences, more especially the *sode-gaki*, in this chap-

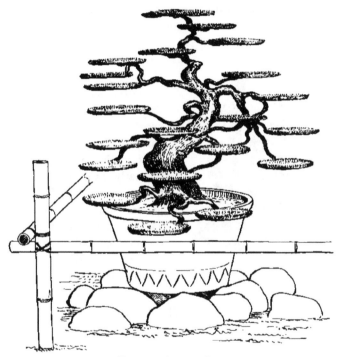

Fig. 281. — Dwarfed Pine.

ter. It was deemed best, however, to include fences of all kinds
under one heading; and this has been done in a previous chapter.
The rustic wells, which add so much to garden effects, might
with equal propriety have been incorporated here; but for similar reasons it was thought best to include with the wells the

19

few brief allusions to water supply and village aqueducts,—and these subjects are therefore brought together under one heading in the chapter which is to follow.

In this chapter on gardens, I regret the absence of general sketches of the garden proper; but the few sketches I had made were too imperfect to hazard an attempt at their reproduction. Moreover, not the slightest justice could have been done to

the thoroughly original character of the Japanese garden, with all its variety and beauty. In lieu of this, however, I have had reproduced a number of views of private gardens, from a Japanese work on the subject published in the early part of the last century,—though, so far as their general arrangement and appearance go, they might have been copied from gardens to be seen in that country to-day.

Fig. 282. — Shrubs wrapped in Straw for Winter.

The first illustration (fig. 283) shows the relation of the various buildings, with the approaches from the street, which is on the left. Here are seen two gateways: the larger one with swinging gates is closed; the smaller one with sliding gate is open. The building with the two little windows and black foundation is the *kura*. The pathway, of irregular slabs of stone, leads around the sides of the *kura* to a second gateway; and beyond this the stone path continues to the *genka*, or main entrance to the dwelling. The drawing is a curious admixture of isometric and linear perspective, with some violent displacements in point of sight and vanishing points, in order to

FIG. 283, SHOWING APPROACHES TO HOUSE. (REPRODUCED FROM "CHIKUSAN TEIZODEN," A JAPANESE WORK.)

show fully the various details within the limits of the plate.
The other illustrations represent respectively a little garden be-

Fig. 284. — Little Garden belonging to the Priests of a Buddhist Temple.
(Reproduced from "Chikusan Teizoden," a Japanese Work.)

longing to the priests' house of a Buddhist temple (fig. 284), a
garden connected with the house of a merchant (fig. 285; the
legend says the owner is a dealer in dress materials and cot-

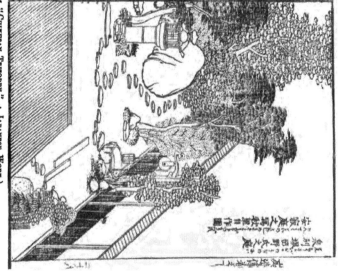

FIG. 285.—GARDEN OF A MERCHANT. (REPRODUCED FROM "CHIKUSAN TEIZODEN," A JAPANESE WORK.)

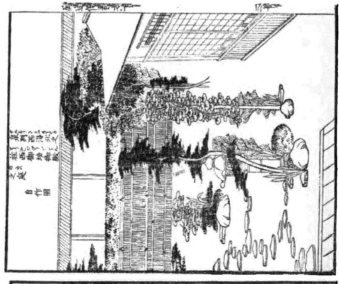

FIG. 286. — GARDEN OF A DAIMIO. (REPRODUCED FROM "CHIKUSAN TRIZODEN," A JAPANESE WORK.)

tons), and a garden connected with the residence of a Daimio (fig. 286). All of these gardens were to be found in Sakai, Idzumi, nearly two hundred years ago, and the more enduring features of some of them may still be in existence. A study of these quaint drawings will enable the reader to recognize the ornamental fences, quaint rocks, rustic wells, *ishi-dōrō*, *chōdzu-bachi*, stone pathways, and curious trees and shrubs so characteristic of the Japanese garden, and so utterly unlike anything with which we are familiar in the geometrical patches we are wont to regard as gardens.

It is a remarkable fact that the various trees and shrubs which adorn a Japanese garden may be successfully transplanted again and again without impairing their vitality. Trees of very large size may be seen, almost daily, being dragged through the streets on their way from one garden to another. A man may have a vigorous and healthy garden under way in the space of a few days, — trees forty or fifty feet high, and as many years old, sturdy shrubs and tender plants, all possessing a vitality and endurance under the intelligent management of a Japanese gardener, which permits them to be transported from one end of the city to the other. If for some reason the owner has to give up his place, every stone and ornamental fence, and every tree and plant having its commercial value, may all be dug up and sold and spirited away, in a single day, to some other part of the town. And such a vicissitude often falls to the lot of a Japanese garden, enduring as it is. The whole affair, save the circular well-hole, may be transported like magic from one end of the country to the other.

CHAPTER VII.

·MISCELLANEOUS MATTERS.

Wells and Water-Supply. — Flowers. — Interior Adornments. — Precautions
against Fire. — Houses of Foreign Style. — Absence of Monuments.

WITH the exception of a few of the larger cities, the water-supply of Japan is by means of wooden wells sunk in the ground. In Tokio, besides the ordinary forms of wells which are found in every portion of the city, there is a system of aqueducts conveying water from the Tamagawa a distance of twenty-four miles, and from Kanda a distance of ten miles or more. It is hardly within the province of this work to call attention to the exceeding impurity of much of the well-water in Tokio and elsewhere in Japan, as shown by many analyses, or to the imperfect way in which water is conveyed from remote places to Tokio and Yokohama. For valuable and interesting papers on this subject the reader is referred to the Journal of the Asiatic Society of Japan.[1]

[1] Professor Atkinson, in the Journal of the Asiatic Society, vol. vi. part i.; Dr. Geerts, ibid., vol. vii. part iii.

Dr. O. Korschelt has made an extremely valuable contribution to the Asiatic Society of Japan, on the water-supply of Tokio. Aided by Japanese students, he has made many analyses of well-waters and waters from the city supply, and shows that, contrary to the conclusions of Professor Atkinson, the high-ground wells are on the whole much purer than those on lower ground. Dr. Korschelt also calls attention to the great number of artesian wells sunk in Tokio, by means of bamboo tubes driven into the ground. The ordinary form of well is carried down thirty or forty feet in the usual way, and then at the bottom bamboo tubes are driven to great depths, ranging from one hundred to two hundred feet and more. He speaks of a number of these wells in Tokio and the suburbs as overflowing. There is one well not far from the Tokio Daigaku which overflows; and a very remarkable sight it is to see the water pouring over a high

The aqueducts in the city are made of wood, either in the shape of heavy square plank tubes or circular wooden pipes. These various conductors are intersected by open wells, in which the water finds its natural level, only partially filling them. These wells are to be found in the main streets as well as in certain open areas; and to them the people come, not only to get their water, but often to do light washing.

The time must soon come when the authorities of Tokio will find it absolutely necessary to establish water-works for the supply of the city. Such a change from the present system would require an enormous expenditure at the outset, but in the

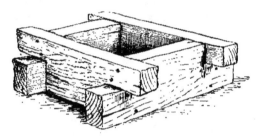

Fig. 287.— Ancient Form of Well-curb.

end the community will be greatly benefited, not only in having more efficient means to quell the awful conflagrations which so frequently devastate their thoroughfares, but also in having a more healthful water-supply for family use. In their present imperfect method of water-service it is impossible to keep the supply free from local contamination; and though the death-rate of the city is low compared with that of many European

well-curb and flooding the ground in the vicinity. He shows that pure water may be reached in most parts of Tokio by means of artesian wells; and to this source the city must ultimately look for its water-supply.

For further particulars concerning this subject, the reader is referred to Dr. Korschelt's valuable paper in the Transactions of the Asiatic Society of Japan, vol. xii. part iii., p. 143.

and American cities, it would certainly be still further reduced
by pure water made available to all.

In many country villages, where the natural conditions exist,
a mountain brook is conducted by a rock-bound canal through
the centre of the village street; and thus the water for culinary
and other purposes is brought directly to the door of every
house on that street.

The wells are made in the shape of barrels of stout staves
five or six feet in height. These taper slightly at their lower
ends, and are fitted one within another; and as the well is dug
deeper the sections are adjusted and driven down. Wells of
great depth are often sunk in this way. The well made in
this manner has the appearance, as it projects above the ground,
of an ordinary barrel
or hogshead partially
buried.

FIG. 288. — STONE WELL-CURB IN PRIVATE GARDEN
IN TOKIO.

Stone curbs of a
circular form are oft-
en seen. An ancient
form of well-curb is a
square frame, made of
thick timber in the
shape shown in fig.
287. The Chinese character for "well" is in the shape of this
frame; and as one rides through the city or village he will often
notice this character painted on the side of a house or over a
door-way, indicating that in the rear, or within the house, a
well is to be found. A picturesque well-curb of stone, made
after this form, is shown in fig. 288, from a private garden
in Tokio.

While the water is usually brought up by means of a bucket
attached to the end of a long bamboo, there are various forms
of frames erected over the well to support a pulley, in which

runs a rope with a bucket attached to each end. Fig. 289 is an illustration of one of these frames. Sometimes the trunk of a tree is made to do service, as shown in fig. 290. In this case the old trunk was densely covered with a rich growth of Japanese ivy.

In the country kitchen the well is often within the house, as shown in the sketch fig. 167 (page 186). In the country, as well as in the city, the regular New England well-sweep is now and then seen. In the

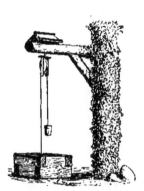

FIG. 289. — WOODEN WELL-FRAME.   FIG. 290. — RUSTIC WELL-FRAME.

southern part of Japan particularly the well-sweep is very common ; one is shown in the picture of a southern house (fig. 54, page 73).

There are many ways of conveying water to villages by bamboo pipes. In Kioto many places are supplied by water brought in this way from the mountain brooks back of the city. At Miyajima, on the Inland Sea, water is brought, by means of bamboo pipes, from a mountain stream at the western end of the village. The water is first conveyed to a single shallow tank, supported on a rough pedestal of rock. The tank is perforated at intervals along its sides and on its end, and

by means of bamboo gutters the water is conveyed to bamboo
tubes standing vertical, — each bamboo having at its top a box
or bucket, in which is a grating of bamboo to screen the water
from the leaves and twigs.   These bamboo tubes are connected
with a system of bamboo tubes under-ground, and these lead
to the houses in the village street below.   Fig. 291 is an illustration of this structure.   It was an old and leaky affair, but
formed a picturesque mass beside the mountain road, covered
as it was by a rich growth of ferns and mosses, and brightened
by the water dripping from all points.

FIG. 291. — AQUEDUCT RESERVOIR AT MIYAJIMA, AKI.

Just beyond this curious reservoir I saw a group of small
aqueducts, evidently for the supply of single houses. Fig. 292
illustrates one of a number of these seen along the road.
Fig. 293 represents one of the old wells still seen in the Kaga
Yashiki, in Tokio, — an inclosure of large extent formerly occupied by the Daimio of Kaga, but now overgrown with bamboo
grass and tangled bushes, while here and there evidences of
its former beauty are seen in neglected groves of trees and in

picturesque ponds choked with plant growth. The buildings of the Tokio Medical College and Hospital occupy one portion of the ground; and the new brick building of the Tokio University, a few dwellings for its foreign teachers, and a small observatory form another group.

Scattered over this large inclosure are a number of treacherous holes guarded only by fences painted black. These are the remains of wells; and by their number one gets a faint idea of the dense community that filled this

FIG. 292. — AQUEDUCTS AT MIYAJIMA, AKI.

area in the days of the Shogunate. During the Revolution the houses were burned, and with them the wooden curbs of the wells, and for many years these deep holes formed dreadful pitfalls in the long grass.

FIG. 293. — WELL IN KAGA YASHIKI, TOKIO.

The effect of rusticity which the Japanese so much admire, and which they show in their gateways, fences, and other surroundings, is charmingly carried out in the wells; and the presence of a well in a garden is looked upon as adding greatly to its beauty. Hence. one sees quaint and picturesque curbs, either of stone and green with plant growth, or of wood and fairly dropping to pieces with decay. One sees literally a moss-covered bucket and well, too; but, alas! the water is not the cold, pure fluid which a New Englander is accustomed to draw from similar places at home, but often a water far from wholesome, and which to make so is generally boiled before drinking. We refer now to the city wells; and yet the country wells are quite as liable to contamination.

Having described in the previous pages the permanent features of the house and its surroundings, a few pages may be properly added concerning those objects which are hung upon the walls as adornments. A few objects of household use have been mentioned, such as pillows, *hibachi,* *tabako-bon,* lamps, candlesticks, and towel-racks, as naturally associated with the mats, kitchen, bathing conveniences, etc. Any further consideration of these movable objects would lead us into a discussion of the bureaus, chests, baskets, trays, dishes, and the whole range of domestic articles of use, and might, indeed, furnish material enough for another volume.

A few pages, however, must be added on the adornments of the room, and the principles which govern the Japanese in these matters. As flowers form the most universal decoration of the rooms from the highest to the lowest classes, these will be first considered.

The love of flowers is a national trait of the Japanese. It would be safe to say that in no other part of the world is the love of flowers so universally shown as in Japan. For pictorial illustration flowers form one of the most common themes; and for decorative art in all its branches flowers, in natural or conventional shapes, are selected as the leading motive. In their light fabrics, — embroidery, pottery, lacquers, wall-papers, fans, — and even in their metal work and bronzes, these charming and perishable objects are constantly depicted and wrought. In their social life, also, these things are always present. From birth to death, flowers are in some way associated with the daily life of the Japanese; and for many years after their death their graves continue to receive fresh floral tributes.

A room in the very humblest of houses will have in its place of honor — the *tokonoma* — a flower-vase, or a section of bamboo hanging from its side, or some form of receptacle suspended from the open portion of the room above, or in front of some ornamental opening in which flowers are displayed. On the street one often meets the flower vendor; and at night, flower fairs are one of the most common attractions.

The arrangement of flowers forms a part of the polite education of the Japanese, and special rules and methods for their appropriate display have their schools and teachers. Within the house there are special places where it is proper to display flowers. In the *tokonoma*, as we have said, is generally a vase of bronze or pottery in which flowers are placed, — not the heterogeneous mass of color comprised in a jumble of flowers, as is too often the case with us; but a few flowers of one kind, or a big branch of cherry or plum blossoms are quite enough to satisfy the refined tastes of these people. Here, as in other matters, the Japanese show their sense of propriety and infinite refinement. They most thoroughly abominate our slovenly methods, whereby a clump of flowers of heterogeneous colors are packed and jammed together, with no room for green leaves: this we call a bouquet; and very properly, since it resembles a ball, — a variegated worsted ball. These people believe in the healthy contrast of rough brown stem and green leaves, to show off by texture and color the matchless life-tones of the delicate petals. We, however, in our stupidity are too often accustomed to tear off the flowers that Nature has so deftly arranged on their own wood stems, and then with thread and bristling wire to fabricate a feeble resemblance to the milliner's honest counterfeit of cloth and paper; and by such treatment, at the end of a few hours, we have a mass equally lifeless.

In their flower-vases, too, they show the most perfect knowledge of contrasts. To any one of taste it is unnecessary to show how inappropriate our gilt and often brilliantly colored flower-vases are for the objects they are to hold. By employing such receptacles, all effects of color and pleasing contrasts are effectually ruined. The Japanese flower-vase is often made of the roughest and coarsest pottery, with rough patches of glaze and irregular contour; it is made solid and heavy, with a good bottom, and is capable of holding a big cherry branch without up-setting. Its very roughness shows off by contrast the delicate flowers it holds. With just such rough material as we use in the making of drain-tiles and molasses jugs, the Japanese make the most fascinating and appropriate flower-vases; but their potters are artists, and, alas! ours are not.

In this connection it is interesting to note that in our country, artists, and others having artistic tastes, have always recognized the importance of observing proper contrasts between flowers and their holders, and until within a very few years have been forced, for want of better receptacles, to arrange flowers in German pottery-mugs, Chinese ginger-jars, and the like. Though these vessels were certainly inappropriate enough, the flowers looked vastly prettier in them than they ever could in the frightful wares designed expressly to hold them, made by American and European manufacturers. What a satire on our art industries, — a despairing resort to beer-mugs, ginger-jars and blacking-pots, for suitable flower-vases! Who does not recall, indeed cannot see to-day on the shelves of most " crockery shops," a hideous battalion of garish porcelain and iniquitous parian vases, besides other multitudinous evidences of utter ignorance as to what a flower-vase should be, in the discordantly colored and decorated glass receptacles designed to hold these daintiest bits of Nature's handiwork?

Besides the flower-vase made to stand on the floor, the Japanese have others which are made to hang from a hook, — generally from the post or partition that divides the *tokonoma* from its companion recess, or sometimes from a corner-post. When a permanent partition occurs in a room, it is quite proper to hang the vase from the middle post. In all these cases it is hung midway between the floor and the ceiling. These hanging flower-vases are infinite in form and design, and are made of pottery, bronze, bamboo, or wood. Those made of pottery and bronze may be in the form of simple tubes; often, however, natural forms are represented, — such as fishes, insects, sections of bamboo, and the like.

The Japanese are fond of ancient objects, and jars which have been dug up are often mutilated, at least for the antiquarian, by having rings inserted in their sides so that they may be hung up for flower-holders.

Fig. 294. — HANGING FLOWER-HOLDER OF BAMBOO.

A curious form of holder is made out of a rugged knot of wood. Any quaint and abnormal growth of wood, in which an opening can be made big enough to accommodate a section of bamboo to hold the water, is used for a flower-vase. Such an object will be decorated with tiny bronze ants, a silver spider's web with bronze spider, and pearl wrought in the shape of a fungus. These and other singular caprices are worked into and upon the wood as ornaments.

20

A very favorite form of flower-holder is one made
of bamboo. The bamboo tube is worked in a variety of ways, by cutting out various sections from
the sides   Fig. 294 represents an odd, yet com-

FIG. 295. — HANGING FLOWER-HOLDER OF BASKET-WORK.

mon shape, arranged for *cha-no-yu* (tea-parties), and sketched at
one of these parties. The bamboo is an admirable receptacle for
water, and a section of it is used for this purpose in many
forms of pottery and bronze flower-holders.

Rich brown-colored baskets are also favorite receptacles for flowers, a segment of bamboo being used to hold the water. The accompanying figure (fig. 295) is a sketch of a hanging basket, the flowers having been arranged by a lover of the tea-ceremonies and old pottery. Many of these baskets are quite old, and are highly prized by the Japanese. At the street flower-fairs cheap and curious devices are often seen for holding flower-pots. The annexed figure (fig. 296) illustrates a form of bracket in which a thin irregular-shaped slab of wood has attached to it a crooked branch of a tree, upon the free ends of which wooden blocks are secured as shelves upon which the flower-pots are to rest. A hole is made at the top so that it may be hung against the wall, and little cleats are fastened crosswise to hold long strips of stiff paper, upon which it is customary to write stanzas of poetry. These objects are of the cheapest description, can be got for a few pennies, and are bought by the poorest classes.

Fig. 296.
Cheap Bracket for
Flower-pots.

For flower-holders suspended from above, a common form is a square wooden bucket, or one made out of pottery or bronze in imitation of this form. Bamboo cut in horizontal forms is also used for suspended flower-holders. Indeed, there seems to be no end of curious objects used for this purpose, — a gourd, the semi-cylindrical tile, sea-shells, as with us, and forms made in pottery or bronze in imitation of these objects.

Quaint and odd-shaped flower-stands are made in the form of buckets. The following figure (fig. 297) represents one sketched at the National Exposition at Tokio in 1877. Its construction was very ingenious; three staves of the lower bucket were continued upward to form portions of three smaller buckets above, and each of these, in turn, contributed a stave to the single bucket that crowned the whole. Another form, made by the same contributor though not so symmetrical, was quite as odd.

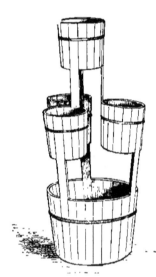

Fig. 297. — Curious Combination of Buckets for Flowers.

Curious little braided-straw affairs are made to hold flowers, or rather the bamboo segments in which the flowers are kept. These are made in the form of insects, fishes, mushrooms, and other natural objects. These are mentioned, not that they have a special merit, but to illustrate the devices used by the common people in decorating their homes. Racks of wood richly lacquered are also used, from which hanging flower-holders are suspended. These objects are rarely seen now, and I have never chanced to see one in use.

In the chapter on Interiors various forms of vases are shown in the *tokonoma.*

My interest in Japanese homes was first aroused by wishing to know precisely what use the Japanese made of a class of objects with which I had been familiar in the Art Museums and private collections at home; furthermore, a study of their houses led me to search for those evidences of household decoration which might possibly parallel the hanging baskets, corner brackets, and especially ornaments made of birch bark, fungi, moss, shell-work, and the like, with which our humbler homes are often garnished. It was delightful to find that the Japanese were susceptible to the charms embodied in these bits of Nature, and that they too used them in similar decorative ways. At the outset, search for an object aside from the bare rooms seemed fruitless enough. At first sight these rooms appeared absolutely barren; in passing from one room to the other one got the idea that the house was to be let. Picture to yourself a room with no fire-place and accompanying mantel, — that shelf of shelves for the support of pretty objects; no windows with their convenient interspaces for the suspension of pictures or brackets; no table, rarely even cabinets, to hold bright-colored bindings and curious bric-à-brac; no side-boards upon which to array the rich pottery or glistening porcelain; no chairs, desks, or bedsteads, and consequently no opportunity for the display of elaborate carvings or rich cloth coverings. Indeed, one might well wonder in what way this people displayed their pretty objects for household decorations.

After studying the Japanese home for a while, however, one comes to realize that display as such is out of the question with them, and to recognize that a severe Quaker-like simplicity is really one of the great charms of a Japanese room. Absolute cleanliness and refinement, with very few objects in sight upon which the eye may rest contentedly, are the main features in household adornment which the Japanese strive after, and which they attain with a simplicity and effectiveness that we can never hope to reach. Our rooms seem to them like a curiosity shop, and "stuffy" to the last degree. Such a maze of vases, pictures, plaques, bronzes, with shelves, brackets, cabinets, and tables loaded down with bric-à-brac, is quite enough to drive a Japanese frantic. We parade in the most unreasoning manner every object of this nature in our possession; and with the

periodical recurrence of birthday and Christmas holidays, and the
consequent influx of new things, the less pretty ones already
on parade are banished to the chambers above to make room for
the new ones; and as these in turn get crowded out they rise
to the garret, there to be providentially broken up by the children, or to be preserved for future antiquarians to contemplate,
and to ponder over the condition of art in this age. Our walls
are hung with large fish-plates which were intended to hold
food; heavy bronzes, which in a Japanese room are made to rest
solidly on the floor, and to hold great woody branches of the
plum or cherry with their wealth of blossoms, are with us often
placed on high shelves or perched in some perilous position over
the door. The ignorant display is more rarely seen of thrusting
a piece of statuary into the window, so that the neighbor across
the way may see it; when a silhouette, cut out of stiff pasteboard,
would in this position answer all the purposes so far as the
inmates are concerned. How often we destroy an artist's best
efforts by exposing his picture against some glaring fresco or
distracting wall-paper! And still not content with the accu-
mulated misery of such a room, we allow the upholsterer and
furnisher to provide us with a gorgeously framed mirror, from
which we may have flashed back at us the contents of the room
reversed, or, more dreadful still, a reverberation of these horrors through opposite reflecting surfaces, — a futile effort of
Nature to sicken us of the whole thing by endless repetition.[1]

  That we in America are not exceptional in these matters of
questionable furnishing, one may learn by listening to an English
authority on this subject, — one who has done more than any
other writer in calling attention not only to violations of true
taste in household adornment, but who points out in a most rational way the correct paths to follow, not only to avoid that

---

[1] The pier-glass is happily unknown in Japan; a small disk of polished metal represents the mirror, and is wisely kept in a box till needed!

which is offensive and pretentious, but to arrive at better methods and truer principles in matters of taste. We refer to Charles L. Eastlake and his timely work entitled "Hints on Household Taste." In his animadversions on the commonplace taste shown in the furnishing of English houses, he says " it pervades and vitiates the judgment by which we are accustomed to select and approve the objects of every-day use which we see around us. It crosses our path in the Brussels carpet of our drawing-room; it is about our bed in the shape of gaudy chintz; it compels us to rest on chairs, and to sit at tables which are designed in accordance with the worst principles of construction, and invested with shapes confessedly unpicturesque. It sends us metal-work from Birmingham, which is as vulgar in form as it is flimsy in execution. It decorates the finest modern porcelain with the most objectionable character of ornament. It lines our walls with silly representations of vegetable life, or with a mass of uninteresting diaper. It bids us, in short, furnish our houses after the same fashion as we dress ourselves, — and that is with no more sense of real beauty than if art were a dead letter." Let us contrast our tastes in these matters with those of the Japanese, and perhaps profit by the lesson.

In the previous chapters sufficient details have been given for one to grasp the structural features of a Japanese room. Let us now observe that the general tone and color of a Japanese apartment are subdued. Its atmosphere is restful; and only after one has .sat on the mats for some time do the unostentatious fittings of the apartment attract one's notice. The papers of the *fusuma* of neutral tints; the plastered surfaces, when they occur equally tinted in similar tones, warm browns and stone-colors predominating; the cedar-board ceiling, with the rich color of that wood; the wood-work everywhere modestly conspicuous, and always presenting the natural colors undefiled by the painter's miseries,—these all combine to render the room quiet and refined to the last degree. The floor in bright contrast is covered with its cool straw matting,—a uniform bright surface set off by the rectangular black borders of the mats. It is such an infinite comfort to find throughout the length and breadth of that Empire the floors covered with the unobstrusive straw matting. Monotonous some would think: yes, it has the monotony of fresh air and of pure water. Such a room requires but little adornment in the shape of extraneous objects; indeed, there are but few places where such objects can be placed. But observe, that while in our rooms one is at liberty to cover his wall with pictures without the slightest regard to light or effect, the Japanese room has a recess clear and free from the floor to the hooded partition that spans it above, and this recess is placed at right angles to the source of

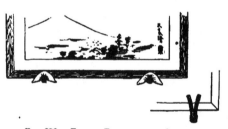

light; furthermore, it is exalted as the place of highest honor in the room, — and here, and here alone, hangs the picture. Not a varnished affair, to see which one has to perambulate the

FIG. 298.—FRAMED PICTURE, WITH SUPPORTS.

apartment with head awry to get a vantage point of vision, but a picture which may be seen in its proper light from any point of the room. In the *tokonoma* there is usually but one picture exposed,—though, as we have seen, this recess may be wide enough to accommodate a set of two or three.

Between the *kamoi*, or lintel, and the ceiling is a space say of eighteen inches or more, according to the height of the room; and here may sometimes be seen a long narrow picture, framed in a narrow wood-border, or secured to a flat frame, which is concealed by the paper or brocade that borders the picture. This picture tips forward at a considerable angle, and is supported on two iron hooks. In order that the edge of the frame may not be scarred by the iron, it is customary to interpose tri-angular red-crape cushions. A bamboo support is often substituted for the iron hooks, as shown in the sketch (fig. 298). The picture may be a landscape, or a spray of flowers; but more often it con-sists of a few Chinese characters em-bodying some bit of poetry, moral precept, or sentiment, — and usually the characters have been written by some poet, scholar, or other distinguished man. The square wooden post which comes in the middle of a partition between two corners of the room may be adorned by a long, narrow, and thin strip of cedar the width of the post, upon which is painted a picture of some kind. This strip, instead of being of wood, may be of silk and brocade, like a *kakemono*, having only one *kaze obi* hanging in the middle from above. Cheap ones may be of straw, rush, or

FIG. 299. — HASHIRA–KAKUSHI.

thin strips of bamboo. This object, of whatever material, is called *hashira-kakushi*, — literally meaning " post-hide." If of wood, both sides are decorated; so that after one side has done duty for awhile the other side is exposed. The wood is usually of dark cedar evenly grained, and the sketch is painted directly on the wood. Fig. 299 shows both sides of one of these strips.

The decoration for these objects is very skilfully treated by the artist; and while it might bother our artists to know what subject to select for a picture on so awkward and limited a surface, it offers no trouble to the Japanese decorator. He simply takes a vertical slice out of some good subject, as one might get a glimpse of Nature through a slightly open door, — and imagination is left to supply the rest. These objects find their way to our markets, but the bright colors used in their decoration show that they have been painted for the masses in this country. The post upon which this kind of picture is hung, as well as the *toko-bashira*, may also be adorned with a hanging flower-holder such as has already been described.

A Japanese may have a famous collection of pictures, yet these are stowed away in his *kura*, with the exception of the one exposed in the *tokonoma*. If he is a man of taste, he changes the picture from time to time according to the season, the character of his guests, or for · special occasions. In one house where I was a guest for a few days the picture was changed every day. A picture may do duty for a few weeks or months, when it is carefully rolled up, stowed away in its silk covering and box, and another one is unrolled. In this way a picture never becomes monotonous. The listless and indifferent way in which an American will often regard his own pictures when showing them to a friend, indicates that his pictures have been so long on his walls that they no longer arouse any attention or delight. It is true, one never wearies in contemplating the work of the great masters; but one should remember that all pictures are not masterpieces, and that by constant exposure the effect of a picture becomes seriously impaired. The way in which pictures with us are crowded on the walls, — many of them of necessity in the worst possible light, or no light at all when the windows are muffled with heavy curtains, — shows that the main interest centres in their embossed gilt frames, which are conspicuous in all lights. The principle of constant exposure is certainly wrong; a good picture is all the more enjoyable if it is not forever staring one in the face. Who wants to contemplate a burning tropical sunset on a full stomach, or a drizzling northern mist on an empty one? And yet these are the experiences which we are often compelled to endure. Why not modify our rooms, and have a bay or recess, — an alcove in the best possible light, — in which one or two good pictures may be properly hung, with fitting accompaniments in the way of a few flowers, or a bit of pottery or bronze? We have never modified the interior arrangement of our house in the slightest degree from the time when it was shaped in the most economical way as a shelter in which to eat, sleep, and die, — a rectangular kennel, with necessary holes for light, and necessary holes to get in and out by. At the same time, its inmates were saturated with a religion so austere and sombre that the possession of a picture was for a long time looked upon as savoring of worldliness and vanity, unless, indeed, the subject suggested the other world by a vision of hexapodous angels, or of the transient resting-place to that world in the guise of a tombstone and willows, or an immediate departure thereto in the shape of a death-bed scene.

Among the Japanese all collections of pottery and other bric-à-brac are, in the same way as the pictures, carefully enclosed in brocade bags and boxes, and stowed away to be unpacked only when appreciative friends come to the house; and then the host enjoys them with equal delight. Aside from the heightened enjoyment sure to be evoked by the Japanese method, one is spared an infinite amount of chagrin and misery in having an unsophisticated friend become enthusiastic over the wrong thing, or mistake a rare etching of Dante for a North American savage, or manifest a thrill of delight over an object because he learns incidentally that its value corresponds with his yearly grocery bill.

Nothing is more striking in a Japanese room than the harmonies and contrasts between the colors of the various objects and the room itself. Between the picture and the brocades with which it is mounted, and the quiet and subdued color of the *tokonoma* in which it is hung, there is always the most refined harmony, and such a background for the delicious and healthy contrasts of color when a spray of bright cherry blossoms enlivens the quiet tones of this honored place! The general tone of the room sets off to perfection the simplest spray of flowers, a quiet picture, a rough bit of pottery or an old bronze; and at the same time a costly and magnificent piece of gold lacquer blazes out like a gem from these simple surroundings, — and yet the harmony is not disturbed.

It is an interesting fact that the efforts at harmonious and decorative effects which have been made by famous artists and decorators in this country and in England have been strongly imbued by the Japanese spirit, and every success attained is a confirmation of the correctness of Japanese taste. Wall-papers are now more quiet and unobtrusive; the merit of simplicity and reserve where it belongs, and a fitness everywhere, are becoming more widely recognized.

It is rare to see cabinets or conveniences for the display of bric-à-brac in a Japanese house, though sometimes a lacquer-stand with a few shelves may be seen, — and on this may be displayed a number of objects consisting of ancient pottery, some stone implements, a fossil, old coins, or a few water-worn fragments of rock brought from China, and mounted on dark wood stands. The Japanese are great collectors of autographs, coins, brocades, metal-work, and many other groups of objects; but these are rarely exposed. In regard to objects in the *tokonoma*, I have seen in different *tokonoma*, variously displayed, natural fragments of quartz, crystal spheres, curious water-worn stones, coral, old bronze, as well as the customary vase for flowers or the incense-burner. These various objects are usually, but not always, supported on a lacquer-stand. In the *chigai-dana* I have also noticed the sword-rack, lacquer writing-box, *makimono*, and books; and when I was guilty of the impertinence of peeking into the cupboards, I have seen there a few boxes containing pottery, pictures, and the like, — though, as before remarked, such things are usually kept in the *kura*.

Besides the lacquer cabinets, there may be seen in the houses of the higher class an article of furniture consisting of a few deep shelves, with portions of the shelves closed,

Fig. 300. — WRITING-DESK.

forming little cupboards. Such a cabinet is used to hold writing-paper, toilet articles, trays for flowers, and miscellaneous objects for use and ornament. These cases are often beautifully lacquered.

The usual form of writing-desk consists of a low stool not over a foot in height, with plain side-pieces or legs for support, sometimes having shallow drawers; and this is about the only piece of furniture that would parallel our table. The illustration (fig. 300) shows one of these tables, upon which may be seen the paper, ink-stone, brush, and brush-rest.

In the cities and large villages the people stand in constant fear of conflagrations. Almost every month they are reminded of the instability of the ground they rest upon by tremors and slight shocks, which may be the precursors of destructive earthquakes, usually accompanied by conflagrations infinitely more disastrous.   Allusion has been made to the little portable engines with which houses are furnished.   In the city house one may notice a little platform or staging with hand-rail erected on the ridge of the roof (fig. 301); a ladder or flight of steps leads to this staging, and on alarms of fire anxious faces may be seen peering from these lookouts in the direction of the burning buildings.   It is usual to have resting

FIG. 301. —STAGING ON HOUSE-ROOF, WITH BUCKET AND BRUSH.

on the platform a huge bucket or half barrel filled with water, and near by a long-handled brush;   and this is used to sprinkle water on places threatened by the sparks and fire-brands, which often fill the air in times of great conflagrations.

During the prevalence of a high wind it is a common sight to see the small dealers packing their goods in large baskets and square cloths to tie up ready to transport in case of fire. At such times the windows and doors of the *kura* are closed and the chinks plastered with mud, which is always at hand either under a platform near the door or in a large earthen jar near the openings.   In private dwellings, too, at times of possible danger, the more precious objects are packed up in a square basket-like box, having straps attached to it, so that it can easily be transported on one's shoulders (fig. 302).

In drawing to a close this description of Japanese homes and their surroundings, I have to regret that neither time, strength, nor opportunity enabled me to make it more complete by a description, accompanied by sketches, of the residences of the highest classes in Japan. Indeed, it is a question whether any of the old residences of the Dai-mios remain in the condition in which they were twenty years ago, or before the Revolution. Even where the buildings re-main, as in the castles of Na-goya and Kumamoto, busy clerks and secretaries are seen sitting in chairs and writing at tables in foreign style; and though in some cases the beautifully dec-

Fig. 302. — Box for Transporting Articles.

orated *fusuma*, with the elaborately carved *ramma* and rich wood-ceiling are still preserved, — as in the castle of Nagoya, as well as in many others doubtless, — the introduction of var-nished furniture and gaudy-colored foreign carpets in some of the apartments has brought sad discord into the former har-monies of the place.

In Tokio a number of former Daimios have built houses in foreign style, though these somehow or other usually lack the peculiar comforts of our homes. Why a Japanese should build a house in foreign style was somewhat of a puzzle to me, until I saw the character of their homes and the manner in which a foreigner in some cases was likely to behave on entering a Japanese house. If he did not walk into it with his boots on, he was sure to be seen stalking about in his stockinged feet, bumping his head at intervals against the *kamoi*, or burning holes in the mats in his clumsy attempts to pick up coals from the *hibachi*, with which to light his cigar.   Not being able to sit on the mats properly, he sprawls about in attitudes confessedly as rude as if a Japanese in our apartments were to perch his legs on the table.   If he will not take off his boots, he possibly finds his way to the garden, where he wanders about, indenting the paths with his boot-heels or leaving scars on the verandah, possibly washing his hands in the *chōdzu-bachi*, and generally making himself the cause of much discomfort to the inmates.

It was a happy idea when those Japanese who from their prominence in the affairs of the country were compelled to entertain the " foreign barbarian," conceived the idea of erecting a cage in foreign fashion to hold temporarily the menagerie which they were often compelled to receive.   Seriously, however, the inelastic character of most foreigners, and their inability to adapt themselves to their surroundings have rendered the erection of buildings in foreign style for their entertainment not only a convenience but an absolute necessity.   It must be admitted that for the activities of business especially, the foreign style of office and shop is not only more convenient but unquestionably superior.

The former Daimio of Chikuzen was one of the first, I believe, to build a house in foreign style in Tokio, and this building is a good typical example of an American two-story house.   Attached, however, to this house is a wing containing a number of rooms in native style.   Fig. 123 (page 142) shows one of these rooms.   The former Daimio of Hizen also lives in a foreign house, and there are many houses in Tokio built by Japanese after foreign plans.

In an earlier portion of this work an allusion was made to the absence of those architectural monuments which are so characteristic of European countries. The castles of the Daimios, which are lofty and imposing structures, have already been referred to. There are fortresses also of great extent and solidity, — notably the one at Osaka, erected by Hideyoshi on an eminence near the city; and though the wooden structures formerly surmounting the walls were destroyed by Iyeyasŭ in 1615, the stone battlements as they stand to-day must be considered as among the marvels of engineering skill, and the colossal masses of rock seem all the more colossal after one has become familiar with the tiny and perishable dwellings of the country. In the walls of this fortress are single blocks of stone — at great heights, too, above the surrounding level of the region — measuring in some cases from thirty to thirty-six feet in length, and at least fifteen feet in height. These huge blocks have been transported long distances from the mountains many miles away from the city.

Attention is called to the existence of these remarkable monuments as an evidence that the Japanese are quite competent to erect such buildings, if the national taste had inclined them in that way. So far as I know, a national impulse has never led the Japanese to commemorate great deeds in the nation's life by enduring monuments of stone. The reason may be that the plucky little nation has always been successful in repelling invasion; and a peculiar quality in their temperament has prevented them from perpetuating in a public way, either by monuments or by the naming of streets and bridges, the memories of victories won by one section of the country over another.

Rev. W. E. Griffis, in an interesting article on " The Streets and Street-names of Yedo,"[1] in noticing the almost total absence of the names of great victories or historic battlefields in the naming of the streets and bridges in Tokio, says: " It

[1] Transactions of the Asiatic Society of Japan, vol. i. p. 20.

would have been an unwise policy in the great unifier of Japan, Iyeyasŭ, to have given to the streets in the capital of a nation finally united in peaceful union any name that would be a constant source of humiliation, that would keep alive bitter memories, or that would irritate freshly-healed wounds. The anomalous absence of such names proves at once the sagacity of Iyeyasŭ, and is another witness to the oft-repeated policy used by the Japanese in treating their enemies, — that is, to conquer them by kindness and conciliation."

CHAPTER VIII.

THE ANCIENT HOUSE.

IT would be an extremely interesting line of research to follow out the history of the development of the house in Japan. The material for such a study may possibly be in existence, but unfortunately there are few scholars accomplished enough to read the early Japanese records. Thanks to the labors of Mr. Chamberlain, and to Mr. Satow, Mr. Aston, Mr. McClatchie, and other members of the English legation in Japan,[1] students of Ethnology are enabled to catch a glimpse of the character of the early house in that country.

From the translations of ancient Japanese Rituals,[2] by Ernest Satow, Esq.; of the *Kojiki*, or "Records of Ancient Matters,"[3] by Basil Hall Chamberlain, Esq.; and an ancient Japanese Classic,[4] by W. G. Aston, Esq., — we get a glimpse of the Japanese house as it was a thousand years or more ago.

Mr. Satow claims that the ancient Japanese Rituals are "the oldest specimens of ancient indigenous Japanese literature extant, excepting only perhaps the poetry contained in the 'Kojiki' and 'Nihongi;'" and Mr. Chamberlain says the

---

[1] Owing to the sensible civil service of England, scholars and diplomates are appointed to these duties in the East; and as a natural result all the honors, — political, commercial, and literary, — have, with few exceptions, been won by Englishmen.

[2] Transactions of the Asiatic Society of Japan, vol. ix. part ii. p. 191.

[3] Ibid., vol. x. Supplement.

[4] Ibid., vol. iii. part ii. p. 121.

"Kojiki" is "the earliest authentic connected literary product of that large division of the human race which has been variously denominated Turanian, Scythian, and Altaïc, and it even precedes by at least a century the most ancient extant literary compositions of non-Aryan India."

The allusions to house-structure in the "Kojiki," though brief, are suggestive, and carry us back without question to the condition of the Japanese house in the seventh and eighth centuries.

Mr. Satow, in his translation of the Rituals, says that the period when this service was first instituted was certainly before the tenth century, and probably earlier. From these records he ascertains that "the palace of the Japanese sovereign was a wooden hut, with its pillars planted in the ground, instead of being erected upon broad, flat stones, as in modern buildings. The whole frame-work, consisting of posts, beams, rafters, door-posts, and window-frames, was tied together with cords, made by twisting the long fibrous stems of climbing plants, — such as Pueraria Thunbergiana (*kuzu*) and Wistaria Sinensis (*fuji*). The floor must have been low down, so that the occupants of the building, as they squatted or lay on their mats, were exposed to the stealthy attacks of venomous snakes, which were probably far more numerous in the earliest ages when the country was for the most part uncultivated than at the present day. . . . There seems some reason to think that the *yuka,* here translated 'floor,' was originally nothing but a couch which ran around the sides of the hut, the rest of the space being simply a mud-floor; and that the size of the couch was gradually increased until it occupied the whole interior. The rafters projected upward beyond the ridge-pole, crossing each other as is seen in the roofs of modern Shin-tau temples, whether their architecture be in conformity with early traditions (in which case all the rafters are so crossed), or modified in accordance with more advanced principles of construction, and the crossed rafters retained only as ornaments at the two ends of the ridge. The roof was thatched, and perhaps had a gable at each end, with a hole to allow the smoke of the wood-fire to escape, — so that it was possible for birds flying in and perching on the beams overhead, to defile the food, or the fire with which it was cooked."

From the "Kojiki" we learn that even in those early days the house was sufficiently differentiated to present forms referred to as temples or palaces, houses of the people, storehouses, and rude huts. That the temples or palaces were more than rude huts is shown by references to the verandah, the great roof, stout pillars, and high cross-beams. They were at least two stories high, as we read of people gazing from an upper story. The peasants were not allowed to build a house with a raised roof frame; that is, a roof the upper portion or ridge of which was raised above the roof proper, and having a different structure. This indicates the existence at that time of different kinds of roofs, or ridges. Fire-places were in the middle of the floor, and the smoke-outlet was in the gable end of the roof protected by a lattice, — as seen in the Japanese country houses of to-day. The posts or pillars of the house were buried deep in the ground, and not, as in the present house, resting on a stone foundation.

The allusions in the "Kojiki," where it says, "and if thou goest in a boat along that road there will appear a palace built like fish-scales," and again, "the ill-omened crew were shattered like tiles," show the existence of tiles at that time. A curious reference is also made to using cormorants' feathers for thatch. There were front doors and back doors, doors to be raised, and windows and openings.

It is mentioned that through the awkwardness of the carpenter the farther " fin " of the great roof is bent down at the corner,—probably indicating wide over-hanging eaves, the corners of which might easily be called " fins." Within the house were mats of sedge, skin, and silk, and ornamental screens to protect the sleepers from draughts of air.[1] The castles had back gates, side gates, and other gates. Some of these gates, at least, had a roof-like structure above, as we read in the " Kojiki," " Come under the metal gate; we will stand till the rain stops."

Fences are also alluded to. The latrine is mentioned several times as being away from the house, and having been placed over running water,—"whence doubtless the name *Kaha-ya;* that is, river-house." This feature is specially characteristic of the latrine, from Siam to Java. This suggestion of early affinities with the Malay people is seen in an ancient Japanese Classic, dating from the tenth century, entitled *Monogatari,* or " Tales of Japan," translated by Mr. Chamberlain,[2] in which we read, "Now, in olden days the people dwelt in houses raised on platforms built out in the river Ikuta." In the " Kojiki " we also read, " They made in the middle of the river Hi a black plaited bridge, and respectfully offered a temporary palace to dwell in." The translator says the significance of this passage is: " They built as a temporary abode for the prince a house in the river Hi (whether with its foundations actually in the water or on an island is left undetermined), connecting it with the main-land by a bridge made of branches of trees twisted together, and with their bark left on them (this is here the import of the word *black*)."

The " Kojiki " mentions a two-forked boat: may this not be some kind of a catamaran? Mention is also made of eating from leaf-platters: this is a marked Malay feature.

---

[1] In Anam I noticed that the bed-rooms were indicated by hanging cloth partitions as well as by those made of matting.

[2] Transactions of the Asiatic Society of Japan, vol. vi. part i. p. 109.

These various statements — particularly those concerning the latrine, and building houses over the water — are significant indications of the marked southern affinities of the Japanese. Other features of similarity with southern people are seen in the general structure of the house.

The principal references which have been made to the "Kojiki" are quoted here for the convenience of the reader. For the history of the origin of this ancient record, methods of translation, etc., the reader is referred to Mr. Chamberlain's Introduction accompanying the translation.

"And the ill-omened crew were shattered like tiles" (p. 8).

"So when from the palace she raised the door and came out to meet him" (p. 34).

"Taking him into the house, and calling him into an eight-foot-spaced large room" (p. 73).

"Do thou make stout the temple-pillars at the foot of Mount Uka in the nethermost rock-bottom, and make high the cross-beams to the Plain-of-High-Heaven" (p. 74).

"I push back the plank-door shut by the maiden" (p. 76).

"Beneath the fluttering of the ornamented fence, beneath the softness of the warm coverlets, beneath the rustling of the cloth coverlet" (p. 81).

The translator says "the 'ornamented fence' is supposed to mean 'a curtain round the sleeping-place.'"

"The soot on the heavenly new lattice of the gable," etc. (p. 105).[1]

"Using cormorants' feathers for thatch" (p. 126).

"The manner in which I will send this sword down will be to perforate the ridge of [the roof of] Takakurazhi's store-house, and drop it through!" (p. 135).

"In a damp hut on the reed-moor, having 'spread layer upon layer of sedge mats, we two slept!'" (p. 149).

"When she was about to enter the sea, she spread eight thicknesses of sedge rugs, eight thicknesses of skin rugs, and eight thicknesses of silk rugs on top of the waves" (p 212).

[1] Satow gives quite a different rendering of this passage.

" So when the grandee of Kuchiko was repeating this august Song [to the Empress], it was raining heavily. Then upon his, without avoiding the rain, coming and prostrating himself at the front door of the palace, she on the contrary went out at the back door ; and on his coming and prostrating himself at the back door of the palace, she on the contrary went out at the front door" (p. 273).

"Then the Heavenly Sovereign, going straight to the place where Queen Medori dwelt, stood on the door-sill of the palace" (p. 281).

> " ' Had I known that I should sleep on the
> Moor of Tajihi, Oh ! I would have brought
> My dividing matting."
>   (p. 288.)

" Then, on climbing to the top of the mountain and gazing on the interior of the country, [he perceived that] there was a house built with a raised roof-frame. The Heavenly Sovereign sent to ask [concerning] that house, saying, ' Whose roof with a raised frame is that ?' The answer was : ' It is the house of the great Departmental Lord of Shiki.' Then the Heavenly Sovereign said : ' What ! a slave builds his own house in imitation of the august abode of the Heavenly Sovereign ! ' — and forthwith he sent men to burn the house [down]" (p. 311).

" Thereupon the grandee Shibi sang, saying, —

> ' The further fin of the roof of the great
> Palace is bent down at the corner.'

When he had thus sung, and requested the conclusion of the Song, His Augustness Woke sang, saying, —

> ' It is on account of the great carpenter's
> Awkwardness that it is bent down at the
> Corner.' "
>   (p. 330.)

In the ancient Japanese Rituals, Mr. Satow finds that the rafters projected upward beyond the ridge-pole of the roof crossing each other, — as is seen in the roofs of modern Shin-tō temples. A curious feature is often seen on the gable ends of the roofs of the Malay houses near Singapore, consisting of projecting pieces crossing each other at the two ends of the roof ;

and these are ornamented by being cut in odd sweeps and curves (fig. 303). Survivals of these crossing rafters are seen in the modern Japanese dwelling; that is, if we are to regard as such the wooden X's which straddle the roof at intervals, as shown in figs. 45 (page 62) and 85 (page 98). A precisely similar feature is seen on the roofs of houses along the river approaching Saigon, and on the road leading from Saigon to Cholon, in Anam (fig. 304).

It has been customary to regard the *tokonoma*, or bed-place, in the Japanese house as being derived from the Aino house. The suggestion of such a derivation seems to me to have no foundation. In the Aino house the solid ground is the floor; sometimes, but not always, a rush mat is spread along the side of the fireplace, which is in the centre of the hut. The slightest attention to comfort would lead the Ainos to erect a platform of boards,—and such a platform is generally found next to the wall in the Aino hut. This platform not only serves as a sleeping-place, but holds also boxes and household goods, as well as such objects as were not suspended to the sides of the houses or from poles stretched across. In no case

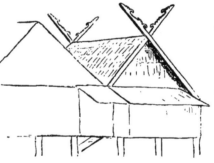

Fig. 303. — MALAY HOUSE NEAR SINGAPORE.

did I see a raised platform protected by a partition, or one utilized solely for a sleeping-place. If it were safe to venture upon any conjecture as to the origin of the *tokonoma*, or if external resemblances had any weight in affinities of structure, one might see the prototype of this feature in the Malay

house. In the Malay villages near Singapore, one may see not
only a slightly raised place for the bed exclusively, but also
a narrow partition jutting out from the side of the wall, not
unlike that which separates the *tokonoma* from its companion
recess (fig. 305).

FIG. 304. — RIDGE OF ROOF IN CHOLON, ANAM.

Whether these various relations pointed out between the
Japanese house and similar features in the Malay house are
of any weight or not, they must be recognized in any attempt to trace the origin of those features in house-structure

FIG. 305. — INTERIOR OF MALAY HOUSE, SHOWING BED-PLACE. SINGAPORE.

which have originated outside of Japan. From all that we
can gather relating to the ancient house of the Japanese, it
would seem that certain important resemblances must be sought
for among the southern nations of Anam, Cochin China, and
particularly those of the Malay peninsula.

Ernest Satow, Esq., in an article on the Shin-tō temples of Ise,[1] which, as the author says, "rank first among all the Shin-tō temples in Japan in point of sanctity, though not the most ancient," has some interesting matter concerning the character of the ancient house. He says : —

"Japanese antiquarians tell us that in early times, before carpenters' tools had been invented, the dwellings of the people who inhabited these islands were constructed of young trees with the bark on, fastened together with ropes made of the rush (*suge*, — Scirpus maritimus), or perhaps with the tough shoots of the wistaria (*fuji*), and thatched with the grass called *kaya*. In modern buildings the uprights of a house stand upon large stones laid on the surface of the earth; but this precaution against decay had not occurred to the ancients, who planted the uprights in holes dug in the ground.

The ground-plan of the hut was oblong, with four corner uprights, and one in the middle of each of the four sides, — those in the sides which formed the ends being long enough to support the ridge-pole. Other trees were fastened horizontally from corner to corner, — one set near the ground, one near the top, and one set on the top, the latter of which formed what we call the wall-plates. Two large rafters, whose upper ends crossed each other, were laid from the wall-plates to the heads of the taller uprights. The ridge-pole rested in the fork formed by the upper ends of the rafters crossing each other. Horizontal poles were then laid along each slope of the roof, one pair being fastened close up to the exterior angle of the fork. The rafters were slender poles, or bamboos, passed over the ridge-pole and fastened down on each end to the wall-plates. Next followed the process of putting on the thatch. In order to keep this in its place, two trees were laid along the top resting in the forks; and across these two trees were placed short logs at equal distances, which being fastened to the poles in the exterior angle of the forks by ropes passed through the thatch, bound the ridge of the roof firmly together.

"The walls and doors were constructed of rough matting. It is evident that some tool must have been used to cut the trees to the required length; and for this purpose a sharpened stone was probably employed. Such

[1] Translations of the Asiatic Society of Japan, vol. ii. p. 119.

stone implements have been found imbedded in the earth in various parts of Japan, in company with stone arrow-heads and clubs. Specimens of the ancient style of building may even yet be seen in remote parts of the country,—not perhaps so much in the habitations of the peasantry, as in sheds erected to serve a temporary purpose.

"The architecture of the Shin-tō temples is derived from the primeval hut, with more or less modification in proportion to the influence of Buddhism in each particular case. Those of the purest style retain the thatched roof; others are covered with the thick shingling called *hiwada-buki*, while others have tiled and even coppered roofs. The projecting ends of the rafters called *chigi* have been somewhat lengthened, and carved more or less elaborately. At the new temple at Kudanzaka in Yedo they are shown in the proper position, projecting from the inside of the shingling; but in the majority of cases they merely consist of two pieces of wood in the form of the letter X, which rest on the ridge of the roof like a pack-saddle on a horse's back, to make use of a Japanese writer's comparison. The logs which kept the two trees laid on the ridge in their place have taken the form of short cylindrical pieces of timber tapering towards each extremity, which have been compared by foreigners to cigars. In Japanese they are called *katsuo-gi*, from their resemblance to the pieces of dried bonito sold under the name of *katsuo-bushi*. The two trees laid along the roof over the thatch are represented by a single beam, called *Munaosae*, or "roof-presser." Planking has taken the place of the mats with which the sides of the building were originally closed, and the entrance is closed by a pair of folding doors, turning not on hinges, but on what are, I believe, technically called 'journals.' The primeval hut had no flooring; but we find that the shrine has a wooden floor raised some feet above the ground, which arrangement necessitates a sort of balcony all round, and a flight of steps up to the entrance. The transformation is completed in some cases by the addition of a quantity of ornamental metal-work in brass."

Coming down to somewhat later times, we find a charming bit of description of the house in an ancient Japanese Classic[1] entitled *Tosa Nikki*, or "Tosa Diary," translated by W.

---

[1] Transactions of the Asiatic Society of Japan, vol. iii. part ii.

G. Aston. This Diary was written in the middle of the tenth century, and is the record of a court noble who lived in Kioto, but who was absent from his home five or six years as Prefect of Tosa. The Diary was a record of his journey home, and the first entry in it was in the fourth year of Shōhei, which according to our reckoning must have been in the early part of 935 A.D., or nearly one thousand years ago. During his absence from home, news had come to him of the death of his little daughter nine years old; and he says, "With the joyful thought, 'Home to Kioto!' there mingles the bitter reflection that there is one who never will return."

The journey home was mostly by sea; and finally, having entered the Osaka River, and spent several days in struggling against the strong current, he reaches Yamazaki, from which place he starts for Kioto. He expresses great delight in recognizing the old familiar landmarks as he rides along. "He mentions the children's playthings and sweetmeats in the shops as looking exactly as when he went away, and wonders whether he will find as little change in the hearts of his friends. He had purposely left Yamazaki in the evening in order that it might be night when he reached his own dwelling." Mr. Aston translates his account of the state in which he found it : —

"The moon was shining brightly when I reached my house and entered the gate, so that its condition was plainly to be seen. It was decayed and ruined beyond all description, — worse even than I had been told. The house[1] of the man in whose charge I left it was in an equally dilapidated condition. The fence between the two houses had been broken down, so that both seemed but one, and he appeared to have fulfilled his charge by looking in through the gaps. And yet I had supplied him, by every opportunity, with the means of keeping it in repair. To-night,

[1] In Mr. Aston's translation this word is printed "heart," but evidently this must be a misprint.

however, I would not allow him to be told this in an angry tone, but in spite of my vexation offered him an acknowledgment for his trouble. There was in one place something like a pond, where water had collected in a hollow, by the side of which grew a fir-tree. It had lost half its branches, and looked as if a thousand years had passed during the five or six years of my absence. Younger trees had grown up round it, and the whole place was in a most neglectful condition, so that every one said that it was pitiful to see. Among other sad thoughts that rose spontaneously to my mind was the memory — ah! how sorrowful! — of one who was born in this house, but who did not return here along with me. My fellow-passengers were chatting merrily with their children in their arms, but I meanwhile, still unable to contain my grief, privately repeated these lines to one who knew my heart."

In this pathetic account one gets a glimpse of the house as it appeared nearly a thousand years ago. The broken fence between the houses; the gateway, probably a conspicuous structure then as it is to-day, in a dilapidated condition; and the neglected garden with a tangle of young trees growing up,—all show the existence in those early days of features similar to those which exist to-day.

The history of house development in Japan, if it should ever be revealed, will probably show a slow but steady progress from the rude hut of the past to the curious and artistic house of to-day, — a house as thoroughly a product of Japan as is that of the Chinese, Korean, or Malay a product of those respective peoples, and differing from all quite as much as they differ from one another. A few features have been introduced from abroad, but these have been trifling as compared to the wholesale imitation of foreign styles of architecture by our ancestors, the English; and until within a few years we have followed England's example in perpetuating the legacy it left us, in the shape of badly imitated foreign architecture, classical and otherwise. As a result, we have scattered over the land, among a few public buildings of good taste, a countless

number of ill-proportioned, ugly, and entirely inappropriate buildings for public use. Had the exuberant fancies of the village
architect revelled in woodsheds or one-storied buildings, the
harm would have been trifling; but the desire for pretentious
show, which seems to characterize the average American, has
led to the erection of these architectural horrors on the most
conspicuous sites, — and thus the public taste is vitiated.

The Japanese, while developing an original type of house,
have adopted the serviceable tile from Korea, and probably
also the economical transverse framing and vertical struts from
China, and bits of temple architecture for external adornments.
As to their temple architecture, which came in with one of
their religions, they had the good sense to leave it comparatively as it was brought to them. Indeed, the temples seem
in perfect harmony with the country and its people. What
shall we say, however, to the taste displayed by the English,
who in the most servile manner have copied foreign styles of
architecture utterly unsuited to their climate and people! In
the space of an English block one may see not only Grecian,
Roman, Italian, and Egyptian, as well as other styles of architecture, but audaciously attempted crosses between some of
these; and the resulting hybrids have in consequence rendered
the modern English town the most unpicturesque muddle of
buildings in Christendom outside our own country.[1]

[1] "It is lamentable to reflect how many monstrous designs have been perpetrated
under the general name of Gothic, which have neither in spirit nor letter realized the
character of Mediæval art. In London these extraordinary ebullitions of uneducated
taste generally appear in the form of meeting-houses, music-halls, and similar places of
popular resort. Showy in their general effect, and usually overloaded with meretricious
ornament, they are likely enough to impose upon an uninformed judgment, which is inca-
pable of discriminating between what Mr. Ruskin has called the 'Lamp of Sacrifice,' —
one of the glories of ancient art, — and the lust of profusion which is the bane of modern
design." — *Eastlake's Hints on Household Taste*, p. 21.

CHAPTER IX.

THE NEIGHBORING HOUSE.

HOUSE OF THE AINO. — OF THE BONIN ISLANDER. — OF THE LOUCHOOAN. — OF THE
KOREAN. — OF THE CHINESE. — CONCLUDING REMARKS.

HAVING got a glimpse, and a slight glimpse only, of the
ancient house in Japan, it may be of interest to consider
briefly the character of the house in neighboring islands forming
part of the Japanese Empire, and also of the house in that
country which comes nearest to Japan (Korea), and from which
country in the past there have been many both peaceful and
compulsory invasions, — compulsory in the fact that when Hideyoshi returned from Korea, nearly three hundred years ago,
after his great invasion of that country, he brought back with
him to Japan colonies of potters and other artisans.

The Ainos of Yezo naturally claim our attention first, because it is believed that they were the aboriginal people of
Japan proper, and were afterwards displaced by the Japanese, —
a displacement similar to that of our North American savages
by the English colonists. Whether the Ainos are autochthonous
or not, will not be discussed here. That they are a savage race,
without written language, — a race which formerly occupied the
northern part of the main island of Japan, and were gradually
forced back to Yezo, where they still live in scattered communities, — are facts which are unquestionable. How far the
Aino house to-day represents the ancient Aino house, and how

many features of the Japanese house are engrafted upon it, are points difficult to determine.

The Ainos that I saw in the Ishikari valley, on the west coast of Yezo, and from Shiraoi south on the east coast, all spoke Japanese, ate out of lacquer bowls, used chop-sticks, smoked small pipes, drank *sake*, and within their huts possessed lacquer boxes and other conveniences in which to stow away their clothing, which had probably been given them in past times by the Japanese, and which were heirlooms. On

Fig. 306. — Aino House, Yezo.

the other hand, they retained their own language, their long, narrow dug-out; used the small bow, the poisoned arrow, and had an arrow-release of their own; adhered to their ancestral forms of worship and their peculiar methods of design, and were quite as persistent in clinging to many of their customs as are our own Western tribes of Indians. That they are susceptible to change is seen in the presence of a young Aino at the normal school in Tokio, from whom I derived some interesting facts concerning archery.

Briefly, the Aino house, as I saw it, consists of a rude framework of timber supporting a thatched roof; the walls being

22

made up of reeds and rush interwoven with stiffer cross-pieces.
Within, there is a single room the dimensions of the house.
In most houses there is an L, in which is the doorway, which
may in some cases be covered with a rude porch. The thatched
roof is well made and quite picturesque, differing somewhat
in form from any thatched roof among the Japanese, — though
in Yamato, as already mentioned, I saw features in the slope
of the roof quite similar to those shown in some of the Aino
roofs.

Fig. 307. — Aino House, Yezo.

Entering the house by the low door, one comes into a room
so dark that it is with difficulty one can see anything. The
inmates light rolls of birch-bark that one may be enabled to see
the interior; but every appearance of neatness and picturesqueness which the hut presented from without vanishes when one
gets inside. Beneath one's feet is a hard, damp, earth floor; directly above are the blackened and soot-covered rafters. Poles
supported horizontally from these rafters are equally greasy and
blackened, and pervading the darkness is a dirty and strong fishy
odor. In the middle of the floor, and occupying considerable
space, is a square area, — the fireplace. On its two sides mats
are spread. A pot hangs over the smoke, for there appears to

be but little fire; and at one side is a large bowl containing
the remains of the last meal, consisting apparently of fish-bones,
large sickly-looking bones, the sight of which instantly vitiates
one's appetite. The smoke, rebuffed at the only opening save
the door, — a small square opening close under the low eaves,
— struggles to escape through a small opening in the angle of
the roof. On one side of the room is a slightly raised floor of
boards, upon which are mats, lacquer-boxes, bundles of nets,
and a miscellaneous assortment of objects. Hanging from the
rafters and poles are bows, quivers of arrows, Japanese daggers
mounted on curious wooden tablets inlaid with lead, slices of
fish and skates' heads in various stages, not of decomposition, as
the odors would seem to imply, but of smoke preservation. Dirt
everywhere, and fleas. And in the midst of the darkness, smoke,
and squalor are the inmates, — quiet, demure, and gentle to the
last degree. Figs. 306 and 307 give an idea of the appearance of
two Aino houses of the better kind, but perhaps cannot be taken
as a type of the Aino house farther north on the island.

Let us now glance at the house of the natives of the
Bonin Islands, or Hachijô, as described by Mr. Dickins and
Mr. Satow.[1] From their communication the following account
is taken: —

"As may readily be supposed, there are no shops or inns on the island,
but fair accommodation for travellers can be obtained at the farmers'
houses. These are for the most part substantially-built cottages of two
or three rooms, with a spacious kitchen, constructed with the timber of
Quercus cuspidata, and with plank walls, where on the mainland it is
usual to have plastered wattles. The roof is invariably of thatch, with
a very high pitch, — necessitated, we were told, by the extreme dampness of the climate, which renders it desirable to allow as little rain as

---

[1] Notes of a visit to Hachijô, in 1878. By F. V. Dickins and Ernest Satow.
Transactions of the Asiatic Society of Japan, vol. vi. part iii. p. 435.

possible to soak into the straw. Many of the more prosperous farmers
have a second building, devoted to the rearing of silkworms, which takes
its name (*kaiko-ya*) from the purpose to which it is destined. There are
also sheds for cattle, usually consisting of a thatched roof resting on
walls formed of rough stone-work. Lastly, each enclosure possesses a
wooden godown, raised some four feet from the ground on stout wooden
posts, crowned with broad caps, to prevent the mice from gaining an entrance. The style resembles that of the storehouses constructed by the
Ainos and Loochooans.

"The house and vegetable-garden belonging to it are usually surrounded by a stone wall, or rather bank of stones and earth, often six
feet high, designed to protect the buildings from the violent gales which
at certain seasons sweep over the island, and which, as we learned, frequently do serious injury to the rice-fields by the quantity of salt spray
which they carry a long distance inland from the shore."

From this general description of the house which incidentally accompanies a very interesting sketch of the physical peculiarities of the island, its geology, botany, and the customs and
dialect of the people, we get no idea of the special features of
the house, — as to the fireplace or bed-place; whether there be
shōji or ordinary windows, matted floor, or any of those details
which would render a comparison with the Japanese house of
value.

As Mr. Satow found in the language of the Bonin Islanders
a number of words which appeared to be survivals of archaic
Japanese, and also among their customs the curious one, which
existed up to within very recent times, of erecting parturition
houses, — a feature which is alluded to in the very earliest records of Japan, — a minute description of the Bonin house with
sketches might possibly lead to some facts of interest.

The Loochoo, or Riukiu Islands, now known as Okinawa
Shima, lie nearly midway between the southern part of Japan
and the Island of Formosa. The people of this group differ

but little from the Japanese,—their language, according to Mr. Satow and Mr. Brunton, having in it words that appear obsolete in Japan. In many customs there is a curious admixture of Chinese and Japanese ways; and Mr. Brunton sees in the Loochooan bridge and other structures certain resemblances to Chinese methods.

The following extract regarding the house of the Loochooans is taken from an account of a visit to these islands, by Ernest Satow, Esq., published in the first volume of the "Transactions of the Asiatic Society of Japan:"—

"The houses of the Loochooans are built in Japanese fashion, with the floor raised three or four feet from the ground, and have mostly only one story, on account of the violent winds which prevail. They are roofed with tiles of a Chinese fashion, very strong and thick. The buildings in which they store their rice are built of wood and thatched with straw. They are supported on wooden posts about five feet high, and resemble the granaries of the Ainos, though constructed with much greater care."

Another extract is here given in regard to the house of the Loochooans, by R. H. Brunton, Esq., published in the "Transactions of the Asiatic Society of Japan"[1]:—

"The streets in the towns present a most desolate appearance. On each side of these is a blank stone wall of about ten or twelve feet high, with openings in them here and there sufficiently wide to admit of access to the houses which are behind. Every house is surrounded by a wall, and from the street they convey the impression of being prisons rather than ordinary dwellings. . . .

"The houses of the well-to-do classes are situated in a yard which is surrounded by a wall ten or twelve feet high, as has been already mentioned. They are similar to the ordinary Japanese houses, with raised floors laid with mats and sliding screens of paper. They are built of wood, and present no peculiar differences from the Japanese style of

[1] Vol. iv. p. 68.

construction. The roofs are laid with tiles, which however are quite different in shape from the Japanese tiles. Over the joint between two concave tiles a convex one is laid, and these are all semi-circular in cross sections. The tiles are made at Nafa, and are red in color; they appeared of good quality. The houses of the poorer classes are of very primitive character. The roof is covered with a thick thatch, and is supported by four corner uprights about five feet high. The walls consist of sheets of a species of netting made of small bamboo, which contain between them a thickness of about six inches of straw. This encloses the whole sides of the house, — a width of about two feet being left in one side as an entrance. There is no flooring in the houses of any description, and there is generally laid over the mud inside a mat, on which the inmates lie or sit."

Considering the presence for so many centuries of strong Chinese influence which Mr. Brunton sees in the Loochooans, it is rather surprising to find so many features of the Japanese house present in their dwellings. Indeed, Mr. Brunton goes so far as to say that the Loochooan house presents no peculiar differences from the Japanese style of construction; and as he has paid special attention to the constructive features of Japanese buildings, we must believe that had differences existed they would have been noted by him.

It seems to me that the wide distribution of certain identical features in Japanese house-structure, from the extreme north of Japan to the Loochoo Islands, is something remarkable. Here is a people who for centuries lived almost independent provincial lives, the northern and southern provinces speaking different dialects, even the character of the people varying, and yet from Awomori in the north to the southernmost parts of Satsuma, and even farther south to the Loochoos, the use of *fusuma*, *shōji*, mats, and thin wood-ceilings seems well-nigh universal. The store-houses standing on four posts are referred to in the description of the Bonin Islanders as well as in that of the Loochooans as resembling those constructed by the Ainos; yet these resemblances must not be taken as indicating a community of origin, but simply as the result of necessity. For travellers in Kamtchatka, and farther west, speak of the same kind of store-houses; and farther south they may be seen in Singapore and Java, — in fact, in every country town in New England; and indeed all over the United States the same kind of store-house is seen. Probably all over the world a store-house on four legs, even to the inverted box or pan on each leg, may be found.

Through the courtesy of Percival Lowell, Esq., I am enabled to see advanced sheets of his work on Korea, entitled "The Land of the Morning Calm;" and from this valuable work the author has permitted me to gather many interesting facts concerning the Korean dwellings. The houses are of one story; a flight of two or three steps leads to a narrow piazza, or very wide sill, which encircles the entire building. The apartment within is only limited by the size of the building; in other words, there is only one room under the roof. The better class of dwellings, however, consist of groups of these buildings. The house is of wood, and rests upon a stone foundation. This foundation consists of a series of connecting chambers, or flues; and at one side is a large fireplace, or oven, in which the fire is built. The products of combustion circulate through this labyrinth of chambers, and find egress, not by a chimney, but by an outlet on the opposite side. In this way the room above is warmed. There are three different types of this oven-like foundation. In the best type a single slab of stone is supported by a number of stout stone pillars; upon this stone floor is spread a layer of earth, and upon this earth is spread oil-paper like a carpet. In another arrangement, ridges of earth and small stones run lengthwise from front to back; on top of this the same arrangement is made of stone, earth, and oil-paper. In the third type, representing a still poorer class, the oven and flues are hollowed out of the earth alone. Mr. Lowell remarks that the idea is a good one, if it were only accompanied by proper ventilation. Unfortunately, he says, the room above is no better than a box, in which the occupant is slowly roasted. Another disadvantage is experienced in the impossibility of warming a room at once. He says: "The room does not even begin to get warm until you have passed through an agonizing interval of expectancy. Then it takes what seems forever to reach a comfortable temperature, passes this brief second of happiness before you have had time to realize that it has attained it, and continues mounting to unknown degrees in a truly alarming manner, beyond the possibility of control." This curious and ingenious method of warming houses is said to have been introduced from China some one hundred and fifty years ago.

A house of the highest order is simply a frame-work, — a roof supported on eight or more posts according to the size of the building; and this with a foundation represents the only fixed structure. In summer it presents a skeleton-like appearance; in winter, however, it appears solid and compact, as a series of folding-doors, — a pair between each two posts, — closes it completely. These are prettily latticed, open outward, and are fastened from within by a hook and knob. By a curious arrangement these doors can be removed from their hinges, the upper parts only remaining attached, and fastened up by hooks to the ceiling. This kind of a house and room is used as a banqueting hall and a room for general entertainment. It may be compared to our drawing-room.

Dwelling-rooms are constructed on quite a different plan. Instead of continuous doors, the sides are composed of permanent walls and doors. The wall is of wood, except that in the poorer house it consists of mud. Says Mr. Lowell: "In these buildings we have an elaborate system of three-fold aperture

closers, — a species of three skins, only that they are for con-
secutive, not simultaneous, use. The outer is the folding-door
above mentioned; the other two are a couple of pairs of sliding
panels, — the survivors in Korea of the once common sliding
screens, such as are used to-day in Japan. One of the pairs is
covered with dark green paper, and is for night use; the other
is of the natural yellowish color of the oil-paper, and is used by
day. When not wanted, they slide back into grooves inside
the wall, whence they are pulled out again by ribbons fastened
near the middle of the outer edge. All screens of this sort,
whether in houses or palanquins, are provided, unlike the Japanese, with these conveniences for tying the two halves of
each pair together, and thus enabling easier adjustment." The
house-lining within is oil-paper. "Paper covers the ceiling,
lines the wall, spreads the floor. As you sit in your room
your eye falls upon nothing but paper; and the very light that
enables you to see anything at all sifts in through the same
material."

It will be seen by these brief extracts how dissimilar the
Korean house is to that of the Japanese. And this dissimi-
larity is fully sustained by an examination of the photographs
which Mr. Lowell made in Korea, and which show among
other things low stone-walled houses with square openings for
windows, closed by frames covered with paper, the frames hung
from above and opening outside, and the roof tiled; also curious
thatched roofs, in which the slopes are uneven and rounding,
and their ridges curiously knotted or braided, differing in every
respect from the many forms of thatched roof in Japan.

The Chinese house, as I saw it in Shanghai and its suburbs, and at Canton as well as up the river, shows differences
from the Japanese house quite as striking as those of the
Korean house. Here one sees, in the cities at least, solid

brick-walled houses, with kitchen range built into the wall, and chimney equally permanent; tiled-roof, with tiled ridges; enclosed court-yard; floors of stone, upon which the shoes are worn from the street; doorways, with doors on hinges; window openings closed by swinging frames fitted with the translucent shells of Placuna, or white paper, the latter usually in a dilapidated condition; and for furniture they have tables, chairs, bedsteads, drawers, babies' chairs, cradles, foot-stools, and the like. The farm-houses of China in those regions that I visited were equally unlike similar houses in Japan.

From this superficial glance at the character of the house in the outlying Islands of the Japanese Empire, as well as at the houses of the neighboring countries, Korea and China, I think it will be conceded that the Japanese house is typically a product of the people, with just those features from abroad incorporated in it that one might look for, considering the proximity to Japan of China and Korea. When we remember that these three great civilizations of the Mongoloid race approximate within the radius of a few hundred miles, and that they have been in more or less intimate contact since early historic times, we cannot wonder that the germs of Japanese art and letters should have been adopted from the continent. In precisely the same way our ancestors, the English, drew from their continent the material for their language, art, music, architecture, and many other important factors in their civilization; and if history speaks truly, their refinement even in language and etiquette was imported. But while Japan, like England, has modified and developed the germs ingrafted from a greater and older civilization, it has ever preserved the elasticity of youth, and seized upon the good things of our civilization, — such as steam, electricity, and modern methods of study and research, — and utilized them promptly. Far different is it from the mother country, where the improvements and methods of other nations get but tardy recognition.

It seems to give certain English writers peculiar delight to stigmatize the Japanese as a nation of imitators and copyists. From the contemptuous manner in which disparagements of this nature are flung into the faces of the Japanese who are engaged in their heroic work of establishing sound methods of government and education, one would think that in England had originated the characters by which the English people write, the paper upon which they print, the figures by which they reckon, the compass by which they navigate, the gunpowder by which they subjugate, the religion by which they worship. Indeed, when one looks over the long list of countries upon which England has drawn for the arts of music, painting, sculpture, architecture, printing, engraving, and a host of other things, it certainly comes with an ill-grace from natives of that country to taunt the Japanese with being imitators.

It would be obviously absurd to suggest as a model for our own houses such a structure as a Japanese house. Leaving out the fact that it is not adapted to the rigor of our climate or to the habits of our people, its fragile and delicate fittings if adopted by us, would be reduced to a mass of kindlings in a week, by the rude knocks it would receive; and as for exposing on our public thoroughfares the delicate labyrinth of carvings often seen on panel and post in Japan, the wide-spread vandalism of our country would render futile all such attempts to civilize and refine. Fortunately, in that land which we had in our former ignorance and prejudice regarded as uncivilized, the malevolent form of the *genus homo* called "vandal" is unknown.

Believing that the Japanese show infinitely greater refinement in their methods of house-adornment than we do, and convinced that their tastes are normally artistic, I have endeavored to emphasize my convictions by holding up in contrast our usual methods of house-furnishing and outside embellishments. By so doing I do not mean to imply that we do not have in America interiors that show the most perfect refinement and taste; or that in Japan, on the other hand, interiors may not be found in which good taste is wanting.

I do not expect to do much good in thus pointing out what I believe to be better methods, resting on more refined standards. There are some, I am sure, who will approve; but the throng — who are won by tawdry glint and tinsel; who make possible, by admiration and purchase, the horrors of much that is made for house-furnishing and adornment — will, with characteristic obtuseness, call all else but themselves and their own ways heathen and barbarous.

GLOSSARY.

In the following list of Japanese words used in this work an opportunity is given to correct a number of mistakes which crept into, or rather walked boldly into, the text. The author lays no claim to a knowledge of the Japanese language beyond what any foreigner might naturally acquire in being thrown among the people for some time. As far as possible he has followed Hepburn's Japanese Dictionary for orthography and definition, and Brunton's Map of Japan for geographical names. Brunton's map, as well as that published by Rein, spells Settsu with one *t*. For the sake of uniformity I have followed this spelling in the text, though it is contrary to the best authorities. It may be added that Ōshiu and Tōtōmi should be printed with a long accent over each *o*.

The words Samurai, Daimio, Kioto, Tokio, and several others, are now so commonly seen in the periodical literature of our country that this form of spelling for these words has been retained. For rules concerning the pronunciation of Japanese words the reader is referred to the Introduction in Hepburn's Dictionary.

Agari-ba . . . The floor for standing upon in coming out of the bath.

Age-yen . . . A platform that can be raised or lowered.

Amado . . . . Rain-door. The outside sliding doors by which the house is closed at night.

Andon . . . . A lamp.

Asagao . . . . A colloquial name for a porcelain urinal, from its resemblance to the flower of the morning-glory.

Benjo . . . . Privy. Place for business.

Biwa . . . A lute with four strings.

Biyŏ-bu . . . A folding screen.

Cha-dokoro . . Tea-place.

Cha-ire . . . . Tea-jar; literally, "tea-put in."

Cha-no-yu . . . A tea-party.

Chigai-dana . . A shelf, one half of which is on a different plane from the other.

Chōdzu-ba . . .	Privy; literally, "hand water-place."
Chōdzu-bachi .	A convenience near the privy for washing the hands.
Chū-nuri . . .	Middle layer of plaster.
Dai-jū-no . . .	A pan for holding burning charcoal, used in replenishing the hibachi.
Daiku	A carpenter.
Daimio	A feudal lord.
Dodai	The foundation-sill of a house.
Dodai-ishi . . .	Foundation stone.
Do-ma	Earth-space. A small unfloored court at the entrance of the house.
Fukuro-dana . .	Cupboard; literally, "pouch-shelf."
Fumi-ishi . . .	Stepping-stone.
Furo	A small culinary furnace, also a bath-tub.
Furosaki biyō-bu.	A two-fold screen placed in front of the furo.
Fusuma	A sliding screen between rooms.
Fū-tai	The bands which hang down in front of a kake-mono; literally, "wind-band."
Futon	A quilted bed-cover.
Ge-dan	Lower step.
Genka	The porch at the entrance of a house.
Geta	Wooden clogs.
Goyemon buro .	A form of bath-tub.
Habakari . . .	Privy.
Hagi	A kind of rush.
Hashira	A post.
Hashira kakushi .	A long narrow picture to hang on post in room; literally, "post-hide."
Hibachi	A brazier for holding hot coals for warming the apartments.
Hibashi	Metal tongs.
Hikite	A recessed catch in a screen for sliding it back and forth.
Hi-no-ki . . .	A species of pine.
Hisashi	A small roof projecting over a door or window.
Hon-gawara . .	True tile.

Ichi-yo-dana	. .	A kind of shelf.
Iri-kawa	. . .	The space between the verandah and room.
Ishi-dōrō	. . .	A stone lantern.
Ji-bukuro	. . .	Cupboard.
Jin-dai-sugi	. .	" Cedar of God's age."
Jinrikisha	. . .	A two-wheeled vehicle drawn by a man.
Ji-zai	. . . .	A hook used for hanging pots over the fire.
Jō-dan	. . . .	Upper step. Raised floor in house.
Kago	. . . .	Sedan chair.
Kaikōsha	. . .	Name of a private school of architecture.
Kake-mono	. .	Hanging picture.
Kaki	. . . . .	Fence.
Kamado	. . .	Kitchen range.
Kami-dana	. . .	A shelf in the house for Shin-tō shrine.
Kami-no-ma	. .	Higher room.
Kamoi	. . . .	Lintel.
Kara-kami	. . .	Sliding screen between rooms.
Kawarake	. . .	Unglazed earthen ware.
Kaya	. . . .	A kind of grass used for thatch.
Kaya	. . . .	Mosquito netting.
Kazari-kugi	. .	Ornamental headed nails.
Kaze-obi	. . .	The bands which hang down in front of the kake-mono ; literally, "wind-band."
Keshō-no-ma	. .	Toilet-room.
Keyaki	. . . .	A kind of hard wood.
Kō-ka	. . . .	Privy ; literally, " back frame."
Koshi-bari	. . .	A kind of paper used for a dado.
Kuguri-do	. . .	A small, low door in a gate.
Kura	. . . . .	A fire-proof store-house.
Kuro-moji-gaki	.	A kind of ornamental fence.
Ma-bashira	. .	Middle post.
Mado	. . . .	Window.
Ma-gaki	. . . .	A fence made of bamboo.
Magari-gane	. .	A carpenter's iron square.
Maki-mono	. .	Pictures that are kept rolled up, not hung.

Maki-mono-dana .	Shelf for maki-mono.
Makura	Pillow.
Miki-dokkuri . .	Bottle for offering wine to gods.
Mochi	A kind of bread made of glutinous rice.
Mon	Badge, or crest.
Mune	Ridge of roof.
Naka-tsubo . .	Middle space.
Nan-do	Store-room. Pantry.
Neda-maruta . .	Cross-beams to support floor.
Nedsumi-bashira	Cross-beam at end of building; literally, " rat-post."
Nikai-bari . . .	Horizontal beam to support second-story floor.
Noren	Curtain. Hanging screen.
Nuki	A stick passed through mortised holes to bind together upright posts.
Nuri-yen . . .	A verandah unprotected by amado.
Oohi-yen . . .	A low platform.
Oshi-ire	Closet; literally, " push, put in."
Otoshi-kake . .	Hanging partition.
Ramma	Open ornamental work over the screens which form the partitions in the house.
Ro	Hearth, or fire-place, in the floor.
Rō-ka	Corridor. Covered way.
Sake	Fermented liquor brewed from rice.
Samisen . . .	A guitar with three strings.
Samisen-tsugi . .	A peculiar splice for joining timber.
Samurai . . .	Military class privileged to wear two swords.
Sashi-mono-ya .	Cabinet-maker.
Setsu-in . . .	Privy; literally, " snow-hide."
Shaku	A wooden tablet formerly carried by nobles when in the presence of the Emperor.
Shaku	A measure of ten inches. Japanese foot.
Shichirin . . .	A brazier for cooking purposes.
Shikii	The lower grooved beam in which the door or screens slide.
Shin-tō	The primitive religion of Japan.

Shita-nuri	. . .	The first layer of plaster.
Shō-ji	. . . .	The outside door-sash covered with thin paper.
Sode-gaki	. . .	A small ornamental fence adjoining a house.
Sudare	. . . .	A shade made of split bamboo or reeds.
Sugi	. . . . .	Cedar.
Sumi-sashi	. . .	A marking-brush made of wood.
Sumi-tsubo	. .	An ink-pot used by carpenters in lieu of the chalk-line.
Sun	. . . . .	One tenth of a Japanese foot.
Sunoko	. . . .	A platform made of bamboo.
Tabako-bon	. .	A box or tray in which fire and smoking utensils are kept.
Tamari-no-ma	. .	Anteroom.
Tansu	. . . .	Bureau.
Taruki	. . . .	A rafter of the roof.
Tatami	. . . .	A floor-mat.
Ten-jō	. . . .	Ceiling.
Te-shoku	. . .	Hand-lamp.
To-bukuro	. . .	A closet in which outside doors are stowed away.
Tokkuri	. . . .	A bottle.
Toko	. . . . .	The floor of the tokonoma.
Toko-bashira	. .	The post dividing the two bays or recesses in the guest-room.
Tokonoma	. . .	A bay, or recess, where a picture is hung.
Tori-i	. . . .	A portal, or structure of stone or wood, erected in front of a Shin-tō temple.
Tsubo	. . . .	An area of six feet square.
Tsugi-no-ma	. .	Second room.
Tsui-tate	. . .	A screen of one leaf set in a frame.
Tsume-sho	. . .	A servant's waiting-room.
Usukasumi-dana	.	A name for shelf; literally, "thin mist-shelf."
Uwa-nuri	. . .	The last layer of plaster.
Watari	. . . .	A passage; literally, "to cross over."
Yane	. . . .	Roof.
Yane-shita	. . .	Roof-beams.
Yashiki	. . . .	A lot of ground upon which a house stands. An enclosure for a Daimio's residence.

Yedo-gawara . .	Yedo tile.
Yen	A coin; equals one dollar.
Yen-gawa . . .	Verandah.
Yen-riyo . . .	Reserve.
Yen-zashiki . .	End-parlor.
Yō-ba	Privy; literally, " place for business."
Yoshi	A kind of reed.
Yoshi-do . . .	A screen made of yoshi.
Yu-dono . . .	Bath-room.
Yuka-shita . . .	The beams supporting the first floor.

INDEX.

AINOS, their houses and customs, 336–339.

Amado, the, their use as storm-doors or at night, 239, 242, 247; their usual form, and accompanying arrangements for ventilation, 247, 248; the single noisy feature of the Japanese house, 248; their various devices for fastening, 248–250; corner-rollers for use in their adjustment, 250; their occasional sliding or swinging doors for night use, 250, 251; their closets, or *to-bukuro*, for storage purposes during day-time, 251, 252.

Ancient House, the, its development as traced in some ancient Japanese records, 323–335; Ernest Satow cited as to the ancient palaces of the Japanese sovereigns, 324, 325; early differentiation in its roof forms, 325, 326; early form of latrine, and its ethnological bearing, 326; its resemblance to the Anam and Malay forms, 330; Ernest Satow cited as to its general character, 331, 332.

Andon, or lamp, its common form, 221; its varieties, 222.

Aqueducts, their occasional use in the cities, 296; their usual method of construction, 297; the insufficiency and poor quality of their water-supply, 297; their construction of bamboo pipes, 299–301; their reservoirs, 300.

Architecture, Japanese, its common terms of framework-construction and dimensions explained, 23 *note;* as intelligently considered, 45–47; sympathy with the Japanese people an essential element of its thorough appreciation, 45, 46; its occasional imposing types, 45, 321; as shown in the temples, 46, 47; its alleged uniformity, 47, 49; absence of books on house-plans and elevations, 47, 48; a few of its most common terms, 106, 107; as compared with our own, 234; its occasional combination with foreign types, 318, 320; as shown in the fortresses, 321; its comparative want of grandeur, 321, 322, its originality of style, 334, 335; its peculiar features as sometimes observed in the surrounding islands, 342, 343; its incorporation of special features from neighboring countries, 346.

Aston, W. G., cited, 323, 333.

Atkinson, Professor, mentioned, 296 *note.*

BALCONIES, their usual occurrence in two-story houses, 244; their varieties of railing, 244–247; instances of artistic design in the perforated panel-form of railing, 245; light bamboo form of railing, 245, 246; more durable forms, 246.

Bamboo, its importance as a Japanese building material, 84; its use in roof-construction, 92, 94–97, 100–104; its peculiar adaptability for artistic decoration, 146, 156, 170, 171; its use in screen and curtain work, 182;

24

University Press : John Wilson & Son, Cambridge.